SEXUALITY AND WAR

"SEXUALITY AND WAR"

Literary Masks of
the Middle East

Evelyne Accad

NEW YORK UNIVERSITY PRESS

NEW YORK AND LONDON

Copyright © 1990 by New York University
All rights reserved
Manufactured in the United States of America

Library of Congress Cataloging-in-Publication Data
Accad, Evelyne.
   Sexuality and war : literary masks of the Middle East / Evelyne
Accad.
      p.   cm. — (Feminist crosscurrents)
   Includes bibliographical references.
   ISBN 0-8147-0595-2 (alk. paper)
   ISBN 0-8147-0615-0 (pbk.)
      1. Arabic fiction—Lebanon—History and criticism.   2. Arabic
fiction—20th century—History and criticism.   3. Lebanese fiction
(French)—History and criticism.   4. Sex in literature.   5. Feminism
in literature.   6. Violence in literature.   7. Lebanon—History—
Civil War, 1975-1976—Literature and the war.   8. Sexual animosity—
Lebanon.   9. Sexual animosity—Arab countries.   I. Title.
II. Series.
PJ8082.A23   1990
892'.736093538—dc20   89-14278
                                         CIP

New York University Press books are printed on acid-free paper,
and their binding materials are chosen for strength and durability.

p 10 9 8 7 6 5 4 3 2 1

Book design by Ken Venezio

Contents

Foreword

Evelyne Accad's study of sexuality and war in the Middle East brings to the surface once again the most basic assumptions of international feminism: confronting the issues particular to any group of women is in the best interest of the liberation of all women, and in the very particularities of race, culture, and national identity there is commonality to women's experience of oppression. Under patriarchal power, sexuality constitutes one of the most personalized forms of domination, ranging from sexual objectification to violence. Sexuality is fundamental to women's control of their own bodies, and how it is socially constructed will in large part determine how women become sexual subjects to themselves—how much they are intimately colonized or what autonomy is left to them. And while sexuality is one of the most unavoidable and radical issues of women's movements, it is the issue that is still the most difficult and painful for women to speak of, write about, and confront because it is often so terrifyingly personal. More than once, in more than one way, its colonization of women has extended into ruptures and fragmentations in the women's movement.

For feminists, coming to terms with liberation ultimately means coming to terms with sexuality. While others have written about and documented rape as a conquering strategy in war and prostitution as an r&r industry for warring men, Evelyne Accad foregrounds the issue of sexuality as being "centrally involved in the motivations of war." Sexuality is causal; it is the conclusion; and when transformed, it can be the hope. But what we learn here is more: coming to terms with militarization, war, and peace means confronting the deployment of sexuality through them. This radical thesis confronts the very cornerstone of war with the most central issue of feminism. Here the novel is taken as a reading of society, one that reveals hidden dimensions in gender power and hierarchy. And what we learn from looking at sexuality and war in the Middle East through their expressions in novels is how men and women look at the same war, see its effects, experience its ravages, sustain hopes for the future through entirely different gendered lenses.

The novel is close to Evelyne Accad. For her it has also been the means by which she has been able to unveil the experiences of being a woman in the Arab world. If she is able to transport us into the reality of women and the war in Lebanon, it is not only because she has struck at the core of the issue in focusing on sexuality but because as a poet, novelist, literary critic, and social analyst her work offers a kind of mosaic that draws these multiple ways of knowing together to bring us into the subjective reality of women in the Arab world in the time of war. Importantly, Evelyne Accad assumes that when this subjective reality is revealed to us, we can and will understand and that will make a difference. She intends for her readers to know and care and want to change. In other works, she has given history to women's place in the recent development of the novel, a relatively new genre of Arab literature. And in the cool evening breeze of the Mediterranean, I have heard her sing the songs she has composed about women, sex, and war in Lebanon as women from fifteen to twenty different countries momentarily transcended with her the national and cultural differences that separated us to be transported into the reality of her and Lebanese women's experiences.

In fact, Evelyne Accad's hope for transforming the situation in the Middle East rests on the assumption that in the particularities, specificities, and diversities that differentiate the situation of women in the Arab world, there is a commonality, a basis for mutual understanding and therefore the possibility that addressing the issue of sexuality in war will resonate for women everywhere. Isolation is endangering. That is why any work that successfully brings the issues of women in any part of the world into a radical feminist international movement must confront multiple hegemonic ideologies that function to distance Western women from the situation of women in the Third World. These issues confronting international feminism are likewise the blockades to political knowledge that Evelyne Accad has had to confront in this work: I am speaking of U.S. national isolationism, Western cultural particularism, Third World masculinist nationalism, and Western feminist reification of differences.

U.S. national isolationism insulates Americans in their individualism from the rest of the world even as they watch the daily horrors of war on television news. This ideology prizes the individual over the community and ensconces individuals in distinct worlds complete with rights and protections that are meant to enable them to remain dissociated from the rest of the world. Ethics of individualism are based on privacy, "minding your own business," and can lead to selfishness, "taking care of No. 1" in a society that experiences very little external threat and therefore seeks only minimal internal cohesion. In their isolation many Americans live as if they can afford not to know and even not to care about what is happening in other parts of the world.

Western liberal particularism, another mode of dissociation from the Third World, finds its logic and justification in what began as a legitimate reaction against the pseudocultural superiority of Western ethnocentrism. But, as usual in the world of male political aggression, the pendulum swung too far back and antiethnocentrism has fostered a Western liberal particularism that says "hands off" to anything produced in Third-World nations or cultures. This simplistic form of cultural relativism handily reinforces difference and separation just when women around the globe are discovering the contrary, the possibilities of international feminist political bonding and unity. It particularizes the war in Lebanon as a centuries-old battle of clans and tribes and disregards the subordination of women through veiling and excision in the Arab world because they represent custom and culture. This liberalism wraps war and sexuality in the inevitability of centuries of cultural tradition and bifurcates any idea of universal human rights from cultural integrity. Then logically, war and sexuality are internal issues of the Lebanese, for women and men in the Arab world. The weight and brunt of exposing these violations must be borne exclusively by its victims, the very ones isolated by American individualism and Western particularism.

Women have been once again caught in the crossfire of male aggression and male antiaggression both in the West and in the Third World. The "hands off" approach of Western liberal particularism coincides with and reinforces Third World masculinist nationalism, which, in telling Western nations that it has no business interfering in the affairs of the Third World, is also telling women of the Third World that to demand rights and to expose male domination are to be disloyal to their country, to violate their culture. Denouncing all women's movements as Western, Third World masculinist nationalism attempts to isolate women in their cultures and identify Western women as their enemy.

Finally, within Western and particularly the American women's movement, genuine efforts to confront racism and bias frequently have been reduced to merely affirming differences among women but in a way that again separates women into their particularities. This Western feminist reification of differences has been pushed to the extent that any basis for collective identity among women as women is rejected in favor of emphasizing that which divides and separates Western white women from women of any color in the Third World. Steeped in American pluralistic values that emphasize individualism and result in U.S. isolationism, this ideology and reification of women's differences reinforce cultural particularism and block genuine efforts to arrive at an international feminism by affirming that indeed women of Third World cultures are different and therefore must be separated unto themselves. Again simplistically, political unity of women has been falsely reduced to sameness.

Evelyne Accad does not confuse feminist collective identity with sameness. She is every bit as much Lebanese as she is woman, and the personal pain of seeing her country torn apart, the agony of losing lifelong friends, and knowing that her family in Beirut lives in daily peril are utterly bound to the political horror of cultural and warring practices that daily destroy women, alienating them from themselves, their bodies, and each other. Accad must be a feminist and a nationalist. Unlike Virginia Woolf, she cannot say "as a woman I have no country," and yet she must reject patriotism, a force of male loyalty that is rooted in patriarchy. To love her country and honor her sex, she turns to nationalism and forges a feminist redefinition of it. Her idea of nationalism is based on a very familiar feminist theme, that the personal is political. Rather than closing off Lebanon in a nationalism that is meant to separate and recreate conditions for future aggressions, the idea of nationalism for her is meant to transcend the patriarchal dichotomies of private/public, inside/outside, and, yes, sexual/political. This nationalism will be founded in a feminist sexual politics. But the hard-line materialist will have difficulty holding up this definition to a nonidealist analysis. For in the final analysis, Accad's feminist idea of nationalism is admittedly utopic, not unreachable, but certainly based on the belief of possibilities for a future that is yet to be conceived. Yet, as a Lebanese woman facing and living through the warring in her homeland, dare she be other than utopian?

Kathleen Barry
Pennsylvania State University

Acknowledgments

The anguish, sadness, and despair over the senseless war and destruction of my beautiful country of birth, Lebanon, is at the core of what led me to write this book. My commitment to women and peace issues have given it its main form and content, and my deep concern about oppression and injustice have marked its tone.

For the institutional and fellowship support that freed me from other resonsibilities, I want to thank the Fulbright Commission, the Social Science Research Council, and the University of Illinois at Urbana-Champaign.

I want to thank all the wonderful women whose encouragement and support uplifted me and gave me the necessary impetus to write this book. I am particularly indebted to Ann Russo, who was the first to see the importance of sexuality in my work and urged me to express and develop ideas she considered vital to women and international feminism. Pat Cramer also provided me with invaluable encouragement. Finding me depressed one day about being told I overemphasize certain points and issues, she remarked that Virginia Woolf had been criticized for the same reasons. Pat corrected my manuscript and encouraged me to develop even further the personal and emotional statements that other readers had found unnecessary and distracting. My deep thanks also go to Kathleen Barry, who provided me with constant and sustaining support. We shared many fruitful and important discussions over common problems, concerns, and issues of international scope. Her intense and powerful commitment is a source of inspiration that has renewed mine. I want to thank Françoise Collin and Marie-Claire Boons for their interest, understanding, and support, especially while I was in Paris, where I wrote much of this book. Françoise Collin was courageous enough to join me in Lebanon over the New Year's holiday in 1988 to interview women and men and to lead several discussions about the war. I am also grateful to my friends Amel Ben Aba and Ilham Ben Milad in Tunisia with whom I have vital discussions and share deep concern over Arab women's issues. The letters Amel and I write each other and the intense moments we live when we meet reinforce my belief in the importance of women's solidarity and sisterhood. My sister Jacqueline Hajjar in Beirut, who spent hours correcting and proofreading my manuscript, also has my gratitude. And I want to thank my two dear friends in Lebanon, Mona Takieddine-Amyuni and Nazik Yared, with whom I have shared so many of these ideas and who have provided me with invaluable insights and comments. These last three women are living the war in Lebanon on a daily basis. Their example of courage, commitment, belief in love and peaceful means, their crossing the divided city at very dangerous times, their teaching, researching, and writing under very difficult conditions—all illustrate the solutions to war implied in this study. These women—and many others too numerous to cite—form an international network of feminism whose values are capable of bringing about the changes necessary for the transformation of society and the achievement of peace.

I want to especially thank my dear friend Paul Vieille, who spent days reading and commenting many of the novels I was reading and studying. He gave me invaluable insights into the "imaginary" of many of the authors. His commitment and understanding of Middle Eastern societies and his relentless study of them over the years give him an acute vision of the relationship between the particular and the global. The importance he places on "letting the people speak for themselves" and being a good listener and observer have taught me a great deal. The discussions we had were a source of discovery and understanding of major aspects of my subject that I would not have seen without his help.

I want to thank my two dear friends Eva Enderlein and Emile Snyder, whose life of commitment, love, and generosity, whose passion for justice, art, and beauty, and whose deep encouragement and understanding of my work, in moments of depression as in moments of great ecstasy, have uplifted me throughout the years and given me the necessary impetus to complete this task. I also want to thank my two friends Guido and Martha Francescato, whose belief in my work and whose sustaining friendship have helped me throughout.

I want to thank all those who read the manuscript and offered invaluable comments and corrections. Among them are: Janie Bond, Fedwa Malti-Douglas, Allen Douglas, Miriam Cooke, Sonya Michel, Zohreh Sullivan, Robert Nelson, Sandra Savignon, Andrée Chedid, and Halim Barakat. And I also want to thank Kitty Moore, senior editor at New York University Press for her interest and encouragement.

Finally, I want to dedicate this book to Mona Takieddine-Amyuni and to her late husband Fouad Amyuni, who died as I was completing this book, innocent victim of the hate and violence denounced in this study, to Nazik and Ibrahim Yared, to Lucien and Huguette Accad, to Jacqueline and Fawzi Hajjar, to Claire Gebeyli, and to all the beautiful women and men who have remained in Lebanon and work for peace and reconciliation, crossing the demarcation line and believing the reunification of the country will take place and that love will triumph.

SEXUALITY AND WAR

Introduction

The war system has brought us to the brink of annihilation, and we still refuse to face the very fundamental feeling it arouses—fear. The society is paralyzed by the masculine suppression of emotion. Surely peace research and world order studies should attend to this paralysis as the first priority in transition. Yet for the most part we continue to close out to the world of feeling and the repositories of that world, feminine values and women.

Betty Reardon, Sexism and the War System

And this city, what is it? A whore. Who could imagine a whore sleeping with a thousand men and continuing to live? The city receives a thousand bombs and continues its existence nonetheless. The city can be summarized by these bombs. . . . When we had destroyed Beirut, we thought we had destroyed it. . . . We had destroyed this city at last. But when the war was declared finished and the pictures of the incredible desolation of Beirut were broadcasted, we discovered we had not destroyed it. We had only opened a few breaches in its walls, without destroying it. For that, other wars would be necessary. (*La petite montagne*, p. 252)

This city is like a great suffering being, too mad, too overcharged, broken now, gutted, and raped like those girls raped by thirty or forty militia men, and are now mad and in asylums because their families, Mediterranean to the end, would rather hide than cure . . . but how does one cure the memory? The city, like those girls, was raped. . . . In the City, this center of all prostitutions, there is a lot of money and a lot of construction that will never be finished. Cement has mixed with the earth, and little by little has smothered most of the trees. If not all. (*Sitt Marie-Rose*, p. 21)

If you had to guess which of these two passages was written by a woman and which by a man, what would your reaction be? In these two images of Beirut, two opposing feelings are being expressed, two contrasting visions emerge. The first wants to get rid of the sinner, the whore, source of all evils, decadence, and the problems of modern existence. The total and violent destruction of the woman is seen as the only way out of an inextricable situation. The second feels sorry for the woman, the city, victim of

1

rape, victim of man's violence. Mediterranean customs are accused. Hypocrisy and the oppression of women are presented as the origin of madness and the destruction of the city.

The first passage is by a man, Elias Khoury, author of *Al-Jabal al-saghir* (*La petite montagne*), the second by a woman, Etel Adnan, author of *Sitt Marie-Rose*. This difference between a man's and a woman's vision of Beirut and their ways of expressing them was even more clearly defined last year at Christmas, as I watched women friends, determined to cross Beirut two or three times a week, pass through the demarcation line—the most desolate, depressing, and often dangerous spot in the city. Most of the time they go on foot, since only a few cars that have special permission are allowed through. They go because they are convinced that by this gesture, real as well as symbolic, Lebanon's reunification will take place. They do this against all logic and under the ironic and sometimes admiring look of men. Men also cross the demarcation line, but it seems to me that fewer men than women make this gesture. Men risk more in crossing the line, since they are more often the victims of kidnappings, assaults, and murders, but men also cross more in the spirit of duty and because of professional interests.

Women friends who cross the demarcation line, defying weapons, militia, and political games, told me how the line has become a meeting place where each morning they look forward to seeing this friend or that. They smile to each other as they walk assuredly through the apocalyptic space of the museum passage (another name for the area because the remains of the museum are located there), conscious that their march is not an ordinary one, that their crossing is a daring act, important to Lebanon's survival.

The aim of this book is to show how sexuality and war are indissolubly linked and to do so through a consideration of novels about the war in Lebanon written by both men and women in French and Arabic. Sexuality has been often left out of analysis about social, economic, and political problems. By *sexuality*, I mean not only the physical and psychological relations between men and women, or the sexual act in itself, but also the customs—Mediterranean, Lebanese, and religious—involved in relations between men and women and the feelings of love, power, violence, and tenderness as well as the notions of territory attached to possession and jealousy. Sexuality is expressed in the symbolic act of crossing the city: it is the bridge between opposing forces.

In order to understand and express this connection between war and sexuality, I have chosen sociological, political, and other recent analyses of the war. I have explored recent feminist interpretations of violence, aggression, war, and women's roles and oppression as well as some men's writings on these topics. All have given me invaluable insights into the relationship between oppression and sexuality. For new and stimulating approaches to these issues, I am particularly indebted to Betty Reardon, Andrea Dworkin, Kathleen Barry, Cynthia Enloe, Virginia Woolf, Cherrie Moraga, Susan Brownmiller, Elisabeth Badinter, Anne-Marie de Vilaine, Nancy Chodorow, Marilyn Waring, Robin Morgan, Yolla Polity Charara, Ilham Ben Ghadifa, Elaine Scarry, Elaine Showalter, Jean Duvignaud, Gérard Mendel, Jean-Marie Muller, Paul Vieille, Ross Poole, Adam Farrar, Bob Connell, Jean-William Lapierre, Wilhelm Reich, Henri Laborit, Michel Foucault, Jean Libis, and others.

In the past twelve years, I have conducted research throughout the Middle East, interviewed women in rural and urban areas about their sexuality, relationships with men (husbands, brothers, sons), relationships with other women, and the special conditions of their lives.[1] I attended conferences such as "Quel féminisme pour le Maghreb (North Africa)?" (Tunisia, 1985), which addressed issues of feminism, nationalism, and, peripherally, sexuality. I taught a course on the role of Arab women in society and literature at the Beirut University College in 1981 and 1984, living the war in Lebanon during those semesters as I had earlier. This research, my discussions with women and men, and my personal experience of these issues have brought me to fresh perspectives on the role of feminism in nationalistic struggles and to the recognition of the inescapable centrality of sexuality in social and political relationships.

I have chosen six novels about the war to illustrate the connections among sexuality, war, nationalism, feminism, violence, love, and power as they relate to the body, the partner, the family, Marxism, religion, and pacifism. These novels do not necessarily represent the entire range of creative works about the war.[2] They were chosen for their significance in terms of the issues under discussion and for their availability in languages understandable to the Western reader. The works, originally written in Arabic or French, are by Lebanese women and men who have lived or are still living in Lebanon. All of the novels chosen are set in Beirut, in the context of the war. ʿAwdat al-taʾir ilal bahr (literally, "Return of the Flying Dutchman to the Sea"; published as *Days of Dust*) by Halim Barakat and *Tawaheen Beirut (Death in Beirut)* by Tawfiq Awwad—works written before the war started in 1975—foreshadow the events. In representations of the war, even though each treats the subject differently, all of the writers show how war and violence have roots in sexuality and in the treatment of women in that part of the world. Most of the characters meet a tragic fate due to the war, but women are the principal victims of both political and social violence. For example, as she tries to gain autonomy and education in the midst of her country's social and political unrest, the heroine of *Death in Beirut*, is seduced, raped, beaten, her face is slashed, her ambitions are smashed. Zahra, in *Hikayat Zahra (The Story of Zahra)* by Hanan al-Shaykh, who tries to find a way out of herself and of the civil war that has just erupted by having a sexual relationship with a sniper, becomes the target not only of his sexual weapon but of his *kalashnikov* (a Russian machine gun) as well. In the end, he kills her. In Etel Adnan's novel *Sitt Marie-Rose*, Marie-Rose is struggling for social justice, Arab women's liberation, and directs a school for the handicapped. She is put to death by Phalangist executioners, who first torture her to get rid of their bad conscience. In *La maison sans racines (House Without Roots)* by Andrée Chedid, Sybil dies from a sniper's bullet at the point of possible reconciliation, where one character had advanced trying to save others, one of whom had been hit by the sniper's death machine as they were starting a peace march. In *Days of Dust*, Pamela, trying to find herself by helping the refugees and protesting against American imperialism, loses herself in a frustrating relationship with the male protagonist. And in *La petite montagne*, the female characters are destroyed, disappear, or are trapped in disgustingly hateful marriage routines.

In addition to the relationship between war and sexuality, I examined the positive and negative actions and resolutions male and female characters take and the differences and similarities between male and female protagonists, between male and female authors, and between those writing in Arabic and in French. I also try to assess the necessary changes Lebanon must undergo to solve its tragedy and to become, once again, the area for democratic tolerance and freedom, a role it had had in the region and which is so much needed in that part of the world.

The questions I am often asked when treating and illustrating my topic are: Is literature an adequate field to understand political and social realities? Can novels be used as social, anthropological, and political documents? What about the imagination, the fantasy of the author? What about his or her "distortions"? My immediate response is to say that creative works are more appropriate than other works. They give us the "total" picture because they not only include all the various fields—social, political, anthropological, religious, and cultural—but they also allow us to enter into the imaginary and unconscious world of the author. In expressing his or her own individual vision, an author also suggests links to the collective "imaginary." (The "imaginary" can be said to be a speculation, with the means at our disposal, about what is possible. Given that "imagination" designates both the contents and the recipient (faculty or capacity), this new term is used to refer to the first of these. Through the imaginary, societies endlessly experiment with new forms of organization, communication, participation, etc., that are not defined by existing institutions. A "figment" of the imaginary is a response to a question that the society has asked itself, whether overtly or not. In all its modalities, the imaginary is an exploration of what is possible.) Thus the author offers an image of his or her society. The tension between individual and collective imagination adds complexities and subtleties not found in more direct scientific documents. Therefore, in my opinion, literature's domain is the most complete. It can make us grasp the whole picture because it is multidisciplinary and multidimensional, and it reflects and articulates the complexities of a situation. In addition, it is artistic and entertaining. It can educate and amuse us at the same time.

A novel has its own internal logic, which can escape both the novelist and "reality." The logic of a novel is that of fantasy. It goes from a reality with one or more characters, or from a certain dimension, and follows their logic to the end. As such, any novel is dated, as the Hungarian critic Georg Lukács, has shown, analyzing it as evolving from a problem of society.[3] At the same time, it carries the logical dimension of this society to the limit, therefore leaving "reality." A novel is recognized as "belonging" to a society at a given time, but it is not a sociological or anthropological work as such. Said differently, it is the imagination of the novelist that is expressed in a novel, but this imagination is of someone who belongs to the society under consideration. The novelist is its witness, even if she or he is not representative in the sociological sense. On the other hand, the novelist is also an actor in her or his society, albeit a privileged one. The imagination of a novelist, expressing itself in a work, marks a generation, a society, in a specific way worth discovering. Thus, the novelist is at once a witness of society, reflecting it in her or his work, and an actor, an agent of transformation. As Raymond Williams articulates this relationship in "Notes on

English Prose," "the society determines, much more than we realize and at deeper levels than we ordinarily admit, the writing of literature; but also . . . the society is not completely, not fully and immediately present until the literature has been written." Hence, literature "can come through to stand as if on its own, with an intrinsic and permanent importance, so that we can see the rest of our living through it as well as it through the rest of our living" (p. 72).

The Arabic novel is a fairly recent phenomenon. *Zaynab,* by the Egyptian writer Muhammad Husayn Haykal, is generally considered the first of the genre. Most of these Arabic works have been written in the context of societies in transition, in a state of stress born of numerous economic and political conflicts. It is a young, often experimental literature that has not yet reached its maturity. As such, it displays a very significant tension between anthropological "realities" and literary solutions. Conflicts created by colonialism, neocolonialism, imperialism, and other forms of oppression and solutions to these conflicts come out in both form and content. Using a genre usually considered European while wanting the destruction of Western models, the novelists work in a contradictory mode. The schizophrenia resulting is often expressed by the authors with originality, in a unique voice that creates its own identity. I have already treated the issue of the relationship between sociological problems and fictional solutions from a critical and sociological perspective in *Veil of Shame: The Role of Women in the Contemporary Fiction of North Africa and the Arab World.* In this study, I want to apply a similar methodology within a theoretical framework that includes not only the sociological and political but also the psychological.

Along with many Third World literatures, Arab literature written in both Arabic and French expression has produced its distinct content, styles, and forms. It has mixed poetry and prose, a sense of time, symbols, and images the Western reader has not always appreciated. For example, when Aimé Césaire wrote *Cahier d'un retour au pays natal* (Return to My Native Land) in the 1940s, he could find no French editor willing to publish it. It was thanks to his friend André Breton, the surrealist poet sensitive to other forms of expression, that the work finally got published and was soon to be recognized as a literary masterpiece, not only for Third World literature but for the world in general.

The Arabic war novel has added its distinctive dimension to a body of literature already quite impressive and fascinating in quantity and quality. War creates such conditions of despair that writing becomes a necessity, an outlet and a catharsis. It helps heal the wounds. It offers an alternative to fighting and destruction. It can become one form of the *active* nonviolent struggles I will talk about throughout this study. The war has seen an appreciable increase in literary productivity, the measure of which becomes quite apparent when one starts putting a bibliography together—without even including all the unpublished works Miriam Cooke has documented in *War's Other Voices.*

The themes and forms of Arab literature have evolved and matured. The problems of living in the war-torn Middle East are so intense, urgent, and horrible that new forms are created to meet the needs. For an author writing in a shelter, while waiting to cross the demarcation line, or while being kept in a basement as a hostage, work has to be done fast and without basic comfort. Short poems, often surrealistic (since they are more difficult to decode), will be a form often used. As in the main corpus, war novels include a blend of poetry and prose, realism and symbolism, but they delight in surrealism, in the absurd, in extreme irony.[4] Such modes of expression become a refuge from the war's cruelty and inhumanity. Through distortions, through irony approaching baroque complexities, through emphasis on the absurd, the author can reverse the war's effects. In this respect, there is a marked similarity between female and male authors and between those writing in Arabic and in French. A notable difference between how women and men authors treat war stems not from the style and techniques, but from the way they view war and the solutions or lack of them they foresee. That is the central topic of this study.

NOTES

1. This research constitutes more than ninety cassettes of taped interviews that I have transcribed and organized for a future publication.
2. For an excellent overview and an in-depth analysis of the novels about the war, see Miriam Cooke's *War's Other Voices: Women Writers on the Lebanese Civil War, 1975–82.*
3. See Georg Lukács, "Realism in Our Time"; *The Theory of the Novel.* See also Fredric Jameson, *The Political Unconscious: Narrative as a Socially Symbolic Act.*
4. See in particular the works of Vénus Khoury-Ghata, Ghada al-Samman, and Rachid al-Daʿif.

PART I

Unveiling Sexuality in War

The connection between admired masculinity and violent response to threat is a resource that governments can use to mobilise support for war.

It has become a matter of urgency for humans as a group to undo the tangle of relationships that sustains the nuclear arms race. Masculinity is part of this tangle. It will not be easy to alter. The pattern of an arms race, i.e. mutual threat, itself helps sustain an aggressive masculinity.

Bob Connell, "Masculinity, Violence and War"

ONE

Sexuality and Sexual Politics: Conflicts and Contradictions for Contemporary Women

But the only hunger I have ever known was the hunger for sex and the hunger for freedom and somehow, in my mind and heart, they were related and certainly not mutually exclusive. If I could not use the source of my hunger as the source of my activism, how then was I to be politically effective?

Cherrie Moraga, *Loving in the War Years*

Sexuality seems to have a revolutionary potential so strong that many political women and men are afraid of it. They prefer to dismiss its importance by arguing that it is not as central as the economic and political factors that are easily recognizable as involving the major contradictions — such as class inequalities, hunger, poverty, lack of job opportunities — that produce revolutions. But sexuality is linked to all these other factors and to get at the roots of the important issues confronting us today, it can no longer be ignored.

I would like to suggest the importance of sexuality and sexual relations and the centrality of sexuality and male domination to the political and national struggles occurring in the Middle East. To illustrate these concepts, I will examine the recent sociological, anthropological, and political studies dealing with aggression, violence, war, and the role of women in the Middle East. I will analyze aspects of nationalism and how they relate to sexuality and to women's traditional roles in society. Finally, I will show how feminist movements are often weakened and threatened by internal dissensions and by subordination to national struggles, the oppressed turning their anger against themselves instead of against the oppressor, in a process described at great length by Frantz Fanon in *Les damnés de la terre*.

Many authors have started looking at these connections, because they realize their importance. Miranda Davies' compilation of articles in *Third World—Second Sex: Women's Struggles and National Liberation* is a good example. In her preface, she states: "As they begin to recognize and identify the specific nature of their double oppression, many women in the Third World realize that, when needed, they may join guerrilla movements, participate in the economy, enter politics and organize trade unions, but at the end of the day they are still seen as women, second-class citizens, inferior to men, bearers of children, and domestic servants" (p. iii). In "Femmes: Une oppression millénaire," Anne-Marie de Vilaine argues that history is founded on a masculine logic, masking the economic and sexual exploitation of women behind political, scientific, or ethical arguments (p. 17). And Jean-William Lapierre, coauthor of the same work, goes along with her analysis, noting: "It is undeniable that half the population of the human race, namely women, have often been neglected by historical knowledge" (p. 18). Such statements emphasize the secondary importance given to sexuality and to women's issues. They indicate how urgent it has become to deal with them as major dilemmas.

Sexuality is much more fundamental in social and political problems than previously thought, and unless a sexual revolution is incorporated into political revolution, there will be no real transformation of social relations. As Andrea Dworkin puts it: "To transform the world we must transform the very substance of our erotic sensibilities and we must do so as consciously and as conscientiously as we do any act which involves our whole lives" (*Marx and Gandhi Were Liberals,* p. 6).

By *sexual revolution* I mean a revolution that starts at the personal level, with a transformation of attitudes toward one's mate, family, sexuality, and society and, specifically, a transformation of the traditional relations of domination and subordination that permeate interpersonal relationships, particularly those of sexual and familial intimacy. Developing an exchange of love, tenderness, equal sharing, and recognition among people would create a more secure and solid basis for change in other spheres of life—political, economic, social, religious, and national—for these are often characterized by similar rapports of domination. As Elisabeth Badinter insightfully expresses:

Equality, which is taking place, gives birth to likeness, which stops war. Each protagonist wanting to be the "whole" of humanity can better understand the Other who has become his or her double. The feelings that unite this couple of mutants can only change in nature. Strangeness disappears, replaced by "familiarity." We may lose some passion and desire, but gain tenderness and complicity, the feelings that unite members of the same family: a mother to her child, a brother to his sister. . . . At last, all those who have dropped their weapons. (P. 245)

By *political revolution,* I mean a revolution primarily motivated by nationalism, in the context of colonialism or neocolonialism. If all of the various political parties trying to dominate a small piece of territory in Lebanon and impose their vision of what Lebanon ought to be were to unite and believe in their country as an entity not to be possessed and used but to be loved and respected without domination, we could work more positively towards resolution, and much of the internal violence, destruction, and conflict would cease. Nationalism—belief and love of one's country—in this context, seems a necessity. This affirmation may sound simplistic, overly optimistic, and naïve given the political forces at stake and the foreign interferences in Lebanon. Nevertheless, I wish to state it and emphasize it throughout this study because I believe it is valid and a real hope for Lebanon's survival, as should become clearer as the study progresses.

I use the term *nationalism* within the perspective stated above and in a way I will elaborate further. Nationalism is a difficult notion about which much is written, much of it conflicting. In both East and West, in old and new concepts of the term, nationalism is a complex component of revolutionary discourse. It can be deployed in all the various facets of political power. For example, nationalism in one extreme form can be fascism. In "Fascisme et mystification misogyne," Thérèse Vial-Mannessier gives a summary of Maria-Antonietta Macciocchi's analysis of fascist ideology in Italy from and throughout the feminine universe. For her, although the collective irrational is at work in all human groups, and although conscious and unconscious forces led the masses from a transcendance of the individual ego into total allegiance to the Italian Nation—to fascism—women, the first victims of this process, adhered to fascist ideology through a masochism ready for all possible sacrifices. According to Macciocchi:

Fascism from its very beginning tried to bring women to an adherence I would describe as masochistic: acceptance, in a death wish [Freud], of all possible solutions. In the name of an immutable ritual, the cult of the dead, widows celebrated their own chastity—expiation in the middle of sculls that the fascists had chosen as their emblem. . . . From this renunciation of life, joy as negation of the self was born, joy in the relationship of women with Power; sacrifice, subordination, domestic slavery, in return for an abstract, wordy, demagogical love of the Chief, the Duce. (P. 156)

Vial-Mannessier's reading of Macciocchi leads her to ask if these forces are not also at work in any social formation. And if so, couldn't this emotional, primitive, and collective power, freed from its mystifying shield, become the necessary element of any political project? She ends with a quotation from Macciocchi's *Les femmes et leurs maîtres* suggesting that, thanks to a new rapport between men and women, a "new continent in history" is being opened up.

While nationalism has been necessary for the young Arab states gaining their autonomy from colonialism, it nevertheless, like fascism, "reclaimed many of the most patriarchal values of Islamic traditionalism as integral to Arab cultural identity as such" as Mai Ghousoub puts it in "Feminism—or the Eternal Masculine—in the Arab World." She states that "the political rights of women, nominally granted by the national state, are in practice a dead letter, since these are military dictatorships of one kind or another, in which the suffrage has no meaning." Her analysis explains how:

Colonialism was lived by the Arabs not simply as a domination or oppression, but as a *usurpation* of power. The principal victims of this complex were to be Arab women. For the cult of a grandiose past, and the 'superiority of our values to those of the West', inevitably led to a suffocating rigidity of family structures and civil codes. Everywhere, under the supposedly modernizing regimes of 'national revolution', the laws governing the domestic and private sphere—marriage, divorce, children—continue to be based on the Shariʿa. The justification of this relentlessly retrogade nexus is always the same. (P. 8)

She adds a very significant remark, one that affected me personally because I, too, have been threatened with it several times in my life: "How many times has every Arab feminist had to listen to men's arrogant refrain: 'Do you want to become like Western women, copying the degenerate society that is our enemy?' " (p. 11). Such comments are meant to make Arab women's criticism of their society weaker, by playing with the political forces at stake, setting them against each other in a tactic of "divide and conquer": East against West, oppressed against oppressor, colonized against colonizer. It is not that these issues are without importance or should not be discussed seriously, but in this context, such remarks show the weakness of the men who make them, their *using* such questions to divert the *real* issue because they are unwilling to look at the problems of their society.

Several definitions of nationalism have recently been given by women writing about war. They often see it in contrast to patriotism. Jean Bethke Elshtain in *Women and War* sees patriotism as attached more to the sense of a political and moral community than to a state and as therefore able to bring out the best in us; nationalism, on the other hand, like the language of war, oversimplifies and can arouse the worse. Miriam Cooke, in *War's Other Voices,* goes along with this definition and sees patriotism as intertwined with female and male images—*patria* as mother earth to whom loyalty is a congenital duty, *pater* as the father who commands loyalty at once gentle and appropriate—while nationalism is a kind of imperialist ideology that imposes uniformity on geographic areas that may be infinitely extended. I would challenge these definitions on the grounds that *patriotism* refers more to *father* than to *mother,* its roots going to patriarchy—rule of the fathers—a concept I hardly want to be loyal to. Even if we could trace it back to the mother, how can such loyalty preserve us from war? A humanist like Camus, when confronted with conflicting loyalties between France and Algeria's independence, declared that between justice and his mother he would choose his mother, France.

Specifically in the case of Lebanon, a country mosaic in ethnic groups and religions, what political entity could help bring it unity? Patriotism? Matriotism? Nationalism? A mixture of many elements? For Georges Corm: "Lebanese culture is a pluralistic, universal one, rich in the best religious traditions of freedom, tolerance and understanding between the various tenants of the Christian and Moslem patrimony. . . . Future generations will be able to have a national culture only if, wanting it, they take good care of this Lebanese patrimony in its true authenticity, meaning its universal pluralism, which each Lebanese ought to know and be proud of" (*Géopolitique du conflit libanais,* p. 245). Here also, *patrimony* refers to *pater, father.* If language has significance beyond the conscious levels of our understanding, should we not be careful with the words we choose? Said differently, is Corm aware that *patrimony* refers to a whole patriarchal structure that needs to be revolutionized?

Other more recent analyses of nationalism see it as closely connected to national economy, which, in the context of today's domination by multinational corporations, transforms the concept into *transnationalism.* A whole issue of *Peuples méditerranéens* is devoted to these relations, asking in its title whether we are witnessing "The End of the National?" [1] Are we going into the era of the transnational? What is the connection among development and consumption as a new way of relating to the world, the urban as a universal form for life, the increase in migrant workers and boundaries of the national? What do the state, the nation, and their specific articulation of the previous capitalist period become? Is a world polity conceivable? Isn't a new bipartition of the world, between those included in production and consumerism and those excluded, occurring, crossing all social formations, substituting for the old center-periphery division between industrialized and Third World countries? Several authors consider these questions and bring to light some important aspects of the national. In "Du transnational au politique-monde," Paul Vieille sees the nation—a solidarity group led by a state aiming at defending the interests of its members against other nation-states—being replaced by transborder solidarities, such as those of Muslims, the disinherited, the poor, the urban masses. This transnational solidarity is not yet structured but works in the feeling and imagination of the masses and transforms the role of the state. Historically, nation-states were constituted against one another. Each state made a nation through a mixture of consensus and violence. The state was defined by a national economy and its redistribution within its borders; its rule was national selfishness. Today, the link between nation and state is being broken. The state is being transnationalized and becoming the place of the political articulation of the space it controls. In a transnational economy, the state no longer functions within national boundaries but on a world scale. The nation enters a crisis; the feeling of belonging falls back on infranational groups, or becomes universalized, or transforms the notion of *nation* itself —which is no longer a political institution, but a cultural choice. The revival and growth of religious identities can be better understood in light of nation-states' failure to fulfill people's needs of belonging to a "national" culture, which, having developed at the time of nation-states, has had little impact on these populations.

Hele Beji in "La métatamorphose nationale: De l'indépendance à l'aliénation," sees the national in constant dramatic roles vying between attraction and rejection of the European model. It is a conflict between nationalism and colonialism still going on today because nationalism has not really established firm foundations. And René Gallissot in "Transnationalisation et renforcement de l'ordre étatique," argues that religious nationalism offers false hopes to the masses who have lost confidence in the nation-state. The state now defines the people as opposed to nationalities that are shared, dispersed (in diasporas), or given minority status. "Transnationalization" or "denationalization" may have to do with this transformation of national feelings on behalf of the interests of the state.

Fouad Ajami, in "The Silence in Arab Culture," analyzes Arab nationalism as a project of the intellectuals. From its very beginning in the late nineteenth century, it is "an idea flung in the face of a political order that was always torn by all sorts of conflicts" (p. 30). Interestingly, he sees Arab nationalism overwhelmed by a "ferocious rebellion dubbed as Islamic fundamentalism." Arab nationalism "never really had a theory of practical action, having inherited the remains of the Ottoman Empire that collapsed during World War I; its principal social glue was the political and cultural ascendancy of urban, orthodox (Sunni) Islam, and for the last four decades, its most frequently proclaimed cause was Palestine" (p. 30). Significantly, the movement originated not in the Arab world but in Iran, showing, according to Ajami, the paralysis of Arab politics.

In light of the more recent developments of nation-states, are we correct in raising this issue in the context of Lebanon? If transnational rules the world, what impact can the national have? Is it not precisely transnationalism that brought the confrontation to its peak in Lebanon, feeding the inside animosities of the various clans from the outside? And if this analysis is correct, can we hope for a solution only from the outside? For me, this inside/outside opposition is closely related to the private/public one as well as to conflicts between professional realms, sexual and political ones, in a way that will become clear throughout this book. I would argue that if we do not work on both, trying to integrate the two in the main struggle for liberation, we are not likely to see tangible results.

In its political organization, Lebanon was not a real nation-state. There was a tribal layer between the state and the families. A culture going beyond ethnic borders grew. Even though the Lebanese state was not a nation-state as such, pluralism—acceptance of others' differences—developed. This is particularly remarkable in view of the political institutions that maintained differences among various communities, reinforced domination of one over others, and institutionalized these relations through a "national agreement." Lebanon became fragile because its political institutions did not represent its people. The domination of ethnic groups became unacceptable when international configurations were changing. Lebanese national identity is linked to the notion of pluralism, acceptance of the other. This is the real hope at the core of the Lebanese tragedy. In Lebanon, both the outside forces—the Syrian and Israeli occupations, the big powers' interferences, the Palestinian desperate struggles—and the inside tribal wars have equally brought the crisis to its peak. It is therefore necessary to work at solving both aspects of the conflict in order to reach results. The resolution of opposition between these two sides can be compared to the feminist association of the otherwise opposed personal and political realms, an association that has acquired even greater meaning in the present Lebanese situation.

In the Middle East, nationalism and feminism have never mixed very well. Women were used in national liberation struggles—in Algeria, Iran, Palestine, to name only a few—only to be sent back to their kitchens after "'independence" had been gained.[2] As Monique Gadant expresses in her introduction to *Women of the Mediterranean:*

Nationalism asked of women a participation that they were quick to give, they fought and were caught in the trap. For nationalism is frequently conservative, even though it appears to be an inevitable moment of political liberation and economic progress which women need to advance along the path to their own liberation. . . . What does it mean for women to be active in political organizations? The example of Algerian women is there to remind all women that participation does not necessarily win them rights. From the point of view of those women contributors who have grown up after a war of liberation, everything is still to be done. (P. 2)

To those who believe that it is utopia to think that feminism and nationalism can ever blend, I would like to first suggest, that it has never been tried, since sexuality has never been conceptualized as being at the center of the problem in the Middle East, and, second, that if an analysis of sexuality and sexual relations were truly incorporated into revolutionary struggle in Lebanon, nationalism could be transformed into a more revolutionary strategy. If women were to demand their rights and a transformation of values and roles in the family at the beginning of national struggles and if national struggles were conceived with different aims that would not perpetuate domination and ownership, we would move toward a different concept of revolution than we have witnessed so far in history. If both aimed at transforming society toward similar values, the often-raised contradiction between nationalism and women's liberation would be erased. If this is utopia, I gladly go along with Jean-William Lapierre's beautifully expressed concept of the role of utopia: for him "utopia is the exploration of the possible" (p. 25).

In most discussions of Third World feminism, sexuality and the privatized oppression of women by men are relegated to secondary issues. When sexuality and/or male domination are raised as significant issues, conflicts arise over the validity of Marxism versus feminism, economic equality versus sexual equality, national revolution versus women's rights, as if each of these sets of concepts must involve opposition—as if the life of one meant the death of the other. For instance, at the "Common Differences: Third World Women and Feminist Perspectives" conference at the University of Illinois in April 1983, a major conflict emerged between those women who believed sexuality and male domination to be central issues and those who believed class and imperialism to be central. Mostly Marxist women, speaking in the name of Third World women, claimed that economic issues, such as food and shelter, were far more important than sex. They accused U.S. lesbians at the conference of over-emphasizing sex, particularly lesbianism. As I listened to these arguments, I felt that they were very "paternalistic" and perhaps irrelevant; first, because sex is one of the basic needs —like food and sleep—in any culture, second, because no mention was made of the spiritual and/or psychological needs for love, affection, and tenderness, intimately connected with sexuality, felt by people in most cultures. To claim that some women live without these needs because of more pressing economic factors seems not only very unfair, but an exercise that only some intellectuals can afford. And third, from my research in the Middle East and North Africa and my analysis of the war in Lebanon, I believe that sexuality and sex-role socialization are intimately connected to national and international conflicts. Ghita El Khayat-Bennaï, the first woman doctor/psychiatrist in Morocco, in her thorough analysis *Le monde arabe au féminin* says: "Women's liberation necessarily goes through their sexual fulfillment, and, if psychoanalysis has been one of the sources for feminism, in spite of all its insufficiencies in terms of women, it is because it allowed the right to desire and pleasure" (p. 258). She notices that it is men's fear of women, in particular of their sexuality, that leads men to subjugate and oppress them. The fascination and horror a man feels for a woman makes him take away the little pleasure she has. El Khayat-Bennaï further claims that Arab societies are the most repressive in terms of sexuality and that Arab societies' decline is closely linked to the female oppression (p. 260).

Many important studies by women and men in the last few years see a link between sexuality and national/international conflicts. Jean-William Lapierre, for example, sees a "deep connection between masculine predominance and the importance of war" (p. 21). According to him, most civilizations are based on conquest and war. "The importance of hunting, then of war in social existence, in economic resources, in cultural models (which valorize the warrior exploits), are at the roots of masculine domination and of women's oppression" (p. 21). He explains how in so-called "modern" societies, politics, industry and business are always a kind of war whereby one (mostly men, and sometimes women imitating men's behavior) must be energetic, aggressive, and strong to be powerful. Still, it is not only capitalist societies that "carry war like clouds carry the storm, but productivism in all its forms, including the so-called 'socialistic' one. In all societies in which economy and politics require a spirit of competition (while its ethic exalts it) women are oppressed" (p. 22).

Contrary to the perspectives of many intellectuals and political women and men involved either in the United States or the Middle East, my interviews with many rural and urban women indicate that sexuality is of utmost concern to women's lives. In fact, it is often women from the most needy levels of society who are the most outspoken on the subject of sex, love, and their relationships to their husbands and family and who, contrary to what some intellectuals have expressed, see the need for change in these areas of their lives. Perhaps it is because they have not interpreted and analyzed their needs from within the framework of patriarchal ways of thinking (such as Marxism, nationalism, capitalism) that they can be so outspoken. For example, in Oran, Algeria, in 1983, I interviewed about half a dozen maids at the hotel where I was staying. Most of them lived in polygamous relationships and had to wear the veil when going out. Most of them expressed revolt against both of these customs, polygamy and the veil, and wished for different conditions for their daughters. In 1978, I visited the hospitals in the United Arab Emirates and conducted interviews with dozens of women living in various oases and remote places. They too expressed to me revolt against their condition—having to produce a child every year with the threat of repudiation or of their husbands taking a younger wife if they did not, and wearing the *burqa* (a stiff, mask-type face cover that leaves purplish-blue marks when one sweats).[3] And in the interviews I had with about a dozen women in Umdurman, Sudan, in 1983, they expressed their unhappiness with the practice of infibulation, their suffering from it, their desire to change customs that mutilate them, for the sake of their daughters, and the difficulties they had faced in their attempts.[4] I am not claiming here representation through numbers, but through the validity of these strong testimonies.

Some women asked me to shut the cassette recorder off when they talked about sexuality, and some burst into tears when talking about intimate experiences in their lives. I wondered, as I listened and talked with women, why there was so much pain in remembering past events in their lives connected with sexuality, yet so much resistance and denial around a political analysis of sexuality? Given the way in which feminist intellectuals have dealt with sexuality, at least at the conferences that I have attended, the issues are far more central than anyone is willing to admit. At the 1985 conference "Quel féminisme pour le Maghreb?" in Tunisia, and at the "Common Differences" conference in Illinois, the topic of sexuality, with all of its ramifications, divided women and created enormous amounts of tension. Women who chose to speak out on sexuality were ostracized by a majority of the other feminist intellectuals. At the conference in Illinois, women viciously attacked one another when addressing the issues of sexuality. One of the participants at the Tunisian conference, Ilham Ben Milad Ben Ghadifa, provided an analysis of the centrality of sexuality and yet of its denial on the part of political women. Because of her analysis and her willingness to speak in such an environment, she felt ostracized and had to leave the country.

At the conference, she began with a discussion of why she had decided to lift the veil of silence regarding her condition, to get rid of autocensorship (a word that acquired great significance when I lived in Tunisia, witnessing its way of killing creativity and freedom in several women to whom I became close): it was so that she would no longer be her own enemy. She felt that Tunisian feminists were silent on three issues: the female body, female relationships, and sexual identity. Silence, she suggested, reigns over the subject of menstruation, virginity, masturbation, pleasure in general, abortion, birth, and the female body as a whole. Moreover, women try to enforce silence on one another with regard to sexual issues. Fear and autocensorship were two key factors preventing women from wanting to explore these issues, silencing women on the topic of sexuality because the subject is too close to home and to their personal lives. As a result, women have become gossips about other women who are open about sexual issues, and this has widened the malaise and tensions. As Ilham put it:

Women's hatred expresses itself in many ways. . . . Feminism and gossiping appear as a contradiction. Unfortunately, it is not so. I was the target of gossip by feminists the preceding year, after my talk on "'Feminism and Fecundity." . . .
They accused me of being a prostitute, a divorcée, a lesbian, a robber of husbands, and a scandal, because I refused maternity! I would like to emphasize how all these accusations are related to sexuality. . . .
Gossiping aims at destroying what one is bothered with and seeks to make one feel more secure. It also expresses anxiety over marginality and tries to disarm one's sense of culpability. . . . Apart from trying to repress the other, because one was

not able to free oneself, gossip has two consequences: (1) it prevents the woman who pronounced it from fulfilling her own desires, therefore of knowing herself deeply; (2) it destroys the woman who uttered it, especially when one adds to it bad conscience and the feeling—more or less diffused—of having made a dangerous concession to society, and to the mother. . . .

Isn't the Third World characterized by a dangerous confusion between individuality and individualism, through a most repressive structure of duty? . . .

One more point I would like to analyze before ending is jealousy in the context of love. The woman who arouses one's jealousy is one we feel is stealing something from us, like our mother stole from us our in-depth being, our body. The more a person lives under repression and unsatisfaction, the greater his or her jealousy will be. As if love and pleasure were a totality threatened when shared. As if what we give to the other has been taken away from us. Jealousy will be increased when the person we envy arouses in us also love and admiration. . . . Jealousy is the expression of a lack of confidence in oneself. . . . One can understand why intellectuals have kept silent in this domain: analysis and rationalization are hardly protections against jealousy.[5]

The topic of feminine relations Ilham raised was charged with meaning. It brought to the surface much of the uneasiness I had felt myself in my relationships with some of the women there. Because I had raised issues about the connection of sexuality to war and to nationalism, I had been the target of gossip, as if to make what I had to say less important and even suspect. I was accused of being CIA, engaging in orgies, and stealing boyfriends. Ilham's speech made me feel less isolated and explained to me some of the problems we face as women who are at once committed to political change and to feminism and sexual freedom.

During the conference, there was little discussion of sexuality. There was no discussion of the issues Ilham raised, as had been the case with other presentations. Rather than take up her points, the discussion centered on issues of language and Arab nationalism. Sexuality was hardly touched upon during the rest of the conference, despite the fact that the conference was to have been: "Quel féminisme pour le Maghreb?" Only one other woman used a frank and personal approach, and when she gave testimony of the deep sexual factors that had led her to feminism, her talk was received with extreme uneasiness. Part of the malaise came from the split between the women themselves, their search for identity and the simultaneous realization of the political, economic, and social tensions created by the crisis the Arab world is undergoing.

The discussion of sexuality and its relationship to political and social conflicts is also silenced through women's unquestioning adherence to dogmatic political systems of thinking. Many nationalist and leftist women at both conferences felt that women should rally behind the already existing movements and ideologies. Yet in these movements, traditional morality often filters through dogmas, setting new barriers between women's sense of obligation and their search for truth and freedom. Yolla Polity Charara provides an incisive analysis of this problem as exemplified in Lebanese politics. According to her, many Lebanese women joined political parties thinking that the condition of women would change. In 1975, during the activities organized for International Women's Year, the Democratic party invited the delegates of the political parties in Lebanon to a meeting aimed at weighing the possibilities for a joint women's action. Women from the Phalangist party, the National Block, the Progressive Socialist party, the Ba‘ath party, the Communist party, as well as others from smaller groups found themselves suspicious and indeed rivals. As Charara puts it: "how could it be possible with so many ideological differences and antagonisms, representing the whole range of political forces in Lebanon, not to be divergent on the details of women's demands?" (pp. 19–20). According to Charara, the party and ideological loyalties made women loath to complain about their fate to other unknown women, and even more so to rivals. The militants among them, when conscious of the discrimination women faced, when they were not themselves token women in the party, preferred to wash their dirty laundry within the family; they refused to question publicly the men of their party, to admit that their men were not the most advanced, the most egalitarian, and the most revolutionary. Thus, in such a context, loyalty to a group became more important than the issues themselves.

These examples show the extent to which adherence to a political party, belief in a dogmatic ideology—even in the name of liberation—and blind commitment to any war strategy can harm women's unity. Instead of being frank with each other, discussing the problems openly, going to the roots in sexuality, in relationships to men, family and society, women hide the sexual source of their conflicts under the pretext of loyalty towards the men or the ideology of their group. As long as women are not ready to shed their masks and masculine discourses, as long as they have not grasped the importance of their solidarity outside of power games, the discovery of their common points for a common struggle and their liberation that can bring the rebirth of society will not take place. As Charara says, women from the various parties could have united on many issues—equality between men and women, optional civil marriage, application of the law on equal pay, generalization of education for girls, better professional training for girls, and extension of crèches—but, given "the anguish provoked by the agenda. . . . There was great reticence in admitting there were problems at all. Thus, if there were few women in the party, this was because women lacked consciousness; if they did not hold responsible positions, this was because they were not sufficiently competent—the party itself did not discriminate. Women found themselves using standard male modes of thought in regard to other women: they talked like men" (p. 23).

The national wars of liberation — in Algeria, Iran, Palestine, to name a few — have shown the negative role ideologies of liberation, even leftist ones, have played in women's movements. Women, used to win victory, were quickly sent back to the homes, the kitchens — their place in history — once the new power was in place. These national struggles were and are necessary, but they occur in the name of ideologies that have not taken root in the daily experiences of the people and of women. As one Palestinian woman, Soraya Antonius, expresses:

I have progressive ideas but I can't implement them fully. . . . Men are my comrades but deep down they don't believe I'm really their equal. Socially we haven't caught up with our political development. . . . I'm 36 and I haven't yet met a man who has really shaken off the old conventions about women. . . . And the leaders are hypocritical about it all. At public meetings they talk about liberating women but they really believe, and some of them say it openly, that a woman does her revolutionary duty by ironing her husband's shirts, cooking his dinner and providing a cosy and restful ambience for the warrior. (Pp. 74–75)

Ghita El Khayat-Bennaï contends that it is "as if revolutions lie in their promises to all women, a guarantee for a change in their condition being included in the revolutionary concept itself. Women always get fooled. The examples are numerous whatever type of revolution, its doctrines and ambitions: the Algerian, the Iranian, the Soviet. . . . The Arab world has only experienced the tomorrows of revolutions that put women back in their ancient place . . . but these revolutions also revealed the profound contradictions hindering Arab women" (pp. 239, 281). This is why I am underlining once more the necessity of combining both nationalism — in order to save a country — and feminism — in order to save women and all of society — for salvation to last, for it to carry on to a world scale.

It is obvious from all of my experiences in the Middle East, as well as in the United States, that sexuality stirs in people reactions that go far deeper than mere intellectual exercises. It brings out gut reactions that go far beyond conscious levels of explanation. It is also evident that sexuality often works together with what may appear as more tangible factors — political, economic, social, and religious choices. It is part of the psychological, physical, and spiritual levels of human existence because these aspects are all mixed with sexuality. As such, it seems quite obvious that if sexuality is not incorporated into the main feminist and political struggles, the struggles for freedom will remain on a very superficial level. A problem cannot be solved without going to its roots.

If women do not begin to see the necessity of dealing with issues of sexuality, more women will feel isolated, rejected, and misunderstood, even within groups leading the struggle for liberation. More will feel pushed to leave for other places in the hope of finding better acceptance and tolerance elsewhere, or they will simply drop out of political struggle. Under the cover of progressive dogmas, some Western and Eastern feminists will continue to speak in the name of all Third World women, triggering in many women a retreat into "national identity" or selfless and sexless political ideology, neither of which speaks to women's experience and struggles in their own lives. What happened at the "Common Differences" conference is an illustration of such reaction. In the name of leftist ideology, some feminists addressed the issues of Third World women for development, food, shelter to take precedence over sexuality. This led to such violent arguments that many women felt caught and pressured into "taking sides," which led some to walk out of the conference. These reactions are expressions for power — a repetition of what historically have been male patterns of behavior. Much of the time women spoke for another group through an already existing dogma, rather than working towards an analysis that could incorporate the pain and suffering women are subjected to in all parts of life.

In this chapter, I have given some definitions of nationalism as it presents itself today and as I would like to see it evolve and work with feminism rather than against it, as it has done so far. Lebanese nationalism, or *Lebanism*, means electing to belong to a culture conceived as pluralistic, as accepting others' differences. The concept of *nation* thereby changes and becomes the popular claim for a political identity from which the state is born. The nation-state built on the war of the sexes is thus transformed.

But recognition of the other also applies to sexual differences, to the relationship between men and women, as well as to the various religious communities. In these terms, a new movement, with a redefined *femihu-*

manism (I am using this expression rather than *feminism* because I believe that both women and men must work together to bring about the changes), working with a reformed nationalism stripped of its male chauvinism, war, and violence, is being conceptualized.

NOTES

1. *Peuples méditerranéens*, 35–36 (1986). See in particular: Yann Moulier Boutang, "Du double visage de la catégorie du transnational"; Laënnec Hurbon, "Les productions des dictatures dans le Tiers-Monde"; Hele Beji, "La métamorphose nationale: De l'indépendence à l'aliénation"; René Gallissot, "Transnationalisation et renforcement de l'ordre étatique"; Serge Latouche, "Les déboires du nouvel ordre économiques international et la transnationalité économique"; Christine Fauré, "Les droits de l'homme, le transnational, et la question des femmes"; Paul Vieille, "Du transnational au politique-monde?"

2. See Miranda Davies' *Third World—Second Sex: Women's Struggles and National Liberation, Third World Women Speak Out:* "The Role of Women in National Liberation Movements," pp. 61–96, in particular, Soraya Antonius' "Fighting on Two Fronts: Conversations with Palestinian Women" and "The Experience of Armed Struggle"; "After the Revolution," pp. 125–72, in particular, "Iranian Women: The Struggle Since the Revolution," by the London Iranian Women's Liberation Group; and "An Autonomous Women's Movement?" pp. 173–94, in particular, "Why an Autonomous Women's Movement?" by the Paris Latin American Women's Group.

3. Miriam Cooke has pointed out to me that *burqa* is made of indigo-impregnated cotton. I purchased one while visiting the Emirates, and to me, it looks more like some thick heavy material. It has two layers: the top one, a kind of cardboard and the next, a thin cloth.

4. As I mentioned earlier, the results of my field research and the interviews I conducted over the last few years would be too large and numerous to incorporate in this book. I am organizing the material, the bulk of which will provide another publication.

5. Ilham Ben Milad Ben Ghadifa, taped unpublished talk. When I wrote Ilham asking if I could mention her by name, or if she preferred to remain anonymous, she replied: "Please get me out of anonymity which weighs on me and is slowly killing me. But what name should I use? Ben Milad—my father's?—Boussen —my mother's?—Ben Ghadifa—my husband's—or just my surname which is not enough? How does one solve this problem?"

TWO

An Occulted Aspect of the War in Lebanon

'Personal' relations are so basic to the dynamics which sustain the military's grip on social policy that militarism cannot be pushed back so long as dominance, control and violence are considered 'natural' ordering principles in relations between men and women—i.e. so long as patriarchy is deemed 'normal'.

Cynthia Enloe, *Does Khaki Become You?*

At a very deep level feminism is recognized as a powerful peace force—not only in the sense of the term as an intervention in a course of violence, but more significantly as a vital energy for peace. Feminism is a force for the transcendence of organized violence, violence rooted in sexism, strengthened by sexist values, and perpetuated by male-chauvinist behavior.

Betty Reardon, *Sexism and the War System*

The importance of incorporating a discourse on sexuality when formulating a revolutionary feminist theory became even more evident as I started analyzing and writing about the Lebanese war. The war itself seems closely connected with the way people perceive and act out their sense of love and power, as well as their sense of relationship to their partners, to the family, and to the general society. The argument has often been made that women's issues detract from the war effort, that wars create such conditions of despair that women's issues are unimportant within this context, and that if the "right" side in a war were to win, women's problems would automatically be solved. I would like to argue the reverse. I would suggest that sexuality is centrally involved in motivations to war, and if women's issues were dealt with from the beginning, wars might be avoided, and revolutionary struggles and movements for liberation would take a very different path. Justice cannot be won in the midst of injustice.

The whole range of oppression women suffer in the Middle East— forced marriage, virginity, and the codes of honor, claustration, the veil, polygamy, repudiation, beating, lack of freedom and the denial of the possibility to achieve their aims and desires in life (some of which practices motivated me to run away from Lebanon at the age of twenty-two)—are closely connected to the *internal* war in Lebanon (I am not referring to the Israeli and Syrian occupations, nor to the foreign interferences). There are at least seventeen political parties—with many subdivisions—fighting each other in Lebanon. Each of these parties has different interests; each tries to dominate a small piece of territory and impose its vision of Lebanon onto that territory. For example, some of the Christian groups believe they are the descendants of the Phoenicians, admire the Crusaders, and generally have tended to be pro-West, while some of the Moslem groups believe Lebanon belongs to the Arab world and as such ought to be Moslem and Eastern. As Halim Barakat expresses it in *Lebanon in Strife:*

The different Lebanese religious communities identify with, and to a great extent model themselves after, different outside groups. On the whole, the Christian Lebanese, and more particularly the Maronites, have looked to the Western nations for protection, inspiration, and education. . . . Some Christian Lebanese have aspired to model Lebanon after Switzerland, others after France. There are also those who call for a Mediterranean unity and consider Arab unity an unrealistic endeavor. It is fair, however, to say that many Christian Lebanese have contributed to the rebirth of Arab culture and some of them are strongly alienated from the West. On the other hand, and on the whole, the affinities of Moslem Lebanese are with the Arab nation. They have identified with other Arab countries and adopted Arab causes as their own. (P. 40)

Barakat fails to tell us what this Arab nation is all about. He is overconfident concerning Arab causes, most specifically the Palestinian one, the so-called Arab cause par excellence. But the Arab countries (the Arab nation?) only paid lip-service to their "dear" cause and abandoned it when it was in most need of support, during the Israeli invasion of Lebanon. Fathia Saoudi, a Palestinian nurse who lived through the siege, wonders: "But where is Arab oil? We do not have the slightest drop to run the operating machines. Why don't they have the courage to send a tanker to Beirut? But perhaps Arab oil is being used for American planes?" (p. 116). Keeping in mind that Barakat tries to find the causes of the conflict, while Andrée Chedid looks at the makeup of the country, Chedid's assessment of Lebanese culture seems more fair and accurate. She sees "in each Lebanese a double inclination for both Europeanization and Arabization; a complex situation, sometimes contradictory, often harmonized" (*Liban,* p. 116).

Whatever the case may be, each group has tried to dominate the others largely through the control of women in a way I will try to formulate. One of the codes of Arab tribes is *sharaf* (honor), which also means the preservation of girls' virginity to ensure that the women are kept exclusively for the men of their tribe. As Ghita El Khayat-Bennaï explains:

The clan and the tribe, as well as the parental structures linked to it, are characteristic of the Arabo-Moslem civilization. . . . It is very significant that the conjugal couple as a base of the social reality does not exist, but instead, that groups of kinship superior to the immediate family dominate. It is also very significant that in these kinship structures, women's condition should be extremely particular, notably in its links with the conception of honor so much valued in the society. Thus, woman's condition in the midst of the family enlightens all the prejudices and the commonplaces that characterize it, including the crimes of honor, the harem, and the veil. (Pp. 56–57)

Women's lives are regulated not by national laws but by community ones. All legal questions related to individual status are legislated by denominational laws. Each creed has a different legislation. For example, there is no civil marriage in Lebanon. Marriage, divorce, separation, custody of children, and inheritance are resolved according to one's confession, one's religious denomination. A couple is obliged to marry in one of the official religions: Maronite, Greek Catholic, Greek Orthodox, Protestant, Shiʿite, Sunni, or Druze. A couple wanting a civil marriage—because they are from mixed religious communities, say, or atheist—has to go to Cyprus or to another country in order to obtain one. Each of the group's laws, rites, practices, and psychological and sexual pressures aim at keeping their women exclusively for the men of their community. As El Khayat-Bennaï says: "Adding that inside each community, one keeps the women only for oneself and is careful not to have them taken by a rival opposing community, one would have concluded the question of the Lebanese woman" (p. 244). If we want a solution to this horrible war, it seems to me essential to start reforming and revolutionizing such a system that, through religion, divides people into clans and oppresses women to maintain the separation.

Women not only side with the men of their group and feel loyalty for their party rather than other women, they also divide themselves and are divided according to various community groups. In Barakat's view, the sources of the civil war include loyalty of the Lebanese to their sectarian, kinship, and local communities, rather than to the country as a whole; increasing legitimization of the sectarian system; and nonseparation of religion from the state, which has prevented the adoption of secularism and civil marriage, among other causes (*Lebanon in Strife*, p. 189). Women's roles and the way sexuality is lived are closely connected to this system. If the different religious groups were to unite on common beliefs—such as the existence and love of Lebanon, the separation of religion and state, a reform of the educational system—they could move towards dialogue rather than deadly strife. And this can take place with a basic change of values, the development of feelings of love, sharing, forgiveness, tolerance, and acceptance of the other.

Violence nourishes itself on the Lebanese confessional system. Throughout his study Georges Corm documents how aggressiveness and violence are founded on the structure of the communities. He analyzes how violence increases and becomes uncontrollable in the present Lebanese situation: "once started, this violence becomes cumulative, especially in a society where the dead must be revenged, and in light of a failing State. In the kidnappings and counterkidnappings, the reprisals and counterreprisals, sometimes spontaneous, sometimes organized, a ruthless amplification of violence follows, where those who have started the death machine disappear in the anonymity of the militias; in fact, the militias not only commit acts of barbary on the territories they control, but often instigate them" (*Géopolitique du conflit libanais*, p. 97).

Arab society in general, and Lebanese society in particular, has always had pride in the *zaʿim* (leaders, chief, hero). The *zaʿim* is the macho man par excellence. He embodies not only all the usual masculine values of conquest, domination, competition, fighting, and boasting, but also that of *shatara* (cleverness). *Shatara* refers to an ability to succeed and get what one wants, even through lying and perfidy. *Zaʿim* and *shatara* are concepts much valued in tribal society. The Lebanese war has transformed the *zaʿim* into the *askari* (man-with-the-gun, militiaman). The *askari* has technical military training, and his goal is the "self-preservation" of his group. In addition to his military role and his socioeconomic function, he has played and continues to play a role that is most violently destructive of his country and therefore of his sexuality as well. He uses weapons of war to destroy and seize control of one region or of another group. He participates in looting to benefit his family and to extend the range of his influence. Given the extension of his influence, he builds a system of wealth distribution and gains even more power. Material goods and gains are obtained through his gun and other war arsenals. It is a "primitive" system, and it involves a vicious destructive cycle, rather than a self-preserving one. The more men desire omnipotence and the control of others, the more weapons are used. The means of conquest are given a value in proportion to their success. The gun, the machinegun, the canon—all masculine sexual symbols—are put forward and used to conquer and destroy. As Adam Farrar argues, there is a kind of *jouissance,* which means pleasure in a sexual sense, in war:

One of the main features of the phenomenology of war is the unique intensity of experience. War experience is exactly the converse of alienation. In war, the elimination of all the norms of intersubjectivity produces, not alienation, but the most intense *jouissance.* The machining of events on the plane of intensity (to use the Deleuzian image), the form of desire, is utterly transformed. Power no longer consists in the capacity to redeem the warrants of communicative intersubjectivity. It consists in the ability of the spear, the sword, the gun, napalm, the bomb etc. to manifest 'in a blast of sound and energy and light' (or in another time, in the blood of a severed limb or a disembowelled body), the merest 'wish flashing across your mind like a shadow.' (P. 66)

Quoting an article by William Broyles in *Esquire* entitled "Why Men Love War," Farrar explains that war for men is at some terrible level the closest thing to what childbirth is for women: the initiation into the power of life and death (p. 61). Elisabeth Badinter makes the same connection between the experience of childbirth and war:

The word *ponos,* designating endured pain, applies as much to a young man learning to harden himself as to the pains of childbirth. In this struggle, the woman inverts certain signs of virility. "In order to confront war and to gain access to the status of citizen, the Greek man buckles up; while a woman in labor, on the contrary, loosens her belt. . . . Nevertheless, even reversed, the sign connecting maternity to combat is there." In both cases, man and woman suffer and risk death. Enough to raise themselves to the same level of transcendance. Enough to make the resemblances win over the differences. Across two activities apparently opposed, men and women live a common experience that unites them in the same concept of Humanity rather than isolating them in their sexual specificity. (P. 96)

What Badinter does not pick up is the fundamental difference between creating life in the act of childbirth and destroying it in that of war. Relating the two within a human concept is too general to be of value. Even if the two experiences could be brought together, they would divide rather than unite man and woman. In such an analysis, the victims are not noticed and differentiated.

In the Middle East, the meaning and importance given to a military weapon and to the sexual weapon are equal. Man uses his penis the way he uses his gun: to conquer, control, and possess. Lebanese macho society must be unveiled and condemned because in the present system, men try to obtain material goods and territory, not in order to enjoy them, not out of need, but to enlarge their domain and authority. Similarly, sexual relations are not built on pleasure, tenderness, or love, but on reproduction, the preservation of girls' virginity (the so-called honor of the family), the confinement and control of women for the increase in male prestige, and the overestimation of the penis. Lapierre has shown that this phenomenon exists in almost all civilizations (pp. 21–22). And Bob Connell sees a relationship among masculinity, violence, and war. He says that it is not by chance that the great majority of soldiers are men—of the 22 million people under arms in the world in 1976, 20 million of them were men. "Most of the police, most of the prison warders, and almost all the generals, admirals, bureaucrats and politicians who control the apparatus of coercion and collective violence are men. Most murderers are men. Almost all bandits, armed robbers, and muggers are men; all rapists, most domestic bashers; and most people involved in street brawls, riots and the like" (p. 4). But such an association should be attributed not to biology, which would absolve men of responsibility in terms of some masculine "destiny," but rather to cultural and institutional factors. As Connell argues:

It is very important that much of the actual violence is not isolated and individual action, but is institutional. Much of the poofterbashing [Australian slang for attacking homosexuals] is done by the police; much of the world's rape is done by soldiers. These actions grow readily out of the 'legitimate' violence for which police forces and armies are set up. . . . The state uses one of the great discoveries of modern history, rational bureaucratic organization, to have policy-making centralized and execution down the line fairly uniform. Given this, the state can become the vehicle of calculated violence based on and using hegemonic masculinity. Armies are a kind of hybrid between bureaucracy and masculinity. (Pp. 8–9)

For Connell, it becomes a matter of urgency to analyze and understand how masculinity is entangled in all that threatens the survival of humanity. "Violence is not just an expression; it is a part of the process that divides different masculinities from each other. There is violence within masculinity; it is constitutive" (p. 8).

How violence is expressed in the opposition between religious-confessional culture and national culture has been very well explained by Corm, who sees in the Lebanese confessional system a culture of dissension based on racism, destructive of freedom of expression, encouraging prejudices, and exercising tyranny imposed by the force of weapons. "The strange thing in this affair is that the culture of dissension could have convinced a good number of Lebanese that there can be no existence nor salvation for themselves and their possessions outside of the politicized community setting, when in fact, the sad reality shows, without any question, that the beginning of community games and pursuing them, were and remain the main factors of Lebanon's destruction" (*Géopolitique*, pp. 220–28).

Lebanese society, currently composed of all its disparate groups and individuals, values them, believing they will save the society and guarantee its survival. Yet, in reality, they are leading the society more and more towards death and destruction. The Lebanese people are blinded by their immediate needs, and by values they have been taught to take pride in. The whole system must be changed and rethought. Betty Reardon's words in *Sexism and the War System* are apt in this context:

What I am advocating here is a new world order value, reconciliation, and perhaps even forgiveness, not only of those who trespass against us, but primarily of ourselves. By understanding that no human being is totally incapable of the most reprehensible of human acts, or of the most selfless and noble, we open up the possibilities for change of cosmic dimensions. Essentially this realization is what lies at the base of the philosophy of nonviolence. If we are to move through a disarmed world to a truly nonviolent one, to authentic peace and justice, we must come to terms with and accept the other in ourselves, be it our masculine or our feminine attributes or any of those traits and characteristics we have projected on enemies and criminals, or heroes and saints. (P. 94)

If the attitudes of the people do not undergo profound transformations—radical changes in the way they perceive power and love—there can be no solution to the inextricable dilemma Lebanon is going through. Again, as Reardon puts it:

The fundamental willingness to use violence against others on which warfare depends is conditioned by early training and continuous socialization in patriarchal society. All are taught to respect authority, that is, fear violence. . . . Boys and men are encouraged to become more fierce, more aggressive when they feel fear. Fear in men is channeled into aggression, in women into submission, for such behaviors are necessary to maintain patriarchal authoritarianism. Aggression and submission are also the core of the basic relations between men and women, accounting, many believe, for women's toleration of male chauvinism. Some assert that these behaviors are the primary cause of all forceful exploitation, and account for perhaps the most significant common characteristic of sexism and the war system: rape. (Pp. 38–39)

Issa Makhlouf, in *Beyrouth ou la fascination de la mort*, discusses rape in the war of Lebanon, a subject no one before him had been willing to expose. He says that it is another facet of the barbarism frequently practiced by militias during massacres and occurring almost everywhere on Lebanese soil.

The fixation of militias on sexual organs affected not only women. Several male cadavers were discovered with their sex cut off and sometimes pushed into their mouths; the simulation of fellatio, generally repressed by morality, is very revealing as a rejection of moral codes. On the other hand, numerous mutilations were practiced on victims, dead or alive. In rape, all forms of violence are combined. All possibilities of death and pleasure are present. All dreams of domination are fulfilled. The victim of rape is the toy of all phantasms and ambitions. Rape is the place of all experimentations. (P. 90)

Susan Brownmiller in *Against Our Will* has shown how rape is a conscious tactic of warfare. Michel Foucault has written extensively on the connection between death, sex, violence, and male sexuality.[1] In *L'irruption de la morale sexuelle* Wilhelm Reich has analyzed how repressed sexuality based on authoritarian family patterns is at the root of sadistic murders, perversions, psychological problems, and social and political conflicts. And Farrar extends male violence against women to nature: "War is a paradigm of masculinist practices because its pre-eminent valuation of violence and destruction resonates throughout other male relationships: relationships to other cultures, to the environment and, particularly, to women. If the 'masculinism' of war is the explanation for its intractability, then we must follow this path to its conclusion, wherever that may be" (p. 59).

When discussing Lebanon, it is important to mention the outside powers that have played with and on Lebanon, trying to impose their views and interests. Should I, as a reminder, enumerate the countries and world politics with which Lebanon is struggling? The big powers are playing with Lebanon; they believe they are solving some of their conflicts by acting them out through Lebanese fighting factions. The Israeli government uses Lebanon and thinks it benefits from a war that, among other things, proves that peaceful cohabitation among different religions is an impossibility and a myth. It thus reinforces its Zionist power partly through racist dogma. Likewise, the Syrian government thinks it can benefit from this war and use it to alleviate its fear of a conflict with Israel on its own land. It enlarges its territory through what it calls Greater Syria, which includes Lebanon. Some of the other Arab countries' governments, not satisfied to watch, indifferent to the worse aggressions and massacres, throw oil on the fire by arming certain factions, paying snipers whose principal role is to inflict panic among the citizens and render the situation more insecure than can be imagined. Few are the countries that have not sent money, weapons, and even fighters—armies of mercenaries—to maintain a conflict over which they shed crocodile's tears while using it to get rid of their war arsenal's surplus and feed their economies. Many world political powers seem somehow allied in destroying a country that had all the potential of fulfilling Reardon's notion that peaceful cohabitation and acceptance of the other is the path toward lasting world peace. The implications are frightening: if Lebanese integrity and sovereignty are not restored soon, the conflict may spread to the rest of the region and the world.

In such a context, how could Lebanon, barely out of colonization, barely independent for the last twenty-five years, resist all the forces linked to destroy it? How could it find its inside voice that would allow it to transcend its differences and internal conflicts? How could it have a larger vision of what it ought to be, help itself open the path to union in diversity and differences, allow itself to get rid of the elements wanting its annihilation? But is it too late? Have we gone too far to see any hope? As I have tried to suggest, the conflict originates not only from the outside—although that is an important component—but also from the inside. As Corm explains:

Violence in Lebanon has been started and is entertained by the hard militia cells who practice, with the regularity of a clock, the most disgusting religious provocation, especially when a possible settlement appears on the horizon. That these cells are being manipulated by Israel, the Palestinian movements, Iran, and Syria is unquestionable, but such manipulation is finally accepted and covered by the Lords of the Lebanese war who have built their tiny community kingdoms on the blood and ruins of the Lebanese people. The scandal is evidently the acceptance of this situation on an international scale. Honored, spoiled, and received in all the big capitals of the world, the Lords of the Lebanese war exist because they play their role of pawn on the bloody chessboard the Lebanese territory has become. (*Géopolitique*, p. 102)

What Corm's excellent study does not mention is the responsibility the civil population also shares in the conflict. I would argue that if the Lebanese people were to unite successfully and believe in their country; if they would strive *not* to possess a small part of it, but to develop a love for it outside of material interests; if there were a real transformation in their sexual rapport within their families and female-male relationships, with

each person accepting the feminine and masculine side of his or her personality; if we got rid of the codes of honor, the virginity rites, the "forced"
religious marriages, and all the gamut of women's oppression; if change
were sought on all levels—from the personal to the political—if all this
could happen, we could move toward a real solution.

Do these ideas point to any actions one can take in Lebanon? Have any
been tried? If we could find a way to disarm all the various fighting factions,
we would have one immediate and efficient remedy, but it would not be
sufficient to get at the roots of the problems. I see peace marches, hunger
strikes, sit-ins, petitions, appeals to international and national peace organizations, and conferences and talks among the various communities as
real, positive actions in the face of the present bleak situation. Lebanese
women and some men have been very active in this domain. Lebanese
women have often stood between the guns and tried to stop the kidnappings.
Wafa Stephan has documented how women have "tried to appease the
fighters by paying visits to refugee camps and military headquarters and
putting flowers in the nozzles of guns" (p. 3). Women one day tried to
eliminate the militia checkpoints where people were being kidnapped. Going
from East Beirut to West Beirut, from Phalangist checkpoint to Progressive
checkpoint, they were speaking in the names of spouses, mothers, and
sisters. They wanted the butchery to stop. They had built homes, but
contrary to what an Arab proverb says about boys' obligation to make a
positive contribution to home and country, the sons had started destroying
the homeland (Charara, p. 15). They blocked the passageways dividing the
Moslem and Christian sides of the capital, organized all night sit-ins, and
stormed into local TV stations to interrupt the news in order to have their
demands broadcast (Stephan, p. 3).

Numerous delegations of women were sent to various conferences
throughout the world and to the United Nations. Numerous vigils, sit-ins,
conferences, peace marches were organized inside and outside the country.
I witnessed and participated in one of the actions for peace on May 6, 1984,
when I taught at the Institute for Women's Studies in the Arab World of
the Beirut University College in West Beirut. The action was initiated by
Iman Khalifeh, a young woman from the Institute who also worked in the
kindergarten of the school. She woke up one day telling herself: "Enough!
Enough of this useless butchery!" She worked with the population of both
sides of the city. The march was to carry as its sole slogan: No to War, No
to the 10th Year of War! Yes to Life! It was to unite both sides of the city

at the only crosspoint, known as the museum passage or demarcation line. Thousands of people were to participate. But the march was stopped by a "blind" shelling (the word *blind* in Lebanon designates any shelling that does not appear to have precise aims or targets, but that, according to many studies, knows exactly what and why it is hitting) that resulted in many victims, dead and wounded, on both sides. Iman has declared: "I was not introducing an original thought—it was not a new idea. But it was the cry of the 'silent majority' voiced aloud by a people that [sic] suffered and endured nine years of ugly war and by a people who carried no arms to defend themselves but struggled to avoid death, violence and ruin in order to live, to build and to continue to be" (quoted in Leila Abdo, pp. 15–16).

Another significant march was that of the handicapped during the summer of 1987, organized and carried out by Laure Moghaïzel, a woman lawyer and activist in the nonviolence and human rights movements in Lebanon. Asked in an interview what she meant by nonviolence, Moghaïzel replied:

I am not a pacifist. I am revolted, revolted by injustices and violence. This is why I use the term *nonviolence*. There is a nuance. Pacifism is a form of passivity, which nonviolence is not. It is a movement that wants peace and that is making itself known through an opposition of unconditional disarmament. . . . Nonviolence is a struggle, and those who say struggle also say activity, dynamism. . . . It is a political action, sustained and energetic, that refuses to exercise violence. But it should not be confused with love for the other. We are not in the era of love. When there is conflict, there is struggle. Nonviolence is a theory very little known in Lebanon. (Quoted in May Makarem, p. 4)

She goes on to explain the origins of the movement in Gandhi and Martin Luther King, Jr.—to cite only the well-known names[2]—and the differences and similarities of nonviolence in Lebanon. Nonviolent Lebanese are ready to suffer, like Gandhi and Martin Luther King, Jr., but martyrdom is not the aim of nonviolence. Their objective consists in eliminating violence through nonviolence. With dialogue, persuasion, they hope to modify the actions of human beings.

These are some of the positive actions at work in Lebanon. They may appear weak, simple, and utopian in the face of the destructive and violent forces of politics and of history. But history has also shown that the actions of a Gandhi or a Martin Luther King did have an impact on society and on the world. The theoretical framework for the change I am proposing lies in a blend of nationalism, feminism, and nonviolent action.

If nationalism—or Lebanism, meaning electing to belong to a culture conceived as pluralistic, on the political notion of alterity, or acceptance of the other's difference—could unite all the various factions fighting each other under a common aim and belief in the existence and the survival of their country, it could move people toward a real solution. But if nationalism remains at a sexist stage and does not move beyond ownership and possession as final goals, the cycle of hell will repeat itself and the violence will continue. In Lebanon, both nationalism and feminism, indeed, femihumanism—both women and men working together in bringing about a pluralistic society built on recognition of the others' differences, be they religious, sexual, or ethnic—are necessary: nationalism in order to unite Lebanon and feminism in order to change the values upon which social relationships are created and formed. The work must begin at the most personal levels: with changes in attitudes and behavior toward one's mate, one's family, one's sexuality, and ultimately one's community and society. From such a personal beginning, at least some of the internal conflicts might move towards resolution. With a stronger nationhood based in mutual love, rather than possession and domination, Lebanon might be able to push out the external influences and find peace.

This argument is clearly not restricted to Lebanon, but involves most geographical areas afflicted with or having the potential for war—meaning most countries in the world. The ideas about sexuality, its centrality in relations among and between women and men and its relationship to war and national interests, probably make sense in differing degrees everywhere. What makes the situation in Lebanon unique is that there these questions take on huge proportions and are more obvious than elsewhere. Lebanon is a Mediterranean country, highly dominated by Islamo-Arab influences. As such, it carries the code of honor and masculine-macho values, as well as the concomitant condition of women's oppression, to their farthest limits. The tragedy of this situation holds its own answer.

NOTES

1. See in particular Michel Foucault, "Tales of Murder," *I, Pierre Rivière.*
2. It is the British suffrage movement that inspired Gandhi. He was in London in 1906, 1909, and 1911, and he wrote about the suffrage movement. See James Hunt, *Gandhi in London* (New Delhi: Promilla, 1978); and Berenice Carroll, "Women Take Action," *Women's Studies International* 12, 1, (January 1989).

PART II

Women Unmask War

We, daughters of educated men, are between the devil and the deep sea. Behind us lies the patriarchal system; the private house, with its nullity, its immorality, its hypocrisy, its servility. Before us lies the public world, the professional system, with its possessiveness, its jealousy, its pugnacity, its greed. The one shuts us up like slaves in a harem; the other forces us to circle, like caterpillars head to tail, round and round the mulberry tree, the sacred tree, of property. It is a choice of evils. Each is bad. Had we not better plunge off the bridge into the river; give up the game; declare that the whole of human life is a mistake and so end it?

The question we put to you, lives of the dead, is how can we enter the professions and yet remain civilized human beings; human beings that is, who wish to prevent war?

Virginia Woolf, Three Guineas

In *Three Guineas,* Virginia Woolf writes about war and how women and men relate to it. She felt herself a victim of both male culture and its outcome in war, two of which she witnessed in her lifetime. In Woolf's view, it is very difficult for women to understand and write about war since it is an experience foreign to them; fighting has been the man's habit, not the woman's: "The vast majority of birds and beasts have been killed by you, not by us; it is difficult to judge what we do not share. How then are we to understand your problem, and if we cannot, how can we answer your question, how to prevent war?" (p. 6).

According to Pat Cramer, who wrote a beautiful thesis on Virginia Woolf and on Hilda Doolittle, analyzing their writings in connection with the wars, "symptoms of everything that was most wrong about our civilization," Woolf "stresses the personal and political advantages of women's outsider position. She argues that women's exclusion from patriarchal traditions makes them uniquely free of the greed and egotism fostered by those traditions and more willing to criticize them; denied the economic and social rewards for aggression and greed granted to men, women are freer to develop values necessary for peace such as cooperation, equality, and creativity" (p. 56). Woolf believes that in fighting, men get the glory, enjoyment, and satisfaction women do not. She sees entering the professional world—the professions being associated with war—as corrupting, but thinks that only by joining it, yet remaining uncontaminated by its possessiveness, jealousy, pugnacity, and greed, can one abolish the inhumanity, beastliness, horror, and folly of war. War can also be prevented by finding new words and creating new methods. "We can best help you to prevent war not by joining your society but by remaining outside your society but in co-operating with its aim. That aim is the same for us both. It is to assert 'the rights of all—all men and women—to the respect in their persons of the great principles of Justice and Equality and Liberty' " (p. 143). Cramer describes how Woolf seeks alternatives:

For Woolf, to ask how to end war is to challenge the foundations of western civilization and to evaluate all levels of private and public life in terms of their contribution to war. . . . In *Three Guineas,* Woolf focuses primarily on three social institutions—education, the professions, and culture—in order to illustrate the ways in which war-like qualities are fostered in men. She creates the opportunity to challenge these insitutions by imagining a request from a man representing a peace society to sign a manifesto protecting culture and intellectual liberty and two requests for money from a woman who asks her to donate money to help women enter the universities and the professions. As she answers these requests one at a time, she counters each negative description of a patriarchal tradition with a vision of how an outsider's society founded on women's values might meet the social needs in non-patriarchal ways. (P. 57)

Virginia Woolf was haunted by war, injustices, and women's oppression. Her lucidity, intensity of emotions, and awareness led her to such despair, seeing she could not actualize her ideas, that she did "plunge off the bridge into the river." The reasons for her suicide are more complex than her despair and anxieties over war; her feelings of hopelessness and helplessness also came from her personal life and controversies over her writings. Nevertheless, war coincided in both Woolf and Doolittle with moments of intense crisis and depressions.

In the novels by women writers I shall examine in this section—Hanan al-Shaykh's *Hikayat Zahra (The Story of Zahra),* Etel Adnan's *Sitt Marie-Rose,* and Andrée Chedid's *House Without Roots*—is there, as in Virginia Woolf, the notion that war is a man's affair, that women have not had much to do with it, that it is ugly, beastly, that it is best not to join man's world and become contaminated by it? Yet how can one change this world and prevent war? Are women always trapped and caught in unbearable situations over which they have no control? Is death, in one form or another, the only solution? Is suicide one of the alternatives to women's apparently inextricable dilemmas?

The three novels I shall discuss in this part seem to concur with Virginia Woolf, presenting war mainly as a male activity, with women as the ultimate victims of its horror. All three novels represent the situation as very bleak and desperate, leading to violence, destruction and inhumanity. All three end with the death of the female protagonist: one is executed for her ideas, and two are killed by a sniper's bullet. The death of Zahra in *The Story of Zahra* can be interpreted as a kind of suicide, since she goes to the sniper with the fear and exaltation she might be killed.

One of these novels, however, appears a little more hopeful and offers another alternative. It is Andrée Chedid's. In *House Without Roots* a peace march is formed by two women from enemy communities who have understood the significance of such an act: it is one of nonviolent resistance. According to Cramer, in Virginia Woolf's theoretical works and novels, there is also a call for nonviolent active struggles to bring about peace.

To peace strategist Jean-Marie Muller, nonviolence means not only refusing to engage in the escalation of violence by not taking revenge, but also avoiding the provocation to be subjected to violence. It is a strategy of resistance, as he explains in *Stratégie de l'action politique non-violente*. The alternative to violence is neither reconciliation, love, nor peace, but only a nonviolent struggle aiming at fighting against injustice and oppression. With its methods of strikes, boycotts, and civil disobedience, there is an element of constraint in nonviolent struggle. To get an opponent to drop something without using violence is the foundation of nonviolent struggle.

In Etel Adnan's *Sitt Marie-Rose*, there is also an element of such resistance. Marie-Rose courageously stands alone in front of her executioners, ready to die for her beliefs, but not without having first confronted the *chabab* (young men who form a militia gang) with their corrupted values.

THREE

Hanan al-Shaykh: Despair, Resignation, Masochism, and Madness

I wanted to live for myself. I wanted my body to be mine alone. I wanted the place on which I stood and the air surrounding me to be mine alone. . . . Why is it that I am always finding myself in a hurtful situation? . . . Ever since I can remember I have felt uneasy; I have never felt anything else. . . . And I felt as if my heart had left me, for how long I don't know, as I lay, submitting to death, with painful resignation.

Hanan al-Shaykh, The Story of Zahra

Hanan al-Shaykh was born in 1945 and grew up in a strict Shi⁽ite Muslim family from the South of Lebanon. She studied in Beirut and later attended the American College for Women in Cairo, where at the age of twenty-two she wrote her first novel, *Intihar rajul mayit* (Suicide of a Dead Man). She then returned to Beirut, working as a journalist at two magazines, *Al Hasna'* (Beauty), the major women's magazine, and *An Nahar* (The Day) newspaper supplement. On her marriage, she moved to the Arabian Gulf, where her husband worked, and there she wrote her second novel entitled *Faras al-Shaytan* (Satan's She-Horse or The Praying Mantis, an insect common to the South of Lebanon) and her third one, *Wardat al-Sahra'* (The Rose of the Desert, translated as *The Story of Lulua*).

The central character of this novel, Sarah, seems to be an avatar of the author. Like al-Shaykh, she grows up in Southern Lebanon in a Shi⁽ite family, closely watched by her stern and fanatically religious father. Forced to undergo rigorous cleansing and prayer rituals every day of the year, she is savagely beaten for the slightest disobedience and, at the age of twelve, forced to don the thick, black veil of traditional Muslim womanhood. The father's fanaticism is so extreme that, at least in Sarah's eyes, it is responsible for her mother's death: he refuses to be disturbed from his prayers to fetch the doctor.

Although this portrayal is at times shocking, it is not self-pitying. The reason for this becomes clear in the second half of the novel, in which Sarah, now grown and married, goes on a visit to an unnamed desert region. There she meets a woman who is a member of a harem of three wives, and, after gaining her confidence, she gradually learns of the traditional ways and customs of the tribal people. By the end of the novel, Sarah realizes that, oppressive though her own upbringing may have been, she at least was able to see her own life in sufficient perspective to understand its limitations and eventually escape them.

Sarah learns that Lulua, the harem wife, is the youngest of the harem and that all three women are considered barren. The husband took the three wives in the hope of having children, but Sarah quickly perceives the real cause of the women's barrenness: the husband has intercourse with them anally, apparently ignorant of any other technique. The wives, for their part, know so little of their own bodies that they are unable to enlighten him. A similar veil of silence and oppression pervades other aspects of their lives as well. Even after Sarah becomes well acquainted with the oldest woman of the harem, she refuses to remove her veil in Sarah's presence, and Sarah later learns that none of the wives ever removes her veil, let alone undresses, in the husband's presence.

Bewildered by this glimpse of a strange, hidden world, Sarah ends her narrative wondering what would have to be done to break the cycle of ignorance and oppressive tradition that prevents the tribal woman from gaining the slightest perspective on her condition. In 1973 in Beirut, when I questioned Hanan al-Shaykh about the implications of her work, she replied that her only concern was with its aesthetic quality; she was not aware of the feminist message. Nevertheless, the message is there and strong: without at least a rudimentary sense of identity, is it possible to have any sort of rebellion?

With female literacy in many of the areas al-Shaykh's describes at only 5 to 10 percent, the direct effect her literature may have is difficult to assess. The important breakthrough in the case of al-Shaykh's work is that it brings to the literate classes of the Arab world the first open portrayal of the most degrading of the traditional customs as they affect women in *all* classes of society.

Hanan al-Shaykh returned to Lebanon but left when the war broke out in 1975 and settled in London, where she wrote *The Story of Zahra*. Its explicit sexual descriptions, its exploration of taboo subjects, such as family cruelty and women's sexuality and its relation to the war, caused such a scandal that the book was banned in several Arab countries. Nevertheless, it circulated widely in the Middle East. Lebanese and Egyptian critics hailed the work for its strength, depth, and lyrical realism, and Hanan al-Shaykh is recognized as a frontrunner among young writers expanding the scope of the contemporary Arabic novel. Her style is probably the most sensual of Arab women writers. With a sensitivity and an inner tone so far unequaled, she has managed to bring out a voice that is original, warm, and vibrant. The delicacy of her images and the lace-like quality of her descriptions are reminiscent of the French woman writer Chantal Chawaf. Her subject matter brings to light some of the most crucial aspects of sexuality as they relate to social and political problems and, more specifically, to war. It is in this respect I wish to discuss her novel, since it illuminates many of the problems with which this study is concerned.

The novel is divided into two parts. The first one, "The Scars of Peace," is divided in five sections—"Zahra Remembers," "Zahra in Africa," "Uncle," "Husband," "Zahra in Wedlock"—all of which deal with Zahra's mental illness, the result of her oppression as a woman in a society that does not allow women to fulfill themselves as human beings. The second part, "The Torrents of War," shows Zahra overcoming her illness and oppression through the war, but hers is an illusory, temporary freedom that masks the deeper problems of a society unable to solve its conflicts except through violence and death.

Zahra remembers her childhood, her closeness to her mother like "the orange and the navel" (pp. 5, 11, 116, 117)[1]—a sensual, organic image that recurs as a leitmotif throughout the novel. It is a symbol of her feeling as if she were at the center of the earth or back in the womb, a symbol of warmth and of life. Zahra remembers her mother taking her along on her love affairs, feeling love and hatred toward her mother, resenting her for using her as an excuse to go out, deceiving her father. She remembers the fear of her father, his khaki suit, his car, his strong body, his beating of her mother, his blows to her: "I no longer knew what my feelings were, to whom I owed loyalty. All I knew was that I was afraid of my father, as afraid of the blows he dealt her as I was of those he dealt me" (p. 11).

She watches her mother giving the best food and all the meat to her brother, Ahmad, and sometimes to her father. She is not overly resentful of this preferential treatment, perhaps because she observes that her mother does not eat meat either. Her sense of community and closeness to her mother does not, however, give her a sense of solidarity with other women, perhaps because her feelings toward her are so contradictory. Already in her childhood, Zahra is constantly hurt by her mother's abandonment of her every time a man comes along. Therefore, it is not surprising that she never learns to build trust and belief in women's togetherness. In Zahra's life, men seem to matter much more than women. This could be what leads her to madness and death in the end.

Remembering her uncle as someone out of the ordinary, someone who would defy tradition, Zahra visits her uncle in Africa. He lives there in exile from the Nationalist Syrian Political Party (PPS), which believes that Lebanon belongs to the "Greater Syria." She has been corresponding with him and decides to accept his invitation to see Africa. It is a way to free herself from her family and from her past. Yet, as soon as she steps down from the plane and sees him, she realizes that he is not her freedom but another prison. He has a very idealistic notion of his homeland and believes it has come to him in the form of Zahra. He gives her his bed in his bedroom, while sleeping on the couch, and comes every morning very early to wake her up. He wants her full attention and often hugs her in a way that makes Zahra feel very uncomfortable. It brings back all the bad memories from her past: her grandfather's naughty advances in the night— or was it her cousin Kasem's?—her sexual encounters with Malek, a married man, supposedly a friend of the family, who takes advantage of her in a garage, a love-making in which Zahra's "body never once responded to his or experienced ecstasy" (p. 24), but which nevertheless resulted in two abortions. Both acts—sex and abortion—filled her with disgust and contempt; she wonders why she kept going back to that garage: "I still shiver today when I think how I believed it was possible for me to control him and our relationship after my pregnancy and abortion. I thought I could influence him; that was my delusion" (p. 27). She recalls being committed to a mental hospital, receiving electric-shock treatment after Malek lied to her family about her health—her mind had turned blank when she could no longer withstand the strain. And she tells herself: "This is Zahra—a woman who sprawls naked day after day on a bed in a stinking garage, unable to protest at anything, who lies on the old doctor's table" (p. 32).

In Africa, she feels from her uncle the same male aggressiveness that has left the deep scars in her past. And she wishes she could tell him: " 'Uncle, please tell me why you have stretched out by my side.' Oh, how I wish I could have said those words! 'Uncle, if you could hear the beat of my heart, if you could only see the disgust and fury gathered in my soul. If only you knew what my true feelings were. I am at my wits' end, and am annoyed with myself and hate myself because I stay silent. When will my soul cry out like a woman surrendering to a redeeming love?" (pp. 27–28). These last words reveal Zahra's inner self, what she is desperately searching for and what, in the second part of the novel, she thinks she has found in the sniper. It foreshadows events to come.

Instead of voicing her anger, Zahra retreats to the bathroom, as she had done in Beirut, and picks at the pimples on her face. The acne is a symbol of her inner scars, an ugliness by which she hopes to drive away men, only to find out "how the disfiguration actually excited Malek, even as he lay on top of me, penetrating my virginity" (p. 24). In the bathroom she writes her diary. It has become her refuge, "a room of her own."

When she decides to accept a marriage proposal from Majed, a friend of her uncle, her uncle tells her he must be warned of her illness, her fits and shock treatment. To this, Zahra is finally and courageously able to reply— in a whisper, her heart beating heavily, but nevertheless reply—that: "Whatever happened to me was your fault! . . . I never cared for your behaviour towards me. . . . It troubled me until it made me sick" (p. 33). These words should have helped her become free, but when her uncle responds by yelling at her and slamming the door, she freezes and withdraws even more. What can Zahra do against all odds, when even the people closest to her refuse to see what she is going through? How can she break the doors of male aggression slamming words in her mouth?

Zahra marries her uncle's friend, and the following two chapters are told from male perspectives, the uncle's and husband's views of Zahra. This technique is not often used by women writers and even less often by Arab women writers. But Hanan al-Shaykh successfully allows us to enter the two men's worlds. Both are very homesick and idealize Lebanon. Zahra becomes the embodiment of their homeland, a tie with their faraway families. Both see Africa and the blacks in racist terms. But whereas the uncle exhibits a certain amount of sophistication in his social relationships and in his feelings for Zahra—"I felt that Zahra was my key to making contact with my past and present as well as my future. . . . This tired, sad butterfly had alighted on me" (p. 58)—the husband is quite crude and marries Zahra to be "the owner of a woman's body that I could make love to whenever I wished. . . . I have married Hashem's niece and so fulfilled the dream I've had ever since being in the south . . . of marrying the daughter of an illustrious family" (p. 69).

When her husband finds out that Zahra is no longer a virgin, he goes into a fit, his honor and pride deeply wounded: "I thanked God that my mother was far away, far from this mess, and could not ask to see the stained sheets so that she might display them to Zahra's mother, to the neighbours and relatives. I thanked God for my mother's absence, and with it her stinging tongue" (p. 72). It is obvious he considers Zahra merely as merchandise of which he is the sole proprietor. He could care less about her welfare or feelings or about creating a true exchange of love and tenderness that could have saved her from the madness arising again in her, the only "protection" she has from the world's craziness.

Zahra withdraws completely, first by locking herself in the bedroom and bathroom—her eternal refuge since childhood—then by refusing to eat, drink, or talk; she only stares into a void. The final scene of Zahra's madness, described by the husband, shows her receiving his friends and taking the flowers they have brought, sticking them all over the place, drawing a square to place them in, saying she is decorating her mother's picture, hysterically laughing without stop, forcing a gold bracelet he had given her on their wedding day on the friend's arm. But while apparently mad, her actions are actually a ritual by which Zahra once more tries to assert herself and become free. She breaks society's rules by showing an improper attitude towards civility and irreverence towards gifts, and the people who make up this society cannot forgive her. She draws her mother into the ritual, both as an appeal and rejection, for it is her mother who taught her both freedom and servitude. But the husband views her as completely crazy and thinks that his narrative of the scene proves how mad she is.

We then return to Zahra's point of view, first describing her marriage and later the war in Beirut, which I consider the most significant pages of the novel in terms of my topic. In wedlock, Zahra is haunted with freedom and with her inner spirit, her *Qarina:* "I wanted to live for myself. I wanted my body to be mine alone. I wanted the place on which I stood and the air surrounding me to be mine and no one else's" (p. 78). When the situation becomes too painful, she dreams of her *Qarina,* usually projecting all her fears on the spirit. In this split of her personality, she puts off her anxiety by projecting it onto another. She feels trapped, always having to hide her real self, always afraid, always in a painful situation: "Ever since I can remember I have felt uneasy; I have never felt anything else. . . . Why did I let that amazing fear take over every moment of my life? . . . Why did I let it consume me and, bit by bit, make me ravage my face till it looks as it does today?" (Pp. 93, 96).

With these feelings comes the realization that she hates all men. This is a cry of despair that appears in many other novels by Arab women. Ferdaws, in Nawal el Saadawi's *Al-mar'ah 'inda niktat al-sifer (Woman at Point Zero),* when she comes to grips with how she has been used and mistreated, also cries out that she hates all men. But while Ferdaws reaches a point where she grabs the knife turned against her, striking the one who was aiming it at her—in a suicidal gesture, since she forsees she may be condemned— Zahra withdraws, in indifferent madness. Yet she is also killed in the end. Both wish for someone or something to save them, but both fall victim to a society that hides its hypocrisy through the oppression of its women and resorts to violence to solve its conflicts.

Zahra's first reactions to the war are to sleep, eat, and refuse to talk or to be sociable. Though she withdraws even further than before, the war gives her also a sense of relief: "I felt calm. It meant that my perimeters were fixed by these walls, that nothing which my mother hoped for me could find a place inside them. . . . My deep sleeping was a sickness, my devouring huge quantities of food was a sickness, my increasing weight, my wearing only my housecoat for two months on end were sicknesses. The scabs on my face that spread to my neck, to my shoulders, and my not caring about them, were a sickness. My silence was a sickness" (p. 107).

She is filled with despair and disbelief at what is going on in her country: the killings, the kidnappings, the disintegration, the slow death. When she realizes her brother, Ahmad, has joined the fighters, she cannot accept his action and reacts by screaming, grabbing at him, and actually passing out. The father seems to join her in these feelings and shouts at her mother who has just accepted two hundred liras from her son: "Who does he think he is fighting? His brother, his friend, his neighbour! We are all Lebanese, you foolish woman. We are all one family! Lebanon is a small country. . . . I wouldn't touch such cursed money. It belongs to martyrs and orphans. You did wrong in accepting it" (p. 112). This is the first time the father says something sensible. It makes him sympathetic, just as Zahra's uncle is sympathetic when he defends her lack of virginity, telling her husband that times had changed, that such customs were trivial and stupid. This is Hanan al-Shaykh's genius: her ability to show unsympathetic characters uttering wisdom, her ability to create complex personalities.

One day, Zahra looks into the street and sees prisoners taken from the

Christian side. It makes her ill. She tries to prevent the shooting by asking the militiamen she knows to let them go free. Her parents, afraid for her life, drag her back. She weeps. "I sat on, punishing myself, feeling guilty for all the times when I had felt uncomfortable before the war, and for all the misery which I had thought was misery before the war, and the pain I had thought was pain before the war" (p. 114).

For the first time, Zahra starts thinking of someone other than herself and volunteers at the hospital. But she does not last there for more than three days: the smell of blood, the stench, the laments make her ill, and she wonders if leaders of factions ever visited hospitals, and if they did how they could live: "Could they stop themselves thinking of an amputated leg? Or of an eye that had turned to liquid? Or of a severed hand lying there in resignation and helplessness? Why did none of those leaders, as they stood listening to the groans, pledge to put a stop to the war?" (p. 115). Then one night she hears the sounds of the prisoners being shot, and she freezes in despair, painfully resigning, submitting to death, the sounds of the rockets raging above their heads making her scream, scream, scream.

Ahmad is numb. He explains that "to belong to a group makes you part of the war and not a murderer. Your gun isn't a gun, but an object you carry naturally. And the group digests you so that you forget you are an individual" (p. 118). Zahra reacts to these words by weeping hysterically and asking him why he is speaking this way. She believes all the fighters are drugged like Ahmad and his friends; it is the only way they can keep on fighting. She can never understand their logic and watches them laughing like boys in a school dormitory. One day, when she begs him to stop taking the drugs he virtually depends on, he responds:

"The whole of Beirut is ours. We, on the western front, and they our opponents on the eastern front, command between us the buildings and the streets. Nothing that moves or doesn't move is outside our control. We are the force and power and everything! No day passes in which I do not perform an act once prohibited by government or law or mere public opinion. There are other things which I wish to do that are still not approved of, and there is nothing left except drugs. You should praise God that I'm not like those who take a fix of heroin or shoot themselves to pieces." (P. 140)

It is clear that it is not engaging in a worthy cause that interests these fighters, but a feeling of power. Strength, domination, conquest of the city excites them. Belonging to a group gives them a feeling of strength and power they might not have had otherwise. There is also in this statement, an explicit rebellion against authority, an implicit revolt of the sons against the fathers. It is an ironic antipatriarchal element in this highly masculinized culture.

The revolt against authority we find in Ahmad's statement will not change the patriarchal tribal system, because it is fighting against that system with the very same values it is trying to get rid of: masculinity and domination. In almost all the war novels written by men, we find descriptions of masculine relationships connected with war. It is a very significant aspect of warfare, analyzed by authors such as Bob Connell, who are concerned with peace issues.

The disintegration of Lebanese society comes about not only through violence, war, and destruction, but also through what war carries with it: weapons, drugs, a loosening of morality, especially as far as sex is concerned. Zahra watches in shock one day as Ahmad masturbates in her presence. She is shaken by his audacity. She wonders how war could have changed things to the extent "that Ahmad could sit and fondle himself without a thought . . . as if he were on his own. . . . Ahmad, you sit in the next room, fondle your genitals and inhale hashish. You smoke grass and fondle your groin, and can only come back to being yourself after you have killed and robbed, hated and fled" (p. 40). Everything has become permissible in war, even what appears to Zahra as the most shocking behavior.

It is evident from Ahmad's attitude in the war and from his words, that the young men of Beirut are not fighting for a worthy cause but for self-indulgence, for a sick power, for the worst in male values: boasting, cruelty, sadism, competition, *shatara* (clever perfidy), all leading to killing, robbing, drugs, violence, death, and destruction. This corruption stems from a poorly understood and badly lived sexuality in which tenderness, love, generosity, recognition of the other in an exchange of feelings have been erased. Sex for the young men becomes a release of nervous energy, yet it is a perpetuation of the violence they live through war and drugs.

The element of rebellion suggested by daring, shock-laden acts, such as masturbating in front of one's sister, or engaging in sexual activity on a Beirut roof, in the sexually repressive Lebanese society, is not positive. It does not lead to a transformation of repressive values. In the long run, such an attitude reinforces the patriarchal tribal system because it is based on the very same macho behavior it is trying to break. Similarly, in the "sexual revolution" of the 1970s in the West, women, told that in order to free themselves, men, and society, they had to engage in promiscuous "free" sex, like orgies, multiple partners, and pornography, discovered they had been used and fooled. The expected freedom turned into a diversion from a true, genuine, liberating change in the relationships between women and men.

Ahmad is very confused about why he is fighting: one day he says it is for the Shi'ites, the next for the Palestinians (and why should they interfere in Lebanese politics?), another day against the United States and Israel, which want to split the Arabs. When he asks his sister to side with them, she quickly replies: "No, I never carried a rifle on my shoulder or in my thoughts. I am neutral. I see the pain on both sides" (p. 142). Ahmad explains why he uses drugs:

Drugs have given the war a new dimension. I can't really explain it. They help you see the war through a filter that screens the eyes. . . . It cancels out the guns, the rockets, the firing, even though we go on fighting. And if I ask myself what I have accomplished, I answer that I have obeyed my commander's orders and achieved much. *I have not stayed at home with the women.* Whenever I hear it said that this war is almost over without anything being accomplished, I freeze. The end of the war means I will become a shadow in the streets where, with my rifle, I have been master, room by room, building by building, tree by tree. I have been master of the nights as well as of the days. (P. 143; my emphasis)

The use of drugs in the Lebanese war has, in fact, reached alarming proportions. Paul Vieille argues that drug consumption, without necessarily being linked to death or a nihilistic ideology, nevertheless expresses despair and self-destruction. It is no longer a statistically marginal fact. In the United States there are about 35 million drug addicts, and in Western Europe, the numbers are also quite high. The developing countries hold their share of addicts; Lebanon and Iran notably are being devastated by drugs ("Le chaos du monde," p. 22).

It is clear from Ahmad's words that he needs drugs in order to behave the way he does. He despises and scorns women. For him, killing means "masculinity"—not being like women. He is worried about the war ending because it means the end of the sick identity that gives him power and control over others. War has given him a sense of adventure and a way to gain money by robbing and looting. It has given him and his comrades an occupation they did not have before and without which they would not know what to do: "I don't wish for this war to end. I don't want to have to worry about what to do next. The war has structured my days and nights, my financial status, my very self. It has given me a task that suits me, especially since those first months when I was so nervous and afraid. Once those first months were over I became like the cock of the roost, spreading my rampant feathers" (p. 144). Even the image he uses for himself, "cock of the roost," embodies masculine values. Ahmad is proud to belong to this world of men who strut across the city, sure of their power. By enabling them to leave home, war and the city allow them to avoid women's, especially mothers', hold on them.

The speech also expresses the fear of growing up, of taking responsibility for one's life. These militiamen are boys playing at being men, at being soldiers. They are fighting for its own sake, not for an ideal or a cause. Vieille explains how war leads to such attitudes:

War reproduces itself in the imagination of fighters, the youth whose sole future is war: fascination with war, fear and love of death, the war-*jouissance* that liberates one from all prohibitions, while at the same time competing with life, bringing fear of women, fear of life, of daily living. Violence itself conflicts with *jouissance* because it no longer finds reasons for existence—it is pure violence, narcissistic violence. Narcissism does not project itself in authenticity, as in Iran, but in purity of death; it invests itself in the exercise of violence. Finally, it is *jouissance* of violence. *Jouissance* of power over others, but also *jouissance* of power over oneself because the threat of death is always present. ("Le chaos du monde," p. 26)

For Andrea Dworkin such attitudes have yet another meaning:

War purifies, washes off the female stink. The blood of death, so hallowed, so celebrated, overcomes the blood of life, so abhorred, so defamed. The ones who survive the bloodbath will never again risk the empathy with women they experienced as children for fear of being found out and punished for good: killed this time by the male gangs, found in all spheres of life, that enforce the male code. The child is dead. The boy has become a man. (*Pornography*, p. 51)

War also brings looting, and Zahra becomes ill as she watches Ahmad bringing home stolen goods at night and hiding them in their parents' room, their parents having left for the South. She thinks of the owners of these objects and wishes she could return them. She wonders: "Might my returning those spoils be considered an abnormal act, comparable to my daily visits to the building of death where its sniper-privateer awaits me?" (p. 146). Georges Corm explains why the Lebanese youth have lost all sense of values: "By taking part in the destruction and looting, without thought for the consequences such acts have on their future, they are taking revenge on a country that has denied them a dignified existence. . . . The youth, see the doors closed, without outlets, without access to the political, eco-

nomic, or other domains except through ethically and professionally doubt-
ful practices, so it is no surprise if the arrival of armed militias has
constituted the mechanism of recuperation of their revolt" (*Géopolitique du
conflit libanais*, p. 213). Paul Vieille concurs, explaining the paradigm of
dereliction/violence as manifested in the Middle East: "The feeling of
dereliction following a failure, the causes of which cannot be grasped
exactly or be clearly identified, refers to death, calls for death, tends to be
transformed into blind violence reverted against oneself or a made-up enemy. . . . Dereliction tends to develop in the world because the people are
not finding a way out, are finding it difficult to make their expectations
come true. This is probably why the big powers are incapable of putting an
end to wars like the Gulf or even the war in Lebanon" ("Le chaos du
monde," p. 22).

The despair of Lebanese youth is epitomized by Zahra's relationship with
the sniper, the major event of the novel. The reasons she throws herself
into this adventure are not altogether clear to her. The war creates such
contradictions within her she wishes somehow to find an answer—even in
death. The afternoon she first goes to him, she really believes she is walking
to her death: "I anticipated only one thing: hearing a bullet and then falling
dead to the ground like the others the sniper had killed. . . . I could no
longer feel my pulse, and my body moved without thought or sensation. In
that critical moment I said to myself, 'Well, here I am. I am about to lose
myself forever' " (p. 125). It is evident from these lines that Zahra sees
death as liberation. The connection among death, war, and sexuality are
closely associated in her walk toward the sniper. In that respect, her
nihilism parallels Ahmad's and his comrades'. They all seek liberation
through death. But while Zahra submits to it masochistically, as a result of
her life of oppression, Ahmad and his comrades inflict it sadistically on
others.

But it is not only the ambivalence of fear and liberation she feels when
she walks up the stairs for the first time to meet with the sniper. There is
also a kind of excitement at the anticipation of a sex act. In the following
pages, we are told that the sniper was not altogether a stranger to Zahra
since she had already exhibited herself half-naked to him one afternoon,
hanging some clothes on her aunt's roof. There had even been a brief
exchange of words between the two. He seems to know who she is. She has
watched him eat at Abu Jamil's restaurant across from her house.

Hanan al-Shaykh shows the sniper as someone integrated into the life of the street, someone who knows who is who and whom he should shoot. It is not the image of the sniper usually presented to us by the media: a half-crazy loner, paid huge sums of money to shoot at random. Here the sniper is described as a tender man, sensitive, soft-spoken, protected by the gang leaders of the street, perhaps even fed by them, and given a precise assignment.

Zahra's first sexual encounters with the sniper are virtually rapes: he pounces on her, releases himself without consideration for her feelings, pleasure, sensations, or the fact that the bare floor hurts her back and side. But as time goes by and she goes back to him every afternoon, they grow accustomed to each other, she relaxes, and he starts responding to her needs. She experiences orgasm for the fist time in her life and cries out. "My cries became like lava and hot sand pouring from a volcano whose suffocating dust was burying my past life. It blotted out the door to Dr. Shawky's clinic [the doctor who had given her the two abortions in the first part of the novel, before she left for Africa] and the door behind which we hid as my mother clutched at me in panic" (p. 130). The sniper's caresses unwind all the suffering from her past. The orgasm brings to the surface all the feelings she had buried deep inside her; it intensifies them while allowing her to forget them: "My cries as I lay in the dust, responding to the sniper's exploring fingers, contained all the pain and sickness from my past, when I had curled up in my shell in some corner, somewhere, or in a bathroom, hugging myself and holding my breath as if always trying to return to the state of being a foetus in its mother's womb" (p. 131). It is a kind of catharsis. She compares it to electroshock treatment, and the image it conjures up is not positive, forewarning of events to come, coloring Zahra's pleasure with the specter of madness and death. She feels real anxiety over the significance of her act and prospects for the future: "My body had undulated with pleasure as the sniper looked into my eyes. Was he really the sniper, this person who was now standing up and who had, for the first time, taken off his trousers? What had made him into a sniper? Who had given him orders to kill anonymous passers-by? Would I be thought of as the sniper's accomplice now that my body had become a partner to his body?" (p. 132).

It becomes clear that one of Zahra's motivations for going to the sniper that first afternoon had been to divert and prevent him from killing: "I wondered what could possibly divert the sniper from aiming his rifle and startle him to the point where he might open his mouth instead?" (p. 134).

She later asks herself, "What was I here for? Before I came, he would have been picking out his victim's heads as targets, and after I left would be doing the same. Why, every day, did I sneak down that street of death and war and arrive at this place? Could I say I had been able to save anyone, even in those moments when we met and had intercourse? But I couldn't even consider these to hold a reprieve from death for anyone. My visits only replaced his siestas" (p. 137). She had even thought of killing him: "Should I throw a hand-grenade at him? Should I learn to use a gun and aim it at his heart? I became obsessed by the sniper, obsessed with noting down the numbers of those killed by him. I began to hold myself responsible for their deaths" (p. 133).

It seems as though in Zahra's mind the only way to have any kind of control over the elements of death ravaging her country is to become part of this violence through sexuality. She tries to help at the hospital, but is unable to bear the stench and suffering. She tries to halt the militiamen from shooting the prisoners, but is held back by her parents, told she is mad, risking death herself. She tries to convince her brother to stop fighting, taking drugs, and looting, only to see him scorn her and masturbate in front of her. What choices does she really have? In light of all these barriers, her act of going to the sniper becomes more understandable, if not condonable. Like others in the war, Zahra is a victim. Deeply wounded in her past by her family and a society that does not allow its individuals, let alone its women, to fulfill themselves, Zahra's "solution" is to sink even more deeply into sickness and destruction, while thinking she has become "normal and human." Even her assertiveness, her taking an active part by going to the sniper, is the result of her victimization. "This war has made beauty, money, terror and convention all equally irrelevant. It begins to occur to me that the war, with its miseries and destructiveness, has been necessary for me to start to return to being normal and human. . . . The war has been essential. It has swept away the hollowness concealed by routines. It has made me ever more alive, ever more tranquil" (p. 138). According to Margaret Higonnet in "The Double Helix," one of the ironies of the war for women is that it loosens social mores and gives them the opportunity to play more of a role, while perverting all cultural systems— most basically by overturning civilization's prohibitions on killings.

Zahra starts worrying about the future. She would like to ask her lover if he is really a sniper—the problem of the sniper's identity being precisely that he is anonymous, that no one knows whether he is a sniper or not—and what his intentions are, what will become of them when the war ends. But she always puts if off until the next day: "Tomorrow, when I see him again, I will speak frankly. We will discuss everything concerning sniping and marriage. Tomorrow will decide my future. There's nothing I don't want to know. I'm impatient to know everything. Tomorrow will decide my life" (p. 149). Making love and killing become connected, and she associates sniping and marriage. But Zahra can never gather enough courage to ask him the questions that worry her: "I felt incapable of asking about them, even though I was almost suffocating with curiosity. I wanted to know his true name, and what his real feelings were towards me" (p. 150). When he finally talks about his family and where he lives, she is convinced he is lying to her. She wonders how he can be so dishonest when they have had physical intimacy. Is it not a typical question many women all over the world ask themselves? Hanan al-Shaykh knows how to put her finger on some of the most basic problems between men and women. A man does not have to be a sniper to avoid answering questions a woman in love raises, especially when such questions concern their future.

The pimples on Zahra's face have disappeared. The war and love-making have swept away some of the aspects of her painful past that had left scars she thought would never go away. Instead of withdrawing in the bathroom to pinch her face, Zahra runs up to the roof and forgets everything through orgasms she reaches every afternoon in the sniper's arms. Sex becomes a drug. Here the parallel between her brother's use of drugs and her use of sex is evident. She is afraid of it, yet it puts her in a trance that blinds her to everything else:

Ah, the beautiful numbness which I feel after I come. For a few moments it plunges me into total darkness. His closed eyes never witness my ecstasy. . . . Yet I don't want to visit him again, anymore than I want to open the door to Ahmad. I would like to chuck all Ahmad's loot off the roof. I just want to stay in this house. If the bathroom had a lock, I would make that my home. But no, I know I will continue to see him every day, to experience that confusion and fear as my feet barely touch the ground or the stair tiles; will know the smell of his sweat, his piercing eyes, my arms gripping his back, making him bear down on me with his full weight. (P. 147)

The stairs have replaced the bathroom, and sex—it can hardly be called love-making—pinching! Neither one is good for Zahra. Neither one can help her find herself and blossom, but what alternative does she have? She is struggling the best she can, considering her past, with elements way beyond her control.

Meanwhile Zahra also starts feeling tired and dizzy. She wonders if she has cancer, she feels so sick. Her appetite has gone completely. Her mother, who has come back from the South on a visit, tells her she acts like a pregnant woman. Zahra does not worry too much since she has been taking the pill. But we soon find out that she is indeed pregnant, having taken "two pills at once, to guard against our love-making of only three days before, and after that followed the instructions on the package. When I woke up one morning in a pool of blood, it occurred to me that the pills were making my period extra heavy. By the time I started on the second pack, I was taking a pill every night. . . . Before I was through the second pack, I had once more swum in a sea of blood" (p. 158). By the time she finds out she is pregnant, the foetus is already four months old. The child has been conceived in blood. How else could it be, given the context of violence, madness, and destruction? The strength of Hanan al-Shaykh's style comes out in all the horror conveyed by this image of a war child who can only be conceived in a pool of blood, symbol of all of Zahra's previous and present rapes, abortions, electroshock treatments, virginity rites and repairs, sick and painful sex, sadomasochistic relationships, where tenderness, love, equal sharing, honesty, recognition of the other as of oneself are but vain words. All of this is epitomized by the sniper, who uses his sex like his *kalashnikov*: to feel more powerful and in control, to relieve his internal conflicts and violent drives. He may be sexually sensitive in bringing Zahra to an orgasm, but he does not try to understand her.

It is also significant that the doctor Zahra goes to should be one who circumcises young boys. The male circumcision rite conveys the fear of castration, the passage into adulthood, the proof of masculinity. In a strongly macho society like the Lebanese, male circumcision brings to the surface values of domination and conquest, in an affirmation of the male organ. Zahra wonders how such a doctor could know about women's problems. But in such a society, it all seems quite normal: babies and male circumcision, bringing lives in the world and cutting prepuces from the penises to shed off female ambiguity, to make them more masculine, to proclaim masculinity. Everything falls into a "natural" order: women fulfill their roles by being subservient and bringing into the world as many children as possible—preferably boys—and men assume their maleness through a virility stripped of any femininity, carried to the extreme of conquest, domination, *shatara*. They seek to control small pieces of land as they possess women's bodies through rape, defloration rites on the wedding night, violence.

When Zahra finds out no doctor will give her an abortion because she is four months pregnant, all she wants is to die, to commit suicide, and not have to face her family and society: "By the time they found out, I would be laid out for ever—I, and whoever was in my stomach, ready to travel underground into total silence. Above us, the noise, the din, and the fighting would continue between cease-fires. The conventions would continue, marriage would continue, giving birth would continue. And the houses, the rain and sun would all remain. Everything in turmoil; everyone inevitably moving towards the moment when they, too, must be laid out. All became equal in that moment. It must be the same for everyone in the end" (p. 170). The idea of death makes war look like trivia.

As she stands, facing the sniper, telling him about her pregnancy, she wonders why she has to go through all that. It is the eternal question many women all over the world ask themselves: "Why does all this have to happen to me? . . . To whom should I talk? How am I to find a solution, when every solution the earth offers seems ultimately without meaning? . . . Why didn't God lose me Himself? . . . Why do these disasters always come in my direction? It's impossible to guess. I feel lost" (p. 176). The sniper tells her she must get an abortion, and he hands her a banknote. At this point Zahra bursts into tears she cannot control: "I wish I could die at this very moment and have everything disappear with me. I want to lie with my hands clutching my shoulders, my knees touching my chin. I want to curl up as though I am a foetus again. Did we all come into being unprotesting, in error, often without a woman's cry of pleasure at our moment of conception?" (p. 178). This is another one of al-Shaykh's ultimate questions raised through Zahra's voice with poignancy and in despair. Surprised by Zahra's reaction and by her tears, the sniper offers her marriage: "Please listen to me. Please. Sure we'll get married, but please stop acting like this. I beg you" (p. 178). His appeasing words are not altogether convincing; he may not be sincere. When he touches Zahra's belly, praying for the child to "be born a fighter, surrounded by the noise of rockets and bazookas" (p. 179), we shiver with anxiety. How else could a killer conceive of life, except as a perpetuation of death? Can he really accept a woman as a life-giver and unite with her to create life? Is she not merely a vessel, like his country, into which he pours his violence, anger, and hatred?

Zahra is also apprehensive of what the future may hold. What will she tell her parents? How and where will they live when they get married? And all at once, she asks him the ultimate question: Is he really a sniper? His violent reaction—"Sniper? What do you say? You really must be insane! Do you distrust me to that extent? People now distrust their own mothers, their own fathers!" (p. 180)—makes us—Zahra and the reader—quiver with fear. He asserts that he is not, but his anger, bitterness, the redness and frown on his face are alarming signs. If he were innocent, would he need to scream it as he does? Can he really be thinking of a future with Zahra, when his only project is destruction and death? Why has he avoided all her questions so far? And why does he ask her to wait and leave only when the night has fallen? These ominous signs soon become clear.

When she leaves, Zahra is hit by a bullet as she crosses the street. He has killed her. "He kills me with the bullets that lay at his elbow as he made love to me. He kills me, and the white sheets which covered me a little while ago are still crumpled from my presence" (p. 183). The images used for the killing are explicitly sexual. It is the killer's ultimate "lovemaking" to Zahra, a metaphor of the Lebanese dilemma, illustrated with paradoxical images by al-Shaykh's powerful pen. Zahra frees herself sexually through the anarchy that reigns because of the war. She is able to experience orgasm every afternoon in the arms of one of the worst perpetrators of violence in her country. All the taboos fall, as have the barriers and rules of morality; sexuality is loose, stark, brutal, and present, not in love and mutuality, but in domination, power relations, cruelty, masochism and sadism. Zahra's acne and madness are cured. She, who in normal times might have led a traditional life with husband, children, and madness, never experiencing orgasm or any kind of ecstasy, suddenly discovers the possibilities of her vibrant body. But this freedom is not a lasting or positive one because its roots go deep into violence, war, death, and destruction. The sexual acts that free Zahra are not based on tenderness, love, and mutual respect, a recognition of the other's dignity and pleasure as of one's own; the result is not life and love, but death. Zahra becomes the target not only of the killer's sexual weapon but of his *kalashnikov* as well. She is able to tame the first, experience pleasure, and even create life, she can do nothing against the terror of the second, which reduces her to a cadaver.

Rape, as the sniper's first reaction to Zahra, is a way of proving his masculinity through control and domination. Along with his killings, it breaks his society's mores and emphasizes the state of chaos he has become part of. Fear is one of the primary motivations to such acts: fear of life, fear of women, fascination with death and destruction. As he grows accustomed to Zahra's daily visits, fear fades away; he starts responding to her sexual needs by caressing her and to her physical comfort by bringing some sheets. He even becomes tender and shows some emotion. But at the announcement of her pregnancy and her question about his occupation, fear takes hold of him again. He cannot fulfill his promise to marry her and reintegrate them into the "normal" life he daily destroys. He cannot assume the life in her womb. In order to reestablish the chaos, the daily drug and only meaning of his existence, he must kill her.

The death of the child in Zahra's womb gives the only faint hope in the midst of the tragedy: at least the fruit of this violence is also killed by the violence from which it originates. But the implications of such a "solution" are frightening: Is total annihilation the only answer to violence? The answer to violence is not violence but nonviolence. As Jean-Marie Muller puts it in "Signification de la non-violence," "we must find means of action that will not lead us into the mesh of violence, that could quickly take us on a path where we could not master our own violence, and we could become perverted by a logic of destruction, the opposite of what we wish to realize for society and for our children" (p. 27). The process is not an easy one, because as Andrea Dworkin says:

Men develop a strong loyalty to violence. Men must come to terms with violence because it is the prime component of male identity. Institutionalized in sports, the military, acculturated sexuality, the history and mythology of heroism, it is taught to boys until they become its advocates—men, not women. Men become advocates of that which they most fear. In advocacy they experience mastery of fear. In mastery of fear they experience freedom. Men transform their fear of male violence into metaphysical commitment to male violence. Violence itself becomes the central definition of any experience that is profound and significant. (*Pornography*, p. 51)

From this analysis, it becomes evident that war is enmeshed in the fear men have of women. Violence serves to overcome that fear. But violence perpetuates violence and may well lead us to the total destruction of the planet. It becomes of vital importance to discover the connections among these various processes and to look for solutions. Several writers have started doing so. In *Sexism and the War System*, Betty Reardon writes:

The profoundly sexist history of the human species indicates that the socially in-
duced and prescribed separations and differences between the sexes are a very
significant component of the inner psychic constructs. They may well be the psychic
origins of war, sexism, and all structures of violence and oppression. Various feminists have pointed to the oppression of women by men as the first and most fundamental form of structural oppression. . . . It is, I think, of some significance
that psychiatry has pointed out that the enemy always becomes the embodiment of
what we fear or reject in ourselves. We attempt to exorcize our own bad spirits by
projecting them on others. . . . It is widely acknowledged that both sexist society
and the war system are kept in order by the capacity to use or threaten the use of
violence against those others who arouse fear. (P. 7)

The Story of Zahra illuminates some of these processes. The youth in
Lebanon use the war to revolt against tradition and authority, to break the
rules of the fathers and mothers. They want to destroy the old order that
oppresses them. The boys as militiamen rebel against it through cynicism,
sadism, and cruelty. The women—in particular Zahra—achieve a certain
autonomy through masochism and submission to cruelty and violence. Neither men nor women have any kind of vision that can help them out of the
vicious circle: the patriarchal tribal system creates war, war is used to
destroy the authoritarian system, war begets more war.

Instead of destroying the old order and its tribal system of oppression,
the *chabab* gangs reinforce it and lead women a step further down. The
male youth may think they have gained a certain autonomy and freedom in
the exhilaration of fighting, destroying, and looting. Women may feel a
certain freedom in the excitement of sexual pleasure. But like drugs, these
actions create only a temporary, artificial nirvana. They do not really
challenge the basic structure the youth rebels against. They are an outlet,
a diversion from hurt: pain fought with pain, violence attacked with violence, authority questioned with authority, power challenged with power.
The youth seek liberation through death, rather than through life and
creativity, and the outcome is death. Only a different vision could break the
circle of hell.

In this novel, Hanan al-Shaykh gives an account both poignant and
horrifying of the sniping, looting, drugs, killing, destroying, abortion, sadism, masochism, cruelty, and madness of war. She does so in a unique
style that blends sensuality, delicacy, and strength in the imagery with in-
depth psychological analysis of the characters and gives voice to both female
and male points of view. Yet in this novel hope is elusive. Al-Shaykh is not

so keen on suggesting solutions as she is in bringing out the issues and representing the problems in total despair.

NOTE

1. Throughout I will be quoting from the English edition by permission of Readers International, London. © Hanan al-Shaykh, 1986.

FOUR

Etel Adnan: Courage, Engagement, and Self-Sacrifice

Here I am on a battlefield. It's a terrain closed in on all sides where it is absolutely essential that someone dies. Death always designates the presence of a battle. . . . My love had promised me an apple orchard. Today, it's death that's promised me. . . . I am weary. My death, after all, will deprive them of very little. . . . If only I could be sure that they would survive my death for a long time! . . . God, whoever you are, protect the future generations from the genocide that awaits them. I want to make my peace with everyone. . . . I am walled in at the will of my executioners, caught between the finger and the windowpane like a fly. I can no longer stand knowing that I'm about to die.

Etel Adnan, *Sitt Marie-Rose*

Lebanese poet and painter, Etel Adnan wrote her first novel, *Sitt Marie-Rose,* during the siege of the Palestinian camp of Tel al-Zaatar in the summer of 1976. Adnan tells us that Marie-Rose, the main character of her novel, "was not a friend of mine. She was a person I knew. I met her. She was sometimes on Lebanese television" (quoted in Judith Pierce, p. 51). As Miriam Cooke notes, the novel is based on the true story of a Syrian woman who taught in a school for mentally retarded children, but was murdered for her support of the Palestinian cause *(War's Other Voices,* p. 17). In the novel, the Syrian woman becomes Lebanese, and the mentally retarded children deaf mute, because, as Adnan explains:

I consider that the deaf mutes represent the Arab people. . . . I was trying to show how some cultural values which have their good side in time of peace can, in time of war, lead to genocide. . . . This is what I call tribal behaviour. Identification with the group begins as a feeling of solidarity, but as they consider themselves as a group, so they consider other individuals as part of groups. When they are at war, the only solution is total eradication of the enemy, his wife and children. This is the most dangerous aspect in the Middle East. . . . I think my book is about the moral and physical death of a city. It will take a long time to feel innocent in Beirut. (Quoted in Pierce, p. 51)

Adnan feels very strongly about Beirut, where she was born in 1925 to a Syrian Muslim father, a former Ottoman officer, and a Greek Christian mother. She was educated in French schools and later studied philosophy at the Sorbonne in Paris and at Harvard and Berkeley in the United States. She has published six volumes of poetry: *Moonshots, Five Senses for One Death, Jebu* and *Beirut-Hell Express, L'Apocalypse arabe, Pablo Neruda Is a Banana Tree,* and *From A to Z.*

Sitt Marie-Rose is very important for this study because Etel Adnan shows that violence in Arab culture has its roots in badly lived sexuality:

[The Arabs] are moved by a sick sexuality, a mad love, where images of crushing and cries dominate. It's not that they are deprived of women or men if they like, but rather are inhibited by a profound distaste for the sexual thing. A sense of the uncleanliness of pleasure torments them and keeps them from ever being satisfied. Thus, the Arabs let themselves go in a tearing, killing, annihilating violence, and while other peoples, virulent in their own obsession with cleanliness, invent chemical products, they seek a primitive and absolute genocide. (P. 66)[1]

At this moment in the novel the author voices her judgments and her pleas directly. This technique may seem overly didactic and heavy for a novel, but perhaps it is necessary in order to bring the Arab audiences Adnan writes for back to their senses. And Adnan is very talented in raising such awareness when addressing audiences.[2]

Adnan also makes the connection among the war, tribal attitudes, and men's relationship to women, the mother in particular:

[The men] don't feel the opposition between that internal road which leads back to the tribe, and that need that one feels under other skies, to break down the barriers and take a look around, like liberated goats. . . . They only admit to good qualities in their mothers because they remember a well-being in them and around them, which they have never left, even if it were only to go kill birds and other men. The exclusive love of the mother sets the cycle of violence in motion again. (P. 66–67)

For Adnan, mothers clearly have a responsibility for the current events. If they had raised their sons with different values, the sons might have had problems coping with the rest of the society, but in the long run they might have been able to break the cycle of destruction and violence. More than that, the mother triggers violence in her son, because the umbilical cord between them has never been cut. Afraid of his need of her and wanting her approval, the love and hate he feels for her prevent him from growing up, from standing alone. He channels all this antagonism into destructive acts. So much Adnan perceives, but she overlooks the fact that mothers are also victims of the patriarchal-tribal society. They channel their need for power into their sons. Boasting and encouraging the macho in their sons, mothers reinforce their place in the family by perpetuating the system. In Adnan's novel, a woman not afraid to face the boyman's childishness, standing boldly as a judge in front of him, making him see his petty behavior, asking him to change his ways, has to be eliminated.

Ultimately, Sitt Marie-Rose is killed because she is such a woman—too strong a woman. Marie-Rose is the opposite of the *chababs'* mothers who flatter their egos. "A woman who stands up to them and looks them in the eye is a tree to be cut down, and they cut it down. She falls with the sound of dead wood which disappears among the perfidious murmurings of the city, and to the smirking of other women who are satisfied with the male victories" (p. 67). A strong woman frightens them, especially when she speaks of love. "It's fear, not love, that generates all actions here. . . . The citizens of this country are accustomed to fear, fear, the immense fear of not deserving their mother's love, of not being first at school or in the car race, of not making love as often as the other guys at the office, of not killing as many birds as their neighbor" (p. 68). All that shines—competing, boasting, succeeding at any cost—is instilled by mothers, according to Adnan. Again, they thus hold their share of responsibility in the carnage. In spite of this perception of the motive forces of her society, however, Adnan fails to see the impact of modernity, industrialization, and capitalism in making people competitive, in a race for success reaching madness.

Marie-Rose frightens the *chabab* because she stands for all that is contrary to their materialistic view of the world. She is not like their mothers. She does not comfort them, reassure them, reinforce their male egos. She is unlike any woman they could dominate. Neither wife nor mistress, neither mother nor whore, she stands alone for what she believes. She chooses a lonely and brave path she knows might lead to death. She believes she has to pick up the causes of the downtrodden in her country and go all the way, wherever that might lead. The *chabab* have

known from the beginning that they wouldn't be able to conquer either her heart or her mind. The more she spoke to them of love, the more they are afraid. . . . She breaks on the territory of their imaginations like a tidal wave. She rouses in their memories the oldest litanies of curses. To them, love is a kind of cannibalism. Feminine symbols tear at them with their claws. For seven thousand years the goddess Isis has given birth without there being a father. Isis in Egypt, Ishtar in

Bagdad, Anat in Marrakesh, the Virgin in Beirut. Nothing survives the passing of these divinities: they only loved Power, their Brother or their Son. And you expect Marie-Rose to hold her head up in the eyes of the males of this country? (Pp. 68–69)

Adnan brings forward feminine mythology—signs of an important past—to reinforce her thesis. By mentioning female goddesses of the Middle East and North Africa, Adnan reminds the reader and some of the protagonists in the novel that there are feminine figures one can be proud of and whose examples one can follow.

The theme that the war stems from an ancestral fear of women is evident in many of the novels used for this study. Adnan strongly emphasizes it. Men are afraid of women because they give life. Their power, masculinity, and egos are at stake. Their need of conquest and domination can find no sphere of action in this context. Marie-Rose epitomizes the woman they most fear because she stands on her own two feet, unafraid to respond to their questions, and, like the goddesses of their ancestral past, puts in doubt their logic and values and above all speaks of love. She incarnates spiritual values against their decadent materialistic ones.

The novel is divided into two parts: Time I, entitled "A Million Birds," and Time II, "Marie-Rose," divided into three acts, each subdivided into seven small scenes, almost as in a play. It is a classical division of time, as in Greek tragedy. This carefully studied sense of time and space reinforces the message and makes it more poignant and direct. As each sequence piles up its doses of horrors, it adds to the urgency of the events.

Time I opens just before the war and introduces the narrator—probably Etel Adnan herself—and the young Christian men who later join the militia and execute Marie-Rose after "trying" her. In this sequence, they are discussing with the narrator, the writer of the film, how to make a film. The superficiality of the young men's views comes out strongly in the dialogue they have with the writer, who would like to delve deep into the subject. They don't speak the same language. The scene opens with the men viewing the film of a hunting trip they took in Syria. They gain real sensual pleasure from killing birds, and their faces glow as they watch the images of their shooting. They associate killing with fucking, preferring the former. One of these gang *chababs* is described by the narrator: "'He prefers killing to kissing. . . . He prefers jeep-speed-desert-bird-bullet to girl-in-a-bed-and-fuck. . . . None of them has ever found in a woman the same sensation of power he gets from a car. An auto rally is more significant than

ETEL ADNAN 67

a conjugal night, and hunting is better still" (pp. 2–3). Aren't the problems here laid out in plain terms? When relationships between men and women are conceived in terms of power games, conquest, violence, domination, and possessing women like objects, how can one hope to have a society and a country that does not reflect those same anomalies at the political level? In such a context, the movement from hunting birds to killing human beings is direct. By setting this scene just before the war, Adnan shows not only the logic of this connection but also how forms of cruelty could happen anywhere, in the most common people, when their values are materialistic. When values are geared primarily to profit-making, human beings can easily be equated with animals or things.

Adnan reveals men's fear of women and associates their desire to destroy women with their need to destroy the city. This idea also appears in Elias Khoury's *La petite montagne*. Like Khoury, Adnan makes a connection between prostitution and Beirut, figuring the city as a victim of modernity and decadence:

In The City, this center of all prostitutions, there is a lot of money and a lot of construction that will never be finished. Cement has mixed with the earth, and little by little has smothered most of the trees. If not all. From every window what we call this city appears like a huge game of colored blocks consumed by the sun. . . . These volumes form a gigantic pile of building blocks, which gives me [the narrator], each time I see it, a sensation of almost mystic terror. (P. 9)

In Adnan's description, there is fear but also love and compassion for a city represented as the victim of industrial illness. Whereas Khoury wants to destroy this "whore of all whores" who receives forty bullets at once, like a prostitute getting fucked by forty men in one afternoon, Adnan's city is a woman being raped: "This city is like a great suffering being, too mad, too overcharged, broken now, gutted, and raped like those girls raped by thirty or forty militia men, and are now mad and in asylums because their families, Mediterranean to the end, would rather hide than cure . . . but how does one cure the memory? The city, like those girls, was raped" (p. 21).

The male writing of Khoury stands in opposition to Adnan's, even though both use prostitution in relation to the city. Khoury wants to punish the "decadent bitch," source of all evils, to destroy her, while Adnan feels sorry for the victim of a culture that not only inflicts deep, unforgivable wounds, but punishes its victim by incarcerating her and treating her like a mad woman. Adnan puts society and culture on trial, while Khoury accuses women, life, destiny in general. The contrasting vision of these two writers is significant and more complex than my reduction here, and I will pick up these differences for further analysis in the conclusion of this chapter and of this book. I have simplified here the perceptions of the city in order to emphasize the male/female differences. In Adnan, there is a hidden attraction of violence which complicates her overall message for peace.

In Time I, the theme of violence is explored, and the author illustrates its strong attraction:

Violence is absorbed like a consumer product. I [the narrator] understood this need for violence one day in front of an electric wire torn from its socket. In the two holes there remained two little bits of brilliant copper wire which seemed to call out to me. And I wanted to touch them, to reunite them in my hand, to make that current pass through my body, and see what it was like to burn. I resisted only with an extraordinary effort. The whole country is responding without reserve to this call to violence. The pleasure of killing with all the justification one could find for it blooms. (P. 13)

Adnan explicitly says here—that death exerts a strong attraction—while she implicitly says that violence and destruction ought to be eradicated.

Why is violence so strong a magnet? Many explanations have been given, among them Gérard Mendel's in his article "La violence est un langage." A French neuropsychiatrist, Mendel notes that all the patients he treated were nonviolent and nonaggressive in their *acts,* but their conscious or unconscious fantasies were aggressive and destructive. This suggests to him that they did not learn to integrate their childhood aggression in socialized action. For Mendel, all our actions are a mixture of constructive and destructive forces. Without a taming process, a socialization of our aggression, we would remain paralyzed.

In Mendel's view, there are two opposing interpretations of violence: one sees violence as a sign of human and social suffering, of dehumanization stemming from the incapacity to control one's acts; the other sees violence as the "beast" in humans, which must be neutralized at any cost. But if we suppose that violence is a reaction to or effect of dehumanization, wouldn't its neutralization lead to a greater dehumanization—by not allowing the oppressed to express themselves, for example? And isn't the "beast" in humans just an essentialism, a physiological explanation as well as justification of violence?

For Mendel, elements of alienation, dehumanization, identity problems, could begin to give some explanations for the attraction exerted by violence in terms of boredom, depression, fascination with death, fear of reality, fear in general. He gives, as an example, the death toll on French roads: 15,000 a year. Is this not a violence in daily living, a way of channeling one's aggression into the feeling that the driver is all-powerful, master of life and death, "the absolute monarch of an illusory kingdom for which he is ready to sacrifice his and others' lives?" (p. 42).

The male youth in Lebanon have not learned to curb their aggression. They are bored, and they are fascinated with death. Driving their cars like masters of the roads, showing off to prove their "superiority," boasting about their driving in very immature ways, those boys learn to kill, destroy, torture, dismember, and burn without remorse in the war.

According to Adnan, aggression is channeled into destruction and sadism:

The detonations are staccato, dry. Mortars smash like so many rotten melons, and houses fall with a soft sound. Rockets whip against buildings and dynamite explodes like an evil eye. Then there is the machinegun fire, the coded messages of a victorious will. To mark the victory of Death, the city burrows deeper into terror. Soon the city will be nothing but a wrecked shell thrown up on its rocks. Every hour the radio reports blindings, castrations, nylon bags full of cut-up bodies thrown onto public squares, deaths by kitchen knives, a disturbing surgery, torture in a cemetery. (P. 15)

The narrator tells herself "that it would be better to let loose a million birds in the sky over Lebanon, so that these hunters could practice on them, and this carnage could be avoided" (p. 17). This, however, seems to be fighting violence with violence. Hunting may be considered a game or a sport, but it is a cruel and deadly one. In this passage, Adnan seems insensitive to the reality that it is men's callous indifference to nature in general that is also the problem. The earth and the animals suffer too.

Violence is closely related to sexuality and to the war. As in the other novels under study, here the war breaks down ethical institutions, particularly those relating to sexuality. The narrator watches "the young couple who live downstairs making love on the verandah in the middle of the afternoon. Recent events must have stunned them. They never would have been so innocent normally. Maybe they're trying to overcome their anxiety" (p. 17). While al-Shaykh describes such behavior as shocking, Adnan sees it as innocent. At some level, war liberates. Unfortunately, it is not "real" liberation, because set in the context of the war, it adds to chaos. The young couple react to the war rather than acting upon it to change it. Like

Zahra's brother who masturbated in front of her, they only add to the confusion, showing how lost people have become. Time I is significant for its revelation of instinct and its introduction of the city, of the narrator (probably Adnan herself), and of how the narrator feels about the situation.

Time II, a period of twenty-four hours, is broken down into three sequences: an introduction to the various characters; the "trial" of Marie-Rose; and the execution of Marie-Rose. The "chorus" of this tragedy include, paradoxically, the deaf-mutes: they are witnesses of the crime of the execution of Marie-Rose, but cannot say anything about it; they only dance in the end. Marie-Rose is a Christ-like figure, killed for her beliefs because she has loved too much and has espoused the causes of the oppressed of her society. Mounir, the interrogator, is like Pilate; he has joined the Christian militia without strong convictions, and, while he is more sensitive and intelligent than the others and while he has loved Marie-Rose in the past, he is forced to give her up for execution. Tony, one of the executioners, is merciless; he thinks himself as "braver than a lion" (p. 90) and sees Marie-Rose as a whore because she sleeps with a Palestinian and "takes herself seriously." Fouad, another executioner, is "the perfect killer; he suffers from never having killed enough" (p. 2). His language is frightening: "me, I know that might makes right, that the wolf doesn't ask the sheep's permission to eat him, it's his right as a wolf," he says (p. 92). And in a Nazi-like speech that recalls Ahmad's in *The Story of Zahra,* he asserts: "a militia is always right, in all its decisions. . . . I am absolute order, I am absolute power, I am absolute efficiency, I've reduced all truths to a formula of life and death" (p. 37). Bouna Lias, the priest, is more like a Judas; he betrays the real gospel message of love; he refuses to give Marie-Rose extreme unction or benediction; he believes he is defending God's interests on earth. Finally, the narrator closes each of the three movements with profound analysis and prophetic revelations about what is taking place in the novel and, by implication, in the Lebanese war and society, the Arab countries, the fate of the Palestinians, and the world in general.

Some of these remarks are pertinent to this study and suggest parallels to al-Shaykh's perceptions in *The Story of Zahra.* Adnan believes that the war has made the members of the militias discover their identities—identities made up of violence, tribalism, lack of empathy or compassion. "They love destruction because it's a process of peeling away, it makes them believe they're on the road to truth. . . . They love noise, they love turmoil. . . . All they do is run headlong into death" (p. 40). Likewise, Paul Vieille contends that the wars taking place in the Middle East today do not have an understandable logic, but rather seem to take their roots in a death ideology, a fascination with death. "Dereliction has given birth to cynical violence, the cynical use of violence. The thirst for power clan leaders held has subdivided society even more, each small group nowadays fighting for its own power" ("Le chaos du monde," p. 25).

For Adnan women who dare question that identity and those values become

the prey the scouts of the clan hunt and bring back to the fold. This is a common good, be it in Islamic tribes in southern Tunisia, or in Christian tribes from the Lebanese mountains: the trapped gazelle is always shared by all. . . . She [Marie-Rose] was also subject to another great delusion believing that women were protected from repression, and that the leaders considered political fights to be strictly between males. In fact, with women's greater access to certain powers, they began to watch them more closely, and perhaps with even greater hostility. Every feminine act, charitable and seemingly unpolitical ones, were [sic] regarded as a rebellion in this world where women had always played servile roles. Marie-Rose inspired scorn and hate long before the fateful day of her arrest. (P. 101)

Many feminists around the world are noticing this phenomenon: that with women's demands for more equality and freedom, there is an equal rise in misogynist behavior. Angela Davis, in *Women, Race and Class,* says that "the present rape epidemic occurs at a time when the capitalist class is furiously reasserting its authority in the face of global and internal challenges. Both racism and sexism, central to its domestic strategy of increased economic exploitation, are receiving unprecedented encouragement. It is not a mere coincidence that as the incidence of rape has risen, the position of women workers has visibly worsened" (p. 200). And Betty Reardon notices how "the specter of threats to the purse and to traditional definitions of masculinity and femininity that is raised by the terms feminist and women's lib provokes a severe backlash from true male chauvinists, both male and female" (p. 21). For her, it is "no wonder [that] more massive weaponry has developed as more women refuse to remain vulnerable and seek to meet the challenges of equality—even when doing so may mean that they become acknowledged, not only implicit enemies" (p. 45). Indeed, she argues, "Women's equality is so strong a threat to sexist masculine identity that it is perceived as a threat to the very being of man" (p. 46). Marie-Rose, who espouses many of the causes of the oppressed—"first it was educational reform, than it was the typographers' strike, then women's liberation" (p. 35)—becomes the scapegoat of all the frustrations, anger, and desire for revenge the males in her country have accumulated.

Those males are described as the *chabab* mafia, the gang of boys. They are like the *zaᶜims* (leaders) or *askaris* (militiamen) in chapter 1, except that here they are identified mainly within the Christian clan. Adnan paints their lives as a function of their vanity. Parading like wild peacocks, "they hold absolute power that's as cold as their guns. . . . These young boys were exalted by the Crusades. . . . They dreamed of a Christianity with helmets and boots, riding its horses into the clash of arms, spearing Moslem foot-soldiers like so many St. Georges with so many dragons" (pp. 46–48). Adnan has no kind words for such Christianity, and rightly so. The Christians she describes have twisted the true message of Christ—love, humility, justice, peace. She shows the Crusade as directed against the poor: "They bomb the underprivileged quarters because they consider the poor to be vermin they think will eat them. . . . They have perverted Charity at the heart of its root. . . . The spiritual Jerusalem is dead, in their consanguineous marriage, and under the weight of their hatred. It is no longer in the Middle East" (p. 52). She says they have transformed Christ into a tribal prince. For her, though, "Christ only exists when one stands up to one's own brothers to defend the Stranger" (p. 104). Marie-Rose has applied this prescription by espousing the Palestinian cause—the downtrodden in the story—and this is why she is a Christ-like figure.

While Adnan describes the Christian militias and some of the priests, in their travesty of Christianity, in the darkest terms, she glorifies the Palestinian cause. Marie-Rose says, "They represent a new beginning. . . . For once in the History of the Middle East, the wandering of the Palestinian is no longer that of a nomad carrying his tribe in himself, but that of a man alone, uprooted, pursued. They're attempting to break down your [some Lebanese Christians, most specifically the *Kataëb*] values, and in the process are breaking their own necks. They're getting their throats cut by you and your sinister allies. To liberate you" (p. 57). When she approaches death, her romantic notion of them reaches a peak: "Oh how innocent and courageous are these people whose vitality defies death! Will the lights shining in their eyes be extinguished one by one? Must a sinister dawn spread like a shroud over their beloved bodies?" (p. 85). Thus Adnan, while correct in her criticism of the perversion of Christianity, romanticizes to the extent of falsifying the Palestinian cause.

The Lebanese war has shown that the Palestinians are as ruthless, as cruel, as hungry for power, as eager to destroy, as much participants in the massacres, and as macho with their women as the men in the other militias. Listen to what Sakinna Boukhedenna, a young Algerian woman, says about one of them in her *Journal "Nationalité: Immigré(e)"*: "I would like to talk about this Palestinan Aïssa [a man with whom she was going out]. I would like to talk about him because, although he was a phallocrat, this guy had some value. He had an important political past at the service of the just cause of his people, the Palestinian people. . . . The good woman for him, it is the sister, the asexual mother, otherwise a woman is a prostitute. The real woman must never exist from Algeria to Palestine" (p. 91). Boukhedenna shows how men, politically liberated and liberating, may nevertheless be oppressive when it comes to women.

It must be noted here that Etel Adnan's support of the Palestinian cause, at the beginning of the war, was very much in line with what most progressive writers, intellectuals, and artists believed. The creation of the state of Israel in the 1940s in the territories where Palestine used to be pushed out thousands of Palestinians, who became refugees in the surrounding countries—Jordan, Syria, Egypt, Iraq, and most of all Lebanon, where they arrived after also being massacred in Arab countries (during Jordan's Black September, for example). Condemned into exile and living under terrible conditions, they were denied basic rights. They organized militarily in and outside their camps and picked up terrorist and guerilla warfare techniques to advance their cause. This made them less sympathetic, especially in Lebanon where their movement broke down the delicate balance among the various communities. Their intervention in and irruption into Lebanese society was one of the key factors that led to the present Lebanese crisis.

Even the leftist Lebanese intellectuals who came into close contact with the Palestinians and who fought with and for the Palestinian cause, believing it would revolutionize the Arab world, were disillusioned. As Roger Naba'a and Souheil al-Kache note in their dialogue:

—What we lacked was an understanding of the internal mechanism of the function of Palestinian society. . . . We did not understand at the time how much the Palestinian Resistance could close itself within the Palestinian specificity. We thought we could extend it, deconstruct it to reconstruct it.
—They are Palestinian Nationalists who justify their regionalism with other regionalisms: Lebanese, Syrian, etc.! After ten years, I have the right to say this! (P. 149)

These intellectuals here use the same method for which they reproach the Palestinians, albeit through language. Who has the "right" to *use* anyone by extension, deconstruction, and reconstruction? Is this not a manipulation of power through language? Here is a good example of how nationalism can be manipulated for negative results: the Palestinians and Israelis justify terrorist tactics; the Lebanese leftists use similar methods to get rid of nationalism altogether. How could the Lebanese intellectuals not see that the Palestinians, being oppressed and downtrodden, would first need to reestablish their identity before talking about universalism? Ultimately, their aim may be praiseworthy, but the way they go about it is doomed. For violence only begets violence.

As for Etel Adnan, can we excuse her by saying that she wrote this novel at the beginning of the war, when there was still hope in the Palestinian cause as a real revolution? Would this not be falling into the same short-sightedness I criticize in her and the leftist Lebanese intellectuals? Can one afford such short-range visions in the face of a war—and of wars that keep repeating themselves? Is it too demanding to want writers and intellectuals to provide, if not the answers, at least the questions that bring out *all* the veils of society, without partisanship?

Etel Adnan points her accusing finger at the Arab world. It "lies on an operating table. The equipment should be removed, the respirator un-plugged. The patient should be obliged to spit out, not the mucous, but the original illness, not the blood clogging his throat but the words, the words, the swamps of words that have been waiting there for so long" (p. 100). And Beirut is compared to "a huge open wound. If suffering could be measured in ounces and square centimeters, then the suffering of this city was greater than any other city in the century. . . . No one seemed to want to admit that cruelty was a part of a moral cancer that was spreading through the whole Middle East" (p. 103).

As in other novels, the city embodies decadence brought by industrialization, while the sea offers hope, the expectation of renewal and rebirth: "the sea is beautiful, even more so since the blood washed down by the greedy rain opened reddening roads into the sea. It's only in it, in its immemorial blue, that the blood of all is finally mixed . . . this city is nothing but a huge square of cement. . . . They [the militias] only address each other with cannons, machine guns, razors, knives. And the sea, receiving them in an advanced state of decomposition, reconciles them in the void" (pp. 98–99). The symbols of the city and of the sea are completed by that of the sky, which Marie-Rose compares to a bird flying alone "cut down by hunters on the look-out" (p. 100), "those four men set upon that passing bird" (p. 103). The theme of hunters and birds, described at the beginning of the novel, is repeated here. It is no longer part of a movie, but has become a reality. For Marie-Rose, it is better never to rebuild the city if it is to repeat "new banks, new slums . . . start polluting the water again, the fields, the streets, and people's minds" (p. 95).

The most important message of the novel is one of love and peace, and in my evaluation it is the best femihumanist one that can be offered in the midst of the chaos and destruction brought by war. Adnan denounces the love of clan, which is the wrong kind of love practiced by Arabs. For her, "the only true love is the love of the Stranger. When you have cut the umbilical cords that bind you together, you will at last become real men, and life among you will have a meaning" (p. 55). In her view, tribal love can be broken down by love between men and women: "When a man and a woman find each other in the silence of the night, it's the beginning of the end of the tribe's power, and death itself becomes a challenge to the ascendancy of the group" (p. 58). Real love for her is not tribal, jealous, possessive, and exclusive, but reaches out to others. In this world, it is "the unknown, the untried" (p. 100), but Marie-Rose does go so far as loving her executioners and forgiving them: "I want to make my peace with everyone. Even with my captors, I want to make my peace. I can no longer sustain this hatred. It's what brought us to this apocalypse" (p. 86).

Etel Adnan's message—represented through Marie-Rose's attitude before her torturers—illustrates Gandhi's concept of nonviolence: "Nonviolence in its active form consists in goodwill towards all living things. It is pure Love. I have read it in the Hindu Holy Scriptures, in the Bible and in the Qur²an" (Gandhi, quoted in "Religions et non-violence selon Gandhi," p. 53). The fact that Adnan expresses her message through a woman is also significant. It joins what Anne-Marie de Vilaine writes in her essay "La maternité détournée": "My body is the place of certain events; it conveys some meanings that *I* don't necessarily mean. Nonviolence, necessary to a real regeneration of civilization by women as I see it, consists first of all— contrary to what eight thousand years of masculine civilization have taught us—in refusing to have a totalitarian conscience in oneself, to believe that one alone could be right" (p. 31).

Sitt Marie-Rose shows a woman who takes her destiny in her own hands, stands alone and courageously for what she believes, and is not afraid to tell men what is wrong with their values, even when she knows they will kill her for defying them. She is truly visionary. She espouses the causes of the oppressed, not only intellectually, but most of all actively. She understands what an active nonviolent struggle means and goes one step further in consenting to die for her beliefs, even forgiving her executioners. She is a victim, but an expiatory one. Her sacrifice, like Christ's, allows others to live. This is not the Christianity of the *chabab* gangs. But perhaps, as Gandhi says, all religions contain such a core message, however much this message may be distorted in practice.

It is significant that Etel Adnan chooses a woman to incarnate values that may change society and overturn the war. The woman she describes did exist: she lived for the oppressed and gave her life hoping her sacrifice might show the fighters their foolishness. In the novel, Marie-Rose also lives her ideals at the personal level. She leaves a husband who oppresses her and goes to live with a man who respects her, loves her, and encourages her in her struggle and values. The narrator makes it a point to tell us that sexual relationships are at the core of political problems. Didactically made, such observations nevertheless reinforce the notion that when relationships between men and women are conceived in terms of power, violence, domination, possession, and objectification, one cannot hope to have a society and a country that will not reflect those same pitfalls at the political level.

NOTES

1. Throughout I will be quoting from the English edition by permission of the Post-Apollo Press, Sausalito, Calif. © Etel Adnan, 1982.
2. At the conference on "Lebanese Women Witness War," organized by the Arab League in Paris, October 20–22, 1987, she literally brought women from enemy clans together, stirring many emotions when she spoke.

FIVE

Andrée Chedid: Determination, Vision, Endurance, and Belief in Humanity

Kalya advances as if she had always been walking. She is advancing, step by step, since eternity, at the bottom of an immense void. . . . A memorial march, yet so brief. . . . Nothing has yet been said. Angers can still be extinguished. Day might still shine. . . . Painful bodies from all the centuries, from all the corners of the earth rise up all around her. . . . Men covet death. Kalya does not stop walking, holding on to every ray of hope, to elude anxiety, to cross the last distance. . . . Her look goes to the young women with whom she shares thoughts and sensations. . . . She will reach the end. She will reach. There is so much strength in every human creature. So much strength in her.

Andrée Chedid, La maison sans racines

Novelist, poet, and dramatist, Andrée Chedid is an outstanding international literary figure. Of Egyptian-Lebanese origin, she was born in Cairo in 1920, attended boarding schools in Cairo and Paris, received a B.A. from the American University in Cairo, and married Louis Chedid, a medical student, at the age of twenty-one. They spent the next three years (1942–1945) in Lebanon, then moved to Paris in 1946.

Chedid is an extremely prolific writer, having published more than nine novels, sixteen collections of poems, two collections of short stories, two plays, and two essays. Her work has been adapted for the cinema, the television, the theater, and radio. She has been translated into several languages, and her work is taught in high schools, colleges, and universities throughout the world. She has received more than six important prizes, among them the Goncourt de la Nouvelle, the Mallarmé, and the Louise Labé and has remained very humble in spite of her successes. She is also an artist and has exhibited her collages. In addition, she has raised two children and has six grandchildren.

As Bettina Knapp has put it: "Chedid's work is profound and sensitive; her vision innovative in its archetypal delineations; her aesthetic, lyrical, dense, symbolistic, a blend of the real and the unreal, the Occident and the

Middle East. Her protagonists emerge from a universal mold; they are eternal in their philosophical and psychological configurations, for they have stepped into life full-blown from the dream" (p. 7). In all of Chedid's work, we see this blend of East and West, and a search for the meaning of life, death, and love. The language, images, and symbols she uses have their roots within the lands she belongs to: Egypt, Lebanon, France, and now also the United States. The quest emphasized in her themes is universal and archetypal, a beautiful mixture of the spiritual and the physical. Her style and her work within various literary forms show great talent, innovation, rhythm, humor, and a blend of what Knapp calls the "sensual and lush, barren and stark" (p. 80).

The novel I am going to analyze, *La maison sans racines,*[1] is especially important in terms of my study because it shows women's positive role in the war, their efforts to bring peace and to reconcile enemy clans. Their initiative goes along with revolting against the traditional roles society prescribes for them. In this respect, the novel clearly illustrates how sexual roles also define attitudes towards war, violence, and peace. While Chedid lives outside of Lebanon, distance and concern have given her a visionary reading of events there. Women were the ones who started peace marches at various times throughout the war and on both sides, East and West.

The novel is innovative in terms of its technique. Three different stories develop, in different times and places, with the unifying element being the march two young women from two enemy communities have started in the center of the war-torn city. An almost cinematic technique gives us the various events of the three narratives. Rendered with lyricism and humor, they express the desire for life, love, and reconciliation amidst the tragedy of war. In this latest novel, Andrée Chedid has achieved a perfection in her art. The peace march, pulling together the various elements in its eloquent appeal, is handled with the precision of a watchmaker.

The first narrative is about Sybil, who is twelve years old and raised in the United States, and her grandmother Kalya, who is in her fifties and lives in Paris. They have never met but decide to spend their vacation in the country of their ancestors, Lebanon. This visit takes place in 1975, on the eve of the Lebanese tragedy, but it could have happened at any time during the war, except that the two might not have decided to go there for a vacation. The second narrative takes us back to 1932, when Kalya used to come from Egypt to spend her vacation in the Lebanese mountains with other members of her family, including her own grandmother, Nouza. The third narrative constitutes the thread of the novel and gives us its key. Ammal (meaning hope in Arabic) from the Muslim community and Myriam (Arabic for Mary, mother of Jesus in both the Qur'an and the Bible) from the Christian community, daughter of Mario, an adolescent love of Kalya, decide to meet at the center of the city, the place of conflicts, and start a peace march. They have planned for crowds on both sides to join them in their effort.

The novel opens on the square where Myriam and Ammal, wearing similar yellow dresses, scarves, and tennis shoes, have marched to meet and start the peace process. They had planned to get together at the center of the place, "to stretch their hands towards each other, exchange a symbolic kiss, and then shake their yellow scarves in the air to call out all those waiting around them" (p. 57). Crowds of people would only have been waiting for this signal to join them and "ask for the immediate ending of all dissension, of all violence" (p. 58). But as they advance towards each other, one of them is hit by a bullet. Kalya grabs a revolver she had kept in a drawer and walks towards the place to save "the hope the two young women had wanted to carry" (p. 17). She holds the weapon well in sight to prevent any other threat. But what can a revolver do against a *kalashnikov?* The ending is figured in the beginning, foreshadowing the tragedy of events to come. Kalya walks slowly not knowing if it is toward life or death. A sinister silence reigns. The road is long and "filled with all of the earth's anxieties, all its lamentations" (p. 56).

It is as if Kalya is walking backwards. "She is advancing, advancing towards she doesn't know what. Perhaps a happy ending: the two young women rising, hundreds of people gathering around them" (p. 98). While one of the stores in the square has already been completely demolished by a shell or dynamite on the preceding day, she does not want to believe the tragedy has begun. She still wants to believe life will triumph.

The march of this woman recalls many others women have walked throughout the ages. "Kalya is advancing as if she had always been walking. She is advancing step by step, since eternity, at the bottom of a great void. . . . An immemorial walk, yet so brief" (p. 117). She is walking towards the place of truth, "wounded bodies coming from all the centuries, from all the corners of the earth . . . a procession of hope breaking against a cement wall. Men coveting death" (p. 118). She seeks, through the life of the two young women she is trying to save, the survival of a whole country and with it the earth's salvation. There is true strength and determination in this woman marching through a city torn by war.

Beirut becomes the sum of all other cities Kalya rejects, destroyed by war throughout history, of all the prisoners, of all the fields filled up with corpses. "When will the earth stop enduring these tortures? . . . Kalya is advancing inside a nightmare. . . . She could, she would like to be elsewhere, in another country, another world, another road. Is death at the end of that one?" (pp. 161–62). Only one shot had been sufficient to turn everything upside down. It is the sniper, "a killer without a cause" (p. 225), who has done the job. Such an act raises essential questions: "Why shorten this sparkle? . . . What makes man's flesh, the texture of his soul, the density of his heart? Under so many words, acts, scales, where does life breathe?" (p. 226).

This long walk of Kalya allows Chedid to raise key questions about Lebanon, the war, violence. Two pages of unpunctuated lines, each beginning with the word *before,* bring out some of the horrible elements of the war: the divisions of the city, the militias, all the various weapons, the snipers, the massacres, the burnt corpses, the screaming mothers—all these descriptions start with "before," as a wish: "Before the worst becomes the daily bread before the road-block of all fraternities of all dialogues breaks horror devastates submerges before before before . . . " (pp. 215–16). This long unpunctuated passage is like the march, breathless, expressing hope against all odds. But "before" has already become "after," and the pool of blood spreads.

Myriam and Ammal are picked up by an ambulance and we are given to believe they will be saved, "they would heal together, more united, more decided than ever" (p. 228). But Sybil, who has run to join her grandmother on the square, is hit by the sniper's bullet. Kalya falls on the ground in front of "the fatal image, irreversible, which, in one stroke, erased her own life" (p. 247). "Will tomorrow bring the apocalypse, an ocean of madness, or peace?" (p. 248). Why did the little girl have to die? Of what use was the revolver the grandmother was carrying? The last image is of the yellow scarf stained with blood, lifted by the wind across the square, symbol of a union that might yet take place in spite of the tragedy.

This ending is revealing: The two young women from enemy communities who started the peace march are saved, in spite of their wounds. They will be able to carry on the struggle. Kalya, on the other hand, the grandmother who had come to Lebanon haunted by her memories, a photographer by profession, carrying a camera with which she would fix images of past, present, and future, is broken with grief at the sight of her grandchild lying dead on the ground. The revolver she carries is of no use. Why does she accept this weapon in the first place? And why does she hold it in her march? A peace march can only be effective without weapons. Did she not act in the same spirit as Myriam and Ammal? The revolver had been given to her by Georges, Myriam's brother, who, very much opposed to his sister's ideas, believes in fighting and has in fact joined a militia. Why does Kalya take it, and what does she think she can achieve with it? If the weapon is symbolic, would it not have been better if she had carried her camera instead, thus making art triumph over violence? By analyzing the other sequences of the story, I will try to find answers to these questions so vital to my discussion and topic.

Through the relationship Kalya has with Sybil, she relives the one she had with her grandmother, Nouza. It was one of great love and affection. Kalya has not been able to accept her death and comes to Lebanon to recapture the moments lived with her. "When she was six, seven, nine, ten, twelve years old, she would run towards Nouza, who always welcomed her as if it were a feast" (p. 240). She describes her as someone tender and strong, capricious and free. She had watched Nouza sleeping on the couch and felt "as if she were her grandchild" (p. 179). She did not want her to grow old and wanted to take her picture. This is what had triggered in her the desire to be a photographer: wanting to fix Nouza, keep her forever. It was her grandmother who had given her her first camera. Many events from the past are repeated in the present, and it is as if Sybil's death is another death of Nouza. Kalya, who comes to Lebanon to exorcise the pain of that loss, finds it reenacted in Sybil's death. She wishes she could also die: "She does not want to struggle anymore, and rejects the breath that stopped at her lips" (p. 247). The granddaughter becomes the grandmother. The parent-child roles are here reversed, emphasizing the cyclical aspect of Chedid's sense of time, her notion that history repeats itself and that life brings its own renewal.

Nouza had also been offered a revolver in the past, and Kalya, a child at the time, had watched her refuse it. Why did she not repeat her grandmother's refusal? Each time, the weapon is offered by the most macho of men, Farid, Nouza's brother, in her case, and Georges, Myriam's brother, in Kalya's. Both men claim it is for protection. Nouza has the strength to push it away, but Kalya, perhaps due to the war tensions, does not prevent its being dropped in her drawer, and even grabs it to deter the sniper's attack, against all logic — a revolver facing cannons, bombs, heavy artillery, machine guns is completely disproportionate and absurd.

Farid is described as having vivid traits quite typical of the Mediterranean male: "Tyrannical and muddle-headed, short-tempered and sentimental, confirmed player, going from poker to baccara . . . he would cover his listener with curses or excessive praises" (p. 41). Growing old, he had imagined himself at the head of the family tribe, he, the black sheep, giving advice to the other members. Nouza would make fun of him, and he would take revenge on his docile wife, Odette. He liked to dominate. Kalya remembers how upset she got at how he treated his wife. Seeking a quarrel and not daring to impose his aggressiveness on his sister, it was his wife he had rebuked for the menu and the table. Kalya had stood up, asking him not to talk this way to his wife. The lack of encouragment from the other two women—Nouza and Odette—had made Kalya sit back (pp. 64–65). It is Kalya—only a child but already aware of injustices—who gets upset and not Nouza, Farid's sister or Odette, his wife, as would be expected. Here already are Kalya's rejection of women's traditional passive roles and her rebellion against male authority and aggressiveness.

Myriam would also stand up against her brother Georges and his desire to control her. She would refuse to answer his questions about her whereabouts and had decided she "would never allow him to go against her desires, prevent her projects, change her way of seeing things" (p. 142). Georges is a whole-hearted militant in one of the parties, while Myriam and Ammal are seeking to unite all the communities under the same aim (p. 174). When he brings the revolver to Kalya, he explains to her that it is to protect her against murder: "The hope of uniting everybody is a source of tensions, look at history, beautiful ideas have never been sufficient, and bringing together different people in the same place only creates hatred" (p. 199). Kalya tells him she will never use it. But when he asks her if she would use it to protect her grandchild, she does not answer. He interprets her silence for agreement and leaves the weapon in her drawer. At that moment, why doesn't Kalya ask Georges to take it back, as her grandmother had done in the past? Does she really believe she will need it to protect her grandchild and through it Lebanon? Given the tensions, she probably feels she might need it to protect Sybil, but her reaction is an instinctive short-sighted one, as the ending will demonstrate.

The connection between a feeling for one's child and for Lebanon has been made by many female authors. Miriam Cooke and others have shown that women in Lebanon and in particular women writers display a kind of "maternal thinking" toward their country. As Cooke writes, "Beirut Decentrists, early in the war were already beginning to demonstrate a maternal attachment to Lebanon which they came to consider a child, sick and in need. . . . If writers could not awaken in others a sense of responsibility for the preservation and ultimate growth of Lebanon as a land and a people, the child already sick would surely die. The need to stay and provide models of endurance and steadfastness became a sacred duty" (*Women Write War*, p. 21). Does Kalya really believe she can protect the children and the country with a revolver or an even bigger weapon? She is confronted with a dilemma: should she join Myriam and Ammal in their pacifist march and become the next target, or should she meet the violence ripping the country apart revolver in hand, thereby hoping to save innocent lives, most particularly the children's?

Nonviolent action, as defined by Jean-Marie Muller, may help to explain Kalya's action. According to Muller, nonviolence does not mean lack of aggressiveness. A certain amount of aggression is, in fact, necessary, for without it, there can be no mature relationships, and conflicts cannot be solved without there being victims. Nonviolence is a radical *rejection* of violence. It is not passive. "Nonviolent action is a trial of strength and, I would go as far as saying, a constraint" ("Signification de la non-violence," p. 20). Could that be the significance of Kalya's act? Is grabbing the revolver for Kalya an aggressive rejection of violence? And if so, why does her grandchild have to die? Isn't the death of the child a negation of her act of salvation? Would the child have died had she been carrying her camera instead of a gun? What is the ultimate meaning of Sybil's death and of Kalya's march?

Ammal and Myriam believe in *assertive* nonviolent action. But they do not go about it the way Kalya does. They choose a peace march, a stretched-out hand, a symbolic kiss, a lifted scarf, announcement of a mass movement that was to have started. The result of both attempts is death. Could it have been otherwise on the eve of the Lebanese war? How could they go against all the forces linked to bring about the tragedy? What could they do against the *kalashnikov* aimed at the heart of their peace initiative? All those who, in Lebanon, are using nonviolent aggressive tactics to deter the war— such as peace marches, hunger strikes, sit-ins, everyday crossings of the demarcation line—know that their belief in peace and unity will someday triumph over the forces of destruction, even though at present everything looks terribly bleak.

In this novel, the desire for peace and its initiation go along with women's need and desire to be liberated. All the strong and assertive women in the story want to be free, to make their own decisions, not to have their choices made for them. They rise up against injustices and are professionally, and therefore also economically, independent. They refuse the roles assigned to them by society and talk back to the males in their families when they feel the men are impinging on their right to live as they see fit.

Ammal and Myriam, for example, do not want to be like their mothers, "too passive or too restless, who wasted idle lives between somnolence and worldliness" (p. 149). Already in their childhood, they had discussed religion and decided their God was the same even if they prayed to Him differently. They do not accept certain customs. When they are nineteen, they decide to go to other parts of the city and find out for themselves about poverty and class differences. They read a lot, and try to understand the meaning of existence. When they are twenty, "they reject routine and prejudices; they make an agreement against all that separates and divides" (p. 149). One studies law, the other pharmacy. Their families, preferring them to be married, established, with children, hope their studies are only temporary. Ammal and Myriam are going against their fathers, brothers, and all of society, but they know that deep inside many think as they do (pp. 148–50).

Kalya is of the same stock, even though she is thirty years older. Various events of her life show us her determination to be different: her questions about life, love, death, God, existence; her professional choice to be a photographer; her refusal of girls' passive roles; her love of Paris and its symbol of freedom; her love of dancing; her awareness of class differences; the fact that she is privileged and the uneasiness it gives her.

She raises important questions about origins: "What are roots? Far away ties or the ones that get woven across one's existence? Those of an ancestral country rarely visited, or of a neighboring country where one would spend one's childhood, or those of a city where one lived for a number of years?" (p. 79). It is as if Andrée Chedid herself is talking through Kalya and telling us how she feels about roots: "Didn't Kalya choose to be uprooted? Didn't she wish to graft all her various roots and sensitivities? Hybrid, why not? She liked these crossings, meetings, these composite looks which don't block the future nor brush aside other worlds" (p. 79). These lines are at the core of Chedid's message. Unlike many North African writers, such as Driss Chraïbi, Albert Memmi, Abdel-Kebir Khatibi, and Marguerite Taos-Amrouche to name only a few, who have described how divided they feel about being a mixture of cultures, how torn and unhappy it causes them to be—they use expressions such as "bâtard historique" (historical bastard), "aliénation culturelle" (cultural alienation), "être entre deux chaises" (to be between two chairs, not really sitting) uneasiness[2]—Chedid insists on the positive aspects of such hybridization, affirming cosmopolitanism and the enrichment, tolerance, and openess it brings. These values are what Lebanon used to represent and what Kalya has come to seek: "Tenderness for this exiguous land that one could cross in one day; this land so tenacious and fragile. For the memory of impetus, hospitability, harmony of voices" (p. 81). This is a picture of Lebanon that Chedid paints in an essay written before the war: "Land where opposed voices, confronting each other, do their best to remain harmonious. Centuries have marked it with unalterable signs, yet nothing fixed, set, flatly eternal weighs you down here. Very ancient land of wonders, never ceasing to give birth to itself" (*Liban*, p. 6). In other passages of this remarkable essay written with sensitivity and love, Chedid describes how action in Lebanon could be summarized in a phrase: "to live with" (p. 55). Its ethnic complexity reflects its whole history, its miracle of being open to the outside world, its "history of schisms and reconciliations, conquests, humiliations, blood, and tears" (p. 59).

Other questions raised by the novel concern God and the differences and similarities among various religions. As a child, Kalya already raises basic questions about God. She would ask her grandmother, "Would God be immensity? Would He be for all human beings? Would He be without hatred? Would He be kindness itself? God would not be God if He were not all of that grandma, isn't it?" (p. 91). Not knowing how to answer these questions, Nouza would send Kalya to Mitry, a cousin, who explained to her the historical Christian and Moslem quarrels, reconciliations, conquests, humiliations, massacres, blood and tears, how "death had always fascinated men" (p. 92). He would conclude: "Each day of peace is a miracle. Don't forget this thought. Wherever you are, in the depth of sadness, it will help you smile. . . . On this tiny land, everything has taken place: the worse and the best! Admirable but dangerous small land" (p. 94). Kalya admires him for believing in God even though he had passed such lucid judgment. She sees in his faith a thirst for perfection and final purpose. There, as in the questions concerning origins, we see Chedid's spirit of tolerance, love, peace, her belief in heterogeneity, and her need of perfection.

Another event in Kalya's childhood, described with much humor, reveals the little girl's precociousness and her rejection of traditional female behavior. The grandfather, walking on all fours in the living room, would carry on his back all the little boys, bouncing them up and down as he went through all the rooms, pretending to turn into hidden obstacles. Convinced that the girls would cry if they ever fell, he would never offer them the trip. One day Kalya jumps on his back by surprise and asks him to take her on the bumpy trip. She falls on purpose to show him her courage, falling harder than she had expected. Her grandfather, impressed with her behavior, declares she deserved to be named Kalil (a boy's name). Is it this daring side of her Kalya reenacts as she walks, revolver in front of her, to save Ammal and Myriam's peace initiative?

Still another event in Kalya's childhood, this time having to do with class differences, reveals Kalya's character and the nature of her quest in the novel. On a visit to the Cairo cemetery with her grandmother, she is confronted with real poverty in the guardian's children, who follow them in their rags, flies on their eyes. Nouza, giving Kalya her purse, asks her to give them all her coins. But Kalya, ashamed, shocked by her grandmother's light attitude, refuses. She is followed by a little girl her own age, who touches her skirt with ecstasy. Kalya is petrified; she "would like to disappear under the earth; or exchange dresses, kiss her, take her home" (p. 136). Like Ammal and Myriam, Kalya expresses social awareness, an extreme sensitivity to human misery and a desire to remedy the inequity. Is it not this consciousness that leads her to choose Lebanon as a meeting place with Sybil and then decide to be part of the peace process?

She has chosen to live in Paris because, even as a child, she has seen that city as a symbol of freedom. She remembers a summer with her grandmother in Paris. Nouza had hired a governess to walk her over the city, but Kalya, tired of the governess' boredom, had escaped from her attention and run all over many streets and along the Seine before returning to the apartment. When they have to leave the city, she feels "as if their breath, their freedom was being uprooted from them" (p. 159). It is interesting to note that uprootedness is used to describe leaving Paris, precisely the place Chedid has chosen in her life for roots. What does "House Without Roots" stand for? Does it symbolize Kalya herself, a woman strong and as stable as a house, having chosen Paris as the place to live, but belonging to many cultures? A hybrid of many elements like Lebanon? In a discussion with Andrée Chedid, she told me that "House Without Roots" stands for a "free house."[3] So perhaps it also means having no ties at all, belonging to no culture.

Just as Mitry initiates her into religions, Kalya's grandfather explains death to her, in yet another aspect of her quest and adolescent search. As a child, she is revolted at the idea that existence ends. Her grandfather tries to make her see death as "an accomplishment rather than an amputation" (p. 192). It is mortality that makes every event so intense. "What happiness is each drop of happiness when one knows it will all end." (p. 192) This is not a question, but an affirmation of the beauty each precious moment holds. He hopes it can help Kalya live, and he is not mistaken. She always wants to leave, move, and even though she loves Nouza, she does not want to be like her—"her look without clouds bothered her" (p. 171)—or the other women around her. She wants "to feel differently, open her eyes till they burnt" (p. 172).

Later, looking back at her life, Kalya notices that she has not lost her adolescent spirit. In spite of the years, she has maintained the enthusiasms of youth, which "flow from the body to the soul and remain there" (p. 103). She chooses to be a photographer to capture the essence of these values. "Shadows had not blocked her horizon for very long. Life loved her, and asked to be loved in return" (p. 103). Kalya has been happy and fulfilled in her life. How can the march she undertakes in the center of Beirut turn her existence upside down the way it does? She is there, in the middle of hostility and hatred, trying to save the life of two young women, convinced that the peace process should start right there and that it could be initiated by them. Just as she jumps on her grandfather's back and purposefully falls to prove her courage, here she takes a gun she has never used and thinks she would never use in her life, and she moves forward, believing that even if the gun is the only means, she can overcome violence by becoming part of the violence ripping the country apart. Many times throughout her walk, Kalya wonders if she is not dreaming; she touches the cloth of her skirt with her legs to convince herself it is really she who has undertaken the march. Her well-guarded, protected, happy life is suddenly upturned by a reality she never thought existed. It is like a nightmare, and she wishes she could wake up from her bad dreams and face what she thinks is reality.

The death of Sybil marks a point of no return. How will she be able to live after that? Sybil's is not like the other deaths described in her past. The brutality, violence, and absurdity of this death—and the Lebanese war—only lead to utter despair and total chaos.

Having fallen on the ground, Kalya hears echoes of absurd sentences pronounced to her by men: "Everything works out," and "I will find you again one day" (pp. 247, 278). She thought they were lies then, and knows now they are indeed lies. The ending of the novel clearly shows that everything does not work out and that love gone, not captured and nurtured, cannot be refound. The brutality of a violent, unnatural death has emphasized aspects of life that might have remained hidden otherwise. What would Kalya's grandfather have said in the face of such death, he who claimed death made things more urgent and more beautiful? Would he not have bowed down in sorrow and despair before such cruelty? Kalya's march through war-torn Beirut gives meaning to events in her life that otherwise might have seemed banal. And in that respect, the grandfather is right. The beautiful significance of the march would have come out also without the revolver and the death of Sybil. In fact, the march with a camera, for example, and without Sybil's death would have changed the final message from absurdity to hope, without changing the basic structure of the novel. Perhaps that would be too utopian. But doesn't one need to dream and try to realize some utopia in the middle of war's horrors?

The ending of Chedid's essay on Lebanon does show the Lebanese utopia extended to the rest of the world: "Attached to the branches of a very old wisdom, land several times millenial that knew democratic ways much before Greek cities; short platform where races, ideologies, events mixed; brief mirror of what a faraway humanity suddenly faced with tomorrow's world could be: one would wish for this Lebanon a destiny in the stride of a universe where languages, morals, hope, seek a new face. Lebanon, conscious of what hinders it, bold in its aims" (*Liban*, p. 185).

In *La maison sans racines,* women go one step further than Marie-Rose, herself much closer to peace and self-realization than Zahra. Zahra tries to free herself the best way she knows, but she falls victim to the war's cruelty, violence, and sadism without understanding what is happening to and around her. By contrast Marie-Rose, conscious of her society's injustices, commits herself to change; knowing she might die from such a commitment, she nevertheless consents to be a victim and to die if it could help bring about peace and justice. Myriam and Ammal are also conscious of their society's injustices and committed to change them, and they proceed by organizing a peace march, the best strategy possible.

As Marie-Rose, Myriam, and Ammal are aware, transformation must also take place through the choice of a different lifestyle. Unlike Marie-Rose, who first goes through a divorce before finding the person supportive of her endeavors, Ammal and Myriam, as well as Kalya, refuse a traditional marriage and put all their energies into their professions. The women in *La maison sans racines* are truly visionary and revolutionary. They have understood the importance of incorporating a sexual revolution within political change; their march symbolizes that strength. Even if the march fails from a practical point of view, it continues to live symbolically. Its spirit can spread and bring about the changes so much needed. Many peace marches and initiatives in Lebanon express this hope. All those in Lebanon who believe that justice and peace will triumph over violence and destruction and who work silently and courageously to reunite the country will some day see the fruits of their patience.

NOTES

1. I will be quoting throughout from the French edition by permission of Flammarion, Paris. © Andrée Chedid, 1985. All translations are my own.
2. See in particular Isaac Yétiv's thorough analysis in *Le thème de l'aliénation dans le roman maghrébin d'expression française*.
3. Telephone conversation in Paris, June 25, 1988.

SIX

Active Nonviolence Versus Victimization

Since the terms are so hard, and there is nobody in existence whose ruling they need respect or obey, let us consider what other method of persuasion is left to us. Only, it would seem, to point to the photographs—the photographs of dead bodies and ruined houses. Can we bring out the connection between them and prostituted culture and intellectual slavery and make it so clear that the one implies the other, that the daughters of educated men will prefer to refuse money and fame, and to be the objects of scorn and ridicule rather than suffer themselves, or allow others to suffer, the penalties there made visible?

Virginia Woolf, *Three Guineas*

The silence of a shy woman is a wall of resistance. Passive resistance can be as strong as violent reaction—and it can be far more transformative.

Marilyn Waring, *Women, Politics, and Power*

If we apply Virginia Woolf's ideas on war to the novels analyzed in this section, what conclusions can we reach? What choices do women have in their lives and in the face of war? Can they influence their society and change the cycles of violence in which the world seems hopelessly entangled? Or are they forever trapped, victims of situations over which they have no control?

Zahra, in *The Story of Zahra,* enters the world of men by having a relationship with a sniper, one of the worst perpetrators of the violence ripping her country apart. She cannot change such a world, the rules of which are beyond the control of anyone but the leaders of the tribes and of the big powers. This world has reached a state of chaos and disintegration much worse than the one described by Virginia Woolf, in which ideas of education, creativity, and democracy still held some place. What can Zahra do against such odds, she who already suffers from madness, a result of the oppression imposed on her by a society that does not allow its women to choose their lives and be themselves? She does not have the strength of a Marie-Rose, the courage of a Kalya, or the vision of a Myriam or an Ammal. She has suffered from too many incurable wounds in her past to be like them. It would take miraculous healing for her to be able to face the war without being destroyed by it, to find some nonviolent form of resistance instead of becoming a victim once again.

Zahra's reaction to the war and to violence is masochistic. She submits herself to violent sex, thereby trying to forget the outside violence with which she cannot cope. It's like a homeopathic cure she is desperately seeking. By having violence acted out on her own body, she is trying to understand a world of violence that makes no sense to her and hoping to find out who she is and heal some of her wounds. She does manage, for a short period of time, to enjoy sex by discovering orgasm. It makes her temporarily forget the war and her past and present life, and it cauterizes some of her wounds. The fact that she becomes pregnant—even though she has been taking the pill—without realizing it, shows how very little she is in control of her own body and of her sexuality. It is almost as much a mystery as the shells falling around her house every night.

Zahra's desperate need to understand what is going on throws her into the arms of the sniper, the result of which is death. It is the inevitable ending of a life of victimization, a kind of suicide, the choice of throwing oneself off the bridge described by Virginia Woolf. Zahra's vertical—upstairs—walk every afternoon to meet the sniper, versus Kalya's, Ammal's, and Myriam's horizontal—crossing the demarcation line—march, all lead to death. But whereas Zahra's sacrifice results in oblivion and probably more violence and destruction, Kalya's, Ammal's, and Myriam's offers the possibility of future hope and reconciliation, the assurance that somewhere peace will win.

Marie-Rose, in *Sitt Marie-Rose,* also joins the world by engaging herself in worthy causes: helping the oppressed and standing up for justice. In this respect, she does what Virginia Woolf prescribes in her essay: she enters the corrupted world of men, but with different values, thereby seeking to change it without being affected by it. She rejects patriarchal society and a traditional marriage. She wants to be free and remain outside of the cruel power games and the violence ripping her country apart. The result of her attempts is also death and victimization. How else could it be when the overwhelming forces of fanaticism, cruelty, torture, and violence aim at destroying those of love, understanding, humility, helping, and forgiving?

Nevertheless, Marie-Rose's victimization and death are not negative like Zahra's. She has stood up for her belief in love and nonviolence. She has defied the *chabab* gang's perversion and inhumanity. Her victimization involves a Christ-like atonement. She becomes the scapegoat that might, in the long run, help get rid of violence. Such a process is described at great length by René Girard in *La violence et le sacré*, where he argues that the sacrifice allows the community to get together again, to throw away its antagonism, anger, and animosity, and to reconcile itself through the death of its victim. "Sacrifice prevents the germs of violence from developing. It helps men to keep vengeance in line" (p. 33). Yet the scapegoat metaphor also has its terrible aspects. No one ever learns from scapegoats; and why should anyone die for another's evil? It rationalizes violence without really getting rid of it.

But, while Zahra's death may engender more violence and revenge, Marie-Rose's could help stop the cycle, if only the society for which she dies were willing to seek spiritual rather than materialistic values. In Marie-Rose's death, there is an element of active struggle. She does not die only as a victim. Having forgiven her executioners, she also talks back to them and tries to show them their corruption, perversion, and inhumanity. Her strategy, like Jean-Marie Muller's in *Stratégie de l'action politique non violente,* is a struggle against injustice, a struggle that recognizes the rights of the oppressed.

The four main women characters in *La maison sans racines*, Kalya, Sybil, Myriam, and Ammal, all stand up for the principles Virginia Woolf claims could deter war: rejecting the patriarchal system, refusing a traditional family structure, pursuing education, and working in and outside men's world in order to influence and change its values. In addition, they understand the significance of nonviolent active struggle against war. Two of them, from enemy communities, decide to end the animosities by organizing a peace march at the place of confrontation, the demarcation line. Such values and actions are truly visionary and constitute the liberating forces that might bring about the lasting changes so necessary to solve the world's problems, if only they are followed by other members of society.

In accordance with Virginia Woolf, Ammal and Myriam move outside the mainstream of history with a vision and gestures that might seem utopian, considering the political forces at stake. But, as I have shown, such actions are "real," and they constitute the most positive answers to the Lebanese dilemma. The death of Sybil, who had run to join her grandmother at the demarcation line, unlike that of Zahra or Marie-Rose, is not hopeless victimization or expiatory self-sacrifice, but the direct result of Kalya's lack of prudence, her failure to see that a revolver is of no use in such a conflict. This aspect of the ending only reinforces the thesis that nonviolent active struggle is the only viable and hopeful strategy.

PART III

War Unveils Men

Wars are no longer fought in the name of a ruler to be defended; they are fought in the name of the existence of us all; entire populations are raised up to mutually kill each other in the name of the necessity for them to live. Massacres have become vital. Sex well deserves death. It is in this sense, but strictly historical one notices, that sexuality is today crossed by the death instinct.

Michel Foucault, *Histoire de la sexualité*

The close connection between sexuality and violence, common inheritance of all religions, leans on an impressive body of convergences. Sexuality frequently starts in concert with violence, and in its immediate manifestations — kidnappings, rapes, deflorations, sadisms, etc. — and in its far away consequences.

René Girard, *La violence et le sacré*

War is a feast, a kind of total intoxication, an orgy. War unveils the joy of destroying, of annihilating, of killing to the bitter end. They feel like giants, because for a time they have gone beyond what could not be transgressed: death. Through killing, they compensate for their own fear of death. . . . They kill because they are afraid, an immense fear without any object. They kill to exorcise it.

Issa Makhlouf, *Beyrouth ou la fascination de la mort*

Throughout the ages, men have been fascinated with war. At some very deep level, it has been for them a way to prove their existence, an expression, according to Adam Farrar, of "male desire" (pp. 68–70). Desire closely linked to sexuality and the death instinct has been much written about by famous authors such as Sigmund Freud and Jacques Lacan, to name only a few, and lesser-known ones. Sexuality connected with war, oppression, power, aggressiveness has been analyzed in works by a great many authors ranging from Wilhelm Reich to Georges Bataille, Michel Foucault, Henri Laborit, and René Girard. More recent works by men make the connection between masculinity and war (Bob Connell, Adam

Farrar, Ross Poole, among others), as does a whole body of feminist writing (Betty Reardon, Andrea Dworkin, Kathleen Barry, Cynthia Enloe, Virginia Woolf, Susan Brownmiller, Elisabeth Badinter, Nancy Houston, Nancy Chodorow, Elaine Showalter, Margaret Higonnet, Sonya Michel, among others). How these issues can be articulated in today's societies and what avenues can be found for nonviolence and peace as positive forces have been the work of a number of other writers, such as Anne-Marie de Vilaine, Marilyn Waring, Robin Morgan, Yolla Charara, Ilham Ben Milad Ben Ghadifa, Georges Corm, Jean Duvignaud, Paul Vieille, Jean-William Lapierre, Jean-Marie Muller, Gérard Mendel, and others whose ideas are used to illustrate this study.

The difference between male theorists, such as Lacan, Freud, and Bataille, and feminist ones, such as Brownmiller, Dworkin, and Reardon, is that the connection between sexuality and violence does not lead them to want to change men, women, objectification, or the dominant-submissive structures of sexuality; in fact they celebrate it. On the other hand, women and a whole recent body of Australian male theorists—Connell, Farrar, and Poole—want to change these conditions of female oppression and male domination. It shows that the differences in outlook are not so much a result of differences in sex as in culture, in training, in vision and values.

Novels by men show a certain exaltation of war not found in those by women. For example, Halim Barakat in *Days of Dust* describes war as a necessary evil, unavoidable in the historical context of imperialism and oppression. Elias Khoury in *La petite montagne* expresses a certain fascination, even a *jouissance* (pleasure in the sexual sense) with war and its consequences; death and destruction. Tawfiq Awwad in *Tawaheen Beirut* (*Death in Beirut*) shows the direct link between war and the treatment of women, violence being closely connected with society's tensions and problems, but in such a context, revenge becomes the only outlet. For all three authors, war is here to stay. It is part of one's fate. Whether one enjoys it or feels repulsed by it, it is an unavoidable part of destiny. We don't find, as in women's writings, choices and actions aimed at changing this aspect of existence. In male writings, it is war that changes existence and not the other way around—that is, choices in one's existence changing war, or at least aiming at changing war.

The three novels analyzed in this section show the ugliness of war, the physical and mental destruction it causes, yet also reveal a fascination with it and express the notion that it can bring about necessary changes—

historical, social, economical, sexual. Going to war is exalted, especially when it is done for the "right" cause, which in all three novels is the Palestinian one. At the same time, war must be exorcised, its evil must be eradicated, especially when the characters fall victims to it. But the victims of war are not any of the central characters, as they are in the women's novels. They die on the "battlefield," far away from the daily realities, heroes of the causes they fight for. Their death is not a concrete horror, nor is it victimization. Heroic death serves to feed the imagination of the fighters and those civilians dreaming of fighting, and it reinforces the notion that it is all part of the game. Exorcism, or trying to get rid of war's bad aspects, is only an exercise within the overall strategy. It is not grounded in positive actions that could bring about concrete changes.

SEVEN

Tawfiq Yusuf Awwad: Revolution, Ethics, Revenge, and Destiny

We are rising in revolt and it is necessary that we should, but is it inevitable we should kill one another in order to be true revolutionaries? Is it the case that the dream of a new Lebanon will never materialize except through the nightmare of slaying? And are we confident that the nightmare of revolution will result in the realisation of the dream of life and not in the realisation of the continuation of the nightmare perhaps into even more horrible nightmares. There is a great deal of hesitation and great fear. Yes, the revolution is a glorious thing, but killing is contemptible. . . .

Superficially our crisis is political, social, confessional, etc. But this is all completely hypothetical, based on a flight from heaven to earth, from dreams to reality, on doubt in God. In the final analysis, isn't God just a symbol of values? No, I mean the sum total of the values that make man a creature that deserves the name.

The way of my destiny . . . [is] violence, contrary to established and acknowledged laws and codes. I shall fight under any sky against all legal codes and traditions sanctioned by society. I shall stab them with my own hand. Because, in their name, under the sky of my own country, society has denied me the right to life.

Tawfiq Yusuf Awwad, *Death in Beirut*

Tawfiq Yusuf Awwad was born in 1911 in the village of Bharsaf, Lebanon, where he experienced the Ottoman occupation and the famine of World War I, the subjects of two of his important works, a volume of short stories entitled *Al-sabi al-aʿraj* (The Handicapped Boy) and the novel *Al-raghif* (The Loaf). He studied at St. Joseph University in Lebanon and graduated with a law degree in 1934. He founded a journal, *Al-Jadid* (The New), between the two world wars, was a leading advocate of independence for Lebanon under French mandate, and was placed in detention in 1940 because of his views. After independence, he served as a diplomat in Argentina, Iran, Spain, Egypt, Mexico, Japan, Australia, and finally Italy, where he was the Lebanese ambassador to Rome until his retirement in 1975. He was killed in his home during the recent shelling of the mountains by the Syrian forces (summer 1989). The novel I am going to discuss, *Death in Beirut*,

99

was first published in Arabic as *Tawaheen Beirut* and was immediately recognized as a masterpiece by critics and readers who saw in it skill in storytelling, sensitivity in depicting the problems of Arab society, talent in describing the violence and the events in Lebanon's fragile balance, and prescience in the author's forewarning of his country's troubles to come. The book is especially important in terms of my subject because it shows how women's lives, delineated through oppressive traditional customs, are closely connected to the violence and political events occurring in the country.

The story centers on Tamima Nassour, a young Shi'ite Muslim woman from the south of Lebanon. She wants to get an education and goes about it against the will of her brother, Jaber, who is very nasty and violent and does everything to prevent her. Her father has gone to Africa to earn money, and her mother has spoiled her son. Jaber does what he wants, squandering the little money his father sends by gambling, running after women, and showing off. When Tamima goes to Beirut to enter the university, he threatens to kill her (p. 18).[1] But Tamima is strong, rebellious, proud, and determined to do what she wants against all the odds—her brother, society, and even her mother. She seeks various alternatives to reach her aim: she writes her father, asks the man handling the money her father sends to loan her some, only to be told that her father is in jail in Africa, accused of smuggling; she thinks of asking her friend Miss Mary, a nurse, for help, and of getting a job while studying. These are very courageous moves, especially in a society where women are kept in their places, required to be submissive, and play the roles of wives and mothers.

Tamima's free spirit is set in a context of violence and political turmoil. The students in various Lebanese universities have started organizing and striking to protest social and religious injustices as well as Israel's interventions in Lebanon. Demonstrations are taking place in support of or against the Palestinian Fedayeen. Various groups are clashing. As she sets foot on one of the campuses, Tamima is immediately caught in one of the clashes and hit in the head by a stone. Through this wound, she meets Hani, a Christian, with whom she falls in love, but their union is made impossible because of their different religious affiliations. Her wound serves as a symbol of other wounds to come.

Tamima finds a room and a job as a typist in an office of the Beirut Port Worker's Union through Madame Rose, the owner of rooms she also rents to prostitutes for her customers. One of the renters is Ramzi Raad, a well-known writer and journalist whom Tamima had been reading and admiring for a period of time. She has read his book, *Masters and Slaves,* banned in the school she attended in the South. Ramzi has definite ideas about revolution, poetry, education, love, and freedom. Revolution is one of slaves against masters (p. 17), the only valuable poet is Khalil Gibran, having something of the prophet about him (p. 19), Lebanese university education is a matter for revolution, not reform (p. 21), the only sacred thing about love is liberty (p. 34), and "the coming revolt in the world is the revolt of mankind against lies, delusions, charms and tokens that have made man a distorted image of his real self" (p. 34). He seduces Tamima and forces himself on her. In a way she is flattered because of who he is, but, being still a virgin, she is afraid and tries to push him away, screaming: "No! No! No! The only thing she remembered was that she screamed, like someone being murdered" (p. 29). After that rape, she goes back to the village and cries so hard that her mother, thinking it is because of the school fees, gives her some money she had hidden for emergencies. The author remarks, "she was crying because she felt like it" (p. 30), but after the brutality of the sexual scene with Ramzi Raad, I am more inclined to think it is because that first encounter is so crude and brings back memories of other men in her past—whom she later recalls in the narrative—who had tried to force themselves on her. Yet, despite this first experience with him, she continues to see him every Sunday in Beirut, lying to her mother concerning her whereabouts and neglecting her studies because of the affair, although she does pass her baccalaureate with distinction.

Even though Ramzi Raad talks about freedom in his speeches, when it comes to Tamima, it's a different story: he shows signs of jealousy and possession. When she goes to visit him in prison, he tells her she must leave Madame Rose's apartment, that "whore house" as he calls it, and the job she has taken at the port. But Tamima will do neither. After being released from prison, where he was sent for "being a smuggler of ideas" (p. 30), some of his first words, spoken while gulping down whiskey after whiskey, are that he despises women and does not believe in love (p. 71). They are in a darkened café on Hamra—a well-known street in Ras-Beirut —and when Tamima thinks that he will try to pull her to his room afterwards, she remembers a frightening incident in her childhood when she risked death by hanging from the branch of a tree above a gorge, only to be rescued by her mother in the nick of time. Nevertheless, she follows him, as if drawn toward her own death, and she remarks, "Love is ugly after it dies. It is like all corpses and it stinks the way they do" (p. 72). But was there love between them at all? Instead of dying, it's more as though it had never existed.

After refusing Akram Jurdi's—one of Madame Rose's customers—present of a watch, Tamima decides to leave the place and moves in to live with Miss Mary. She admires her friend because she lives independently and earns her own living. Likewise, Tamima wants to be assertive. She asks Hani, her boyfriend, to kiss her and to let her visit his room—two unusual requests in a traditional society where women are supposed to wait for men to make the moves. But Hani is preoccupied with his studies, his ambitions, his village of Deir Mutill, his friends, and the political turmoil in his country. He gets Tamima to participate in the meetings he organizes and often gives her tasks such as reading speeches or taking down the minutes. He makes Tamima laugh (p. 46), and believes what is happening in the country to be madness, Israel being a nightmare—"the latest of the plagues of the Old Testament" (p. 47). He is delighted Ramzi Raad has been sentenced because, he says, "He's an anarchist, spreading doubt about everything, lighting fires, turning liberty into licence" (p. 47). Hani does not like poetry, which he considers to be a drug for the Arabs (p. 48); he thinks all the different ideologies in Lebanon should be put aside in face of the one big threat constituted by Israel (p. 49). He likes the job Tamima gets because it will introduce her to the life of the proletariat and the trade unions (p. 52). He believes it is of vital importance for Muslims and Christians to merge. "Blood ties—that's the question for Lebanon" (p. 77). They are on the Tabarja beach when he talks of this union between the two communities, and he must be thinking of the two of them. Tamima is seized with feelings she cannot quite grasp. Are they fear or joy? She senses the waves pounding inside of her, sees them "dancing a macabre dance under the lash of the wind" (p. 78), and bursts into tears, hiding her face on Hani's chest. Images of birds soaring and dipping between earth, sea, and sky are often associated with Tamima, her desire to fly above the clouds of her life, her need to be free.

Much later, when she makes love with Ramzi Raad, it is Hani she thinks of: "She was there, on that beach. On the other shore of the sea. She had wings, like the sea birds. She soared and dipped with the sea—with the birds, between sea, land and sky" (p. 100). She looks at her sex "her honour, like a beast of prey" (p. 101), an ominous word in the context of Lebanon and the virginity revenge rites. Her sex is also a symbol of a bird trying to fly above the clouds, above the oppressive customs of her country, and being shot down. The bad omen is being fulfilled as she goes down the stairs after a visit to Ramzi Raad. She feels something sharp slashing her face twice and a voice warning: "The next time, I'll kill you, you whore" (p. 101). The blood that fills her mouth has the "bitter sweet taste of life and death" (p. 101). It is Hussein Qammoo'i, her brother's accomplice who has carried out the task assigned to him, washing the family's honor in blood by cutting her face with a razor blade. Overcome with guilt, Tamima immediately thinks that it is the result of her rebellion and that she will have to carry the scars, evidence to everyone of her dishonor. She wishes Hussein had completed his job and killed her. She feels so desperate that she attempts suicide by swallowing iodine. Miss Mary saves her, and Tamima goes to her village in the South to recover. She wonders what she will tell Hani and if she should give him any explanations about the scars.

In her village, Tamima locks herself in her room, refusing to eat or see anyone. Her mother pleads with her. But Tamima screams her anger and revolt at her. She confesses everything that has happened in her life, from Ramzi Raad to Hani, and accuses her of blindly accepting everything from men, of waiting eighteen years for a husband who wouldn't come back, like waiting for death, of looking up to Jaber as a god. Tamima herself has rejected God—"Rejected Him" (p. 121). Her mother reacts to her words by slapping her on the face and slamming the door. The rage between the two women is echoed by the rage of war outside: Israel is bombing the village for the second time. Tamima thinks that for her mother "Death held no terrors except death by bombing. Apart from that, death was fixed, an inescapable rendez-vous towards which she moved quite calmly. It was the food she took in with her daily bread. She shared it with the dead and the living, there in the village cemetery, a few yards away from the house, on the little limestone hill that stood up in the waste land like a serving tray" (p. 121).

When Tamima is able to camouflage her scars under makeup, she returns to Beirut to resume her studies and her job. She realizes that Hani goes out with several beautiful women and that he admires free women, but that deep inside he would want her to keep her chastity till they got married—if he ever proposed to her—so that she could bring her box (meaning virginity) to him and say: "If you please, here it is. Do open it— you with your knowledge and experience with scores of women" (p. 126). We realize what a gap there is between the two of them when, upon her return, they have a conversation and Hani tells her he believes in only one thing—the revolt against the self, a revolution against selfishness and individualism. When she asks him if he believes in God, he tells her that superficially the Lebanese crisis is political, social, and confessional, but that it is really based on doubt in God. "God is one of our great problems. Not the God that Moslems and Christians divide among themselves. . . . That's the God of confessionalism, of politics. . . . Nor the God that stands between us to prevent mixed marriages. . . . I'm talking about the real God" (p. 128). It is obvious from Hani's words that he understands that faith goes beyond the institutions of faith. As for Tamima, she expresses at various moments her revolt against God and her atheism.

The crisis in Tamima's life takes a turn for the worst with her brother Jaber's return from Africa. Jaber mortgages their home to go to Guinea. Tamima receives a letter from her father confirming her worst doubts: Jaber has taken their father's business and money while the father has been in prison, he has squandered it, and he has raped the black half-sister his father had entrusted him with. But, worse for Tamima, he intends to return to Beirut. Tamima feels the bitter taste of blood while reading the letter, the same taste she had felt when her mouth was filled with her own blood after Qammoo'i had slashed her face (p. 135).

Upon his return from Africa, Jaber is even more contemptible than before. He shows off, boasting about his money, car, clothes, and prowess. He goes after prostitutes and is high on pornography, gambling, and drinking. Some of the women whose company he seeks make fun of him, like Odette, who makes him look pitiful by toying with him (pp. 149–50). But others fall prey to his cruelty, like Zennoub, a servant of Madame Rose he had seduced, raped, and impregnated and who, as a result, eventually commits suicide. At the same time he prepares to kill his sister. He wants to slash her from ear to ear with the razor, "that was the traditional way and he would not veer from tradition, no matter what Qammoo'i said. The pistol was for men, in case any man got in his way" (p. 179). He has these thoughts while in a hashish den with a whore, "pondering the prostituted flesh" (p. 181). His double standards and hypocrisy come out in such actions. It is permissible for him to have sex with "easy" women, but his sister's free behavior must be punished. Women are the exclusive possessions of the tribes, and brothers must insure it remains this way.

In the figure of Jaber, Awwad creates one of the ugliest male characters Lebanon has produced and one of the worst perpetrators of the traditions that are rooted in violence and support women's oppression. He would almost be a caricature were it not that he represents some of the most frightening realities of Lebanese men and society. Thinking he might be put in prison for slaughtering his sister, his words are charged with meaning: "Prison? Fine, it's welcome!" Prison was for men. He would go to prison, not on a contemptible charge, like that business of Zennoub, the shepherd's daughter from Akkar, but with his head high, carrying in his right hand the banner of exalted honour" (p. 181). Not only does he boast about the possibility of going to jail for a crime of honor, but he also knows that society and the law will look leniently on his behavior and will quietly praise him for such an act. As for Zennoub, she is not even worth the bother about what the law might do, since she comes from an inferior class and one of the poorest regions in Lebanon.

Hani does propose marriage to Tamima; "he wants to announce to the whole world that Hani Raai, the Christian from Deir Mutill, is going to marry Tamima Nassour, the Shiite Moslem girl from Mahdiyya" (p. 153). Tamima shows him her father's letter and tells him about her worries. She does not confess to him the real reasons for her concern over Jaber's return or reveal the scars she has managed to hide. Hani reassures her. He says that both her brother and Hussein Qammoo'i are going to be put in prison or killed for defrauding the Fedayeen. Hani's real concern is to help rebuild Lebanon. He wants to go to Harvard, specialize in urban planning, and become one of the best engineers. Tamima will travel with him and continue her studies in the same university. They will take jobs in their spare time (p. 153). Tamima wonders if she should tell her mother about their decision to get married and how her village will receive the news. She decides she does not care about them: "the whole world had nothing to do with her. Her life was hers, not theirs. She would live her life just as she wished" (p. 154). But her wishes are one thing, what society will tolerate, another. It is more or less accepted for a Muslim man to marry a Christian, since she has to convert, but for a Christian to marry a Muslim woman is a totally different story. Tamima will soon discover the price she has to pay.

Zennoub's gruesome story comes as a reminder of Lebanese society's cruel traditions amidst the joy of Tamima and Hani and Miss Mary and Akram Jurdi (a lawyer and one of Madame Rose's tenants) in planning their respective weddings. A friendship had developed between Zennoub and Tamima when Tamima was still living at Madame Rose's. Zennoub would take special pleasure in cleaning Tamima's room, and Tamima in teaching her how to read and write. Tamima discovers early on what a difficult life Zennoub has had, when she sees Zennoub's father come to get the meager salary she makes. When Zennoub asks him to buy her a small bracelet out of her total wages, the father's response is to kick her and send her rolling down the steps. Getting up, covered in blood, she screams: "Kill me, go on, kill me! I'd be better off dead" (p. 54). It is the same scream Tamima utters when her brother threatens to kill her and after Qammoo'i slashes her face. Despite their class differences, the two women share a common destiny in sufferings and oppression. This resemblance comes out symbolically in the scene in which the two women try to save some kitttens. Garbage collectors are taking a sadistic pleasure in killing kittens, which try to hide from their cruelty. The cat and one of its kittens manage to escape, and Zennoub and Tamima decide to hide them in Tamima's room. Zennoub's remarks also fit the two women: "How could the kittens that survived manage? Was there some place on the beach rubbish tip where small kittens could hide?" (p. 57). Like the poor kittens, the two women try to hide from their society's rubbish collectors and the violent perpetrators of cruelty and sadism. Their rooms and friends, however, are not enough to protect them.

After Jaber rapes Zennoub and she discovers she is pregnant, she escapes to hide in the South, not in the North where she comes from. But where can she go and what can she do? She roams about, gets abused, and finally raped by three men, one after the other, on her way back to Beirut. She tells Tamima when she finally goes to her for protection and consolation that she wishes her father had finished her off when he was beating her (p. 164). Miss Mary finds out that Zennoub is seven months pregnant and that no doctor will give her an abortion. Zennoub feels that "either way she'd be dead. Her father's knife or the doctor's. . . . It was as if the knives had already cut her. All knives, the doctors' knives and the fathers', were in her heart" (p. 164). Miss Mary tells Tamima to keep her at the apartment for one night and then return her to Madame Rose's. As she leaves the apartment the following day, Zennoub walks back not to Madame Rose's but to Raouche (the pigeon rock overlooking the sea where people commit suicide) and throws herself into the sea. The newspapers comment, "she was pregnant and it is generally believed that she committed suicide to be rid of her shame," and they note that the violator of her chastity had fled and that investigations were in progress to ensure his arrest (p. 165). Tamima feels terrible and responsible for Zennoub's death. She shouldn't have abandoned her and let her go, "the poor, innocent, hunted creature running this way and that in her panic, oppressed by shame, panting, pushed backwards and forwards between Sidon and Beirut, driven by despair from wall to wall—from the walls of houses to the rocks on the beach. And rocks were to be her bed, her coverlet the crows of the land and the creatures of the sea" (p. 174). She would like to kill Jaber for what he has done. She knows she will be one of his next victims.

Tamima decides she wants to be completely honest with Hani and tell him about her relationship with Ramzi Raad before he learns it from someone else. She plans what she will say: "I shan't boast about it like you, I don't need to brag the way you men do about the number of your exploits and conquests" (p. 177). These are sensitive remarks coming from a man of Awwad's generation. It shows he has done a lot of deep thinking about women's problems and men's behavior related to these issues. Listen to some other revolutionary lines he puts in Tamima's mouth: "I prefer to come to you as an honest woman rather than as a sham virgin. . . . I'll take the initiative" (p. 177). But Hani is not as liberal and open as he seems at the beginning. He slaps her when he hears the news; "she raised her hand to her face to wipe away the sting of his blow and she welcomed in the dawn with a stream of tears" (p. 181). Hani's reaction is very disappointing, coming from someone who, throughout, has voiced so many revolutionary ideas about Lebanon—rebuilding it with new values, bringing Christians and Muslims together through blood ties—and who has been concerned for the poor, displayed a wide sense of history, and understood the problems in the Arab world. But when it comes to his private life, Hani is as narrow-minded, as prideful, as stuck up as any other male. He wants freedom and sexual liberation for himself, but his bride-to-be must remain a virgin.

Awwad once more points to the double standards and hypocritical attitudes of Lebanese men. Tamima has the courage to go to Hani and tell him about the loss of her virginity. She did not want to do what scores of other women in her country do—get a virginity repair job by a doctor before the wedding. She has the truly revolutionary idea of wanting to start her life with Hani in honesty and openness. But Hani cannot accept it. The slap he gives her is even worse than the other blows and wounds she has received. It goes much deeper in her psyche; she can do nothing about it, nor cover it with makeup, nor try to forget it. "The mark of the blow of your fist will never disappear. The blows I have received from even my mother and my brother made my blood boil. But I feel your slap on my face as if it were dew; in my heart its echo will reverberate like the bells of Deir Mutill

[Hani's village] until I die" (p. 183). Hani is able to see the political, economical, and religious problems in his country, but he remains blind to the sexual ones. How can these other questions, so intimately related to violence and war, so deeply rooted within sexuality, find solutions when those who are involved in them refuse to see the connection?

Tamima's tribulations are not over yet. As she returns from Hani's home to Miss Mary's apartment, she is fired at, the bullet hitting Miss Mary, who has tried to shield her. Later we learn that Miss Mary dies from her wound. Tamima is saved by a neighbor coming out of his door "who grabbed the criminal and shouted to the girl to run" (p. 182). The comments of passers-by are worth noticing because they reflect Lebanese people's attitudes towards crimes of honor. They are not very surprised: "Someone had fired at his sister. . . . He had wanted to kill her for her *irregular* behavior." (p. 182; my emphasis).

It is the second time that Miss Mary saves Tamima's life, but this time she pays for it with her own. Tamima, desperate over what has happened, decides to join the Palestinian guerrillas. She makes her reasons for doing so clear in her diary, in lines she addresses to Hani:

It's my fate. . . . You remember we spoke in the meeting yesterday about acts of violence, contrary to established and acknowledged laws and codes. That is where I belong. I shall fight under any sky against all legal codes and traditions sanctioned by society. I shall stab them with my own hand. Because, in their name, under the sky of my own country, society had denied me the right to life. When it wanted to rob me of life itself in their name, instead of one crime it committed two—it killed the dearest and most noble and purest of friends and it slew my love. (P. 184)

This ending is rather disappointing. Wounded physically and psychologically by the violent and cruel traditions reigning in her country and by the strongly macho behavior of the men, Tamima reacts by joining other perpetrators of violence. Even if the violence of the Palestinians may be more understandable—as belonging to the down-trodden, the oppressed of the world—it still cannot be condoned. Her motivations are not love, but hate and revenge, and the results will not be constructive but destructive.

In *The Wretched of the Earth*, Frantz Fanon explains the cathartic use of violence by oppressed people who otherwise would turn the effects of their oppression against themselves, becoming masochistic or mentally ill. A psychiatrist for the Algerians, Fanon came to see that he couldn't really help them because their problems stemmed from social and political conditions, and so he became an advocate and leader in the national struggle for liberation. Is this what Awwad is also trying to say through Tamima? Instead of attempting suicide as she does before, or succeeeding like Zennoub, or becoming the target of violence like Miss Mary, she decides to become part of this violence and direct it against others. But is this really a good solution? History has shown that violence only begets violence. And had Fanon lived, would he have been convinced by the results of the national struggle for liberation in Algeria? Would he not have seen it, as Sartre does in "Black Orpheus," as only the first step, moving towards more constructive and universal solutions?[2] Likewise, in *Death in Beirut*, had Tamima joined the Palestinians not to engage in terrorist acts—as she seems to imply—but to help with humanitarian actions or out of love—like Marie-Rose in *Sitt Marie-Rose*—or had she·joined some other type of constructive organization in the country, working for peace through nonviolent acts, would it not have been a more hopeful ending? What is upsetting with Tamima's choice is that she is not struggling to free herself; she becomes like Hani and the other males in her life.

Awwad's work shows how violence is closely connected to the political climate and the treatment of women in Lebanese society. All the major female characters in the novel—Tamima, her mother, Zennoub, Miss Mary—fall prey to the customs and traditions surrounding their lives. Tamima cannot really be free, study as she wants, marry or be with whom she desires, or achieve her aims in life. All the men around her prevent her from doing so: her brother, by trying to stop her from studying and by sending an agent to slash her throat when he finds out about her sexual affair; Ramzi Raad, by forcing himself on her and imposing his views; and even Hani, who seems to love her, but cannot accept the sexual freedom he practices himself. Even the author gives her a fate connected with male violence by having her choose to engage in the Palestinian movement. It does not have to be the only alternative for her life. Why not have her choose a life/peace alternative instead, by having her organize a peace march, for example, engage in any *active* nonviolent action, or work in a consciousness-raising group to help women in large numbers have the courage and collective strength to oppose the men who maintain them in submission and thereby affirm themselves?

Zennoub is cruelly treated as a servant-slave at the mercy of Madame Rose's customers and of her father, to whom she must give all the money she earns. She is sexually and economically abused. Her oppression comes not only from the traditional and cultural customs that confine Tamima, but also from her class identity. Even the feelings of solidarity women like Tamima and Miss Mary express for her are of no use against the strength of male domination and violence. As for Tamima's mother, she is living a slow death, waiting for her husband to return from Africa, subjected to shelling from Israel.

Miss Mary is the only female character who seems to be able to stand on her own two feet, but her kindness and generosity as well as her attempts to help her sisters are what cause her death. She gains some autonomy thanks to her education, her job as a nurse, and her economic independence. But she also falls victim of men's violence, killed by precisely the backward rite she had tried to abolish. In shielding Tamima from the bullet aimed at washing honor in blood, she is trapped in the same mechanism of horror.

In this novel, Awwad shows the backwardness, barbarity, and hypocrisy of Lebanese men's attitudes and practices towards women and how these factors are entangled within the political situation, violence feeding itself on honor and women's oppression. His critique is from a liberal perspective rather than a feminist one; hence, the solution he imagines is one of *equality* for Tamima (she gets to act like a man), not radical change, transformation.

NOTES

1. Throughout I will be quoting from the English edition (London: Heineman, 1976).
2. This is a notion Fanon could not accept in Sartre, with whom he had many discussions without being convinced (see Simone de Beauvoir's *La force des choses,* p. 431). Had he lived longer—he died young of leukemia in the country he hated most, the United States—wouldn't he have seen the validity of Sartre's universal notions?

EIGHT

Halim Barakat: Despair, Fear, Revolt, Tradition, and Heroism

Man creates war, but it becomes independent of his will and re-creates him in a form that it wishes, a form that has absolute control over his old self.
He wanted to be like a wave, to be independent and yet attached, to be free and yet part of something big.
The guerrillas were the only bridge that would take the Arabs to the future, that would take them beyond the walls of the tragedy. And the tragedy was not that they had lost the war but that they had lost it without heroism.

Halim Barakat, *Days of Dust*

Halim Barakat was born in Kafroun, a Syrian village near the Mediterranean and Lebanese border, in 1933, the son of Christian parents who moved to Lebanon when he was still a child. Barakat attended school in Lebanon and earned a degree in sociology from the American University in Beirut. He pursued his studies in the United States, obtaining a doctorate in social psychology from the University of Michigan. He taught at the American and Lebanese universities in Beirut for several years, served as a research fellow at Harvard University, and is presently teaching and doing research at Georgetown University in Washington, D.C. Barakat has published his creative writing in Arabic and scholarly works in English. His fictional writings include a collection of short stories—*Al-samt wal-matar* (Silence and Rain, 1958)—and five novels—*Al-qimam al-khadra³* (The Green Summits, 1956), *Sittat ayyam* (Six Days, 1961), *ʿAwdat al taʾir ilal-bahr* (Return of the Flying Dutchman to the Sea, 1969), *Al-rahil bayn al-sahm wal-watar* (The Trip Between the Arrow and the Musical Chords, 1979), and *Taʾir al-hown* (The Ibis, 1988). His sociological studies include: *River Without Bridges: A Study of the Exodus of the 1967 Palestinian Arab Refugees* (1969), *Lebanon in Strife: Student Preludes to the Civil War* (1977), *Al-ruʾiyat al-ʾijtimaʿi fi al-riwaya al-ʿarabiyya* (Visions of Social Reality in the Contemporary Arab Novel, 1977), *Al-mujtamaʿ al-ʿarabi al-muʿasir* (Arab Society, 1984), and numerous articles in various journals.

The novel I am going to analyze, *Days of Dust,* first published in Beirut in 1969 under the title ʿ*Awdat al-taʾir ilal bahr,* literally translated as "Return of the Flying Dutchman to the Sea," (the word *al-taʾir* carries the idea of a migrating bird)[1] is important in terms of my study because, set in the context of the 1967 war of Israel against the Arabs, it portrays Palestine, the land and the people, as a woman, and describes the relationship of the central character, Ramzy, with women, particularly an American one.[2]

The allegory of the Flying Dutchman is about a ship unable to reach harbor, condemned forever to exile. The captain can break the spell only by finding a woman true to him till death. Every seven years, the Flying Dutchman is permitted to come ashore and search for this woman, but every time, he returns to the sea more desperate and disillusioned. In *Days of Dust,* Palestine is compared to this ship, unable to find anyone who will give it absolute love. Ramzy feels his country is denied death as well as life and has no inspiring leader. "He longed for a leader who would glow with defiance, one who would inspire the people to use their minds and their emotions in a dialogue with themselves and with their leaders—someone who would scream for freedom, straining every nerve and emotion in search of freedom" (p. 27).

The novel is about the drama of an uprooted people, unable to find a harbor of love and peace. It is also about the tragedy of humanity always at war, with various groups trying to dominate the others, the big fish eating the small fish, the aggressive dominating the passive. The symbolism of the woman as the one who must give this love, yet is found unfaithful and incapable of providing it, shows that the clichés about women's fickle nature, their unreliability, remain strong.[3]

The allegory of the ship is accompanied by the popular Palestinian tale of the hyena and by biblical stories. The hyena (or Israel) is the threat that weighs on the bride (or Palestine), who is being carried secretly to a cave to be "gobbled up," a sexual image suggesting rape. The bridegroom (the Palestinian people or Ramzy) is incapable of overcoming the hyena, which dirties everything (it also eats corpses and is therefore associated with death) and castrates him (it pisses on the bridegroom's tail [The novel says that "the hyena pissed on his tail" (p. 24); it's not clear what the tail is] and on his tree, both symbols of the phallus). The spell can only be broken through blood. It is only when the bridegroom hits the stone and his foot (or forehead, it is the same thing) bleeds that he is able to kill the hyena and "gobble up" the bride. The stone is the bride's virginity, the pledge of her fidelity. Through the rupture of her hymen and the flow of her blood, the woman is acknowledged as the sole property of the bridegroom. The honor of the fiancé is not blemished. Only blood, war, can prove that Palestine has remained faithful. Only through the flowing of blood will the Palestinians be able to recapture their lost land and end their exile. The myth of the wandering ship and the myth of the hyena meet here. Both the captain of the ship and the bridegroom are after a "faithful woman."[4]

The novel is presented as a chronicle of the Six-Day War between Israel and the Arabs, set in Beirut and Amman, and involving multiple characters. It is divided into three parts. The first one, "The Threshold," which takes place between June 11 and June 20, 1967, is about Ramzy going to Jordan after the Six-Day War and witnessing the horrors of napalm, which he compares to a nuclear disaster. The second and main section, "Voices Surge and the South Wind Rages," is about the war itself, taking place between June 5 and June 10, 1967. It is divided into six parts, one chapter for each day of the war. The third and last part, "Numerous Days of Dust," returns to the first period of time, the threshold of the war being the end. This section represents the blood and tears of a defeated people. It poses questions about roots and possible solutions. One of the answers is the guerrillas —a "solution" worth analyzing because it is similar to the one found in Awwad and is implied in Khoury and Adnan. The division of time and the structuring of events in six days—the seventh being that of rest—is a classical one, similar to what we found in Adnan. To this is added the biblical—and other religious and mythological—element of perfection: seven is supposed to be the perfect number. Barakat has used the numbers three, six, and seven to organize his material. It is an unusual and effective way of dealing with time and space.

At the threshold of the Six-Day War, Ramzy sees its horror in the refugees and the napalm-burnt patients in the hospitals. He feels as if he were walking through purgatory, that history had reversed itself, showing the ignorance and naïveté of Arabs who let themselves be defeated. He holds himself responsible and wishes that repentance for his sins might somehow shut off the moans of the wounded he can no longer bear to hear. It is not clear why he feels so guilty and what his sins are. He would like to see defiance rather than surrender in "his" (the Palestinian) people. How could he lead them to revolt? Images of climbing a mountain are mixed with those of water and darkness, like the world before creation or after a nuclear disaster. The "dove" that comes down on earth searching for peace is in the shape of napalm—but what does napalm look like? He has done none of the daring acts he is dreaming of. His guilt is of an intellectual torn in his mind, not close enough to the people.

Ramzy expresses his feelings about dereliction and his rejection of those who exclude him. He feels very lonely and searches for a paradise he believes must exist beyond the purgatory where he is presently plunged. He does not ask himself how to overcome defeat. Defeat and misfortune make him think of paradise and purgatory. The ideas of sin and punishment, redemption and reward are always present. It is a universe of good and evil, a religious universe, even if Ramzy has rejected formal religion.

From the very beginning, an American woman, Pamela, is associated with sadness and Ramzy's loneliness. She brings hope and saves Ramzy from despair. The universe they create is one of "the two of us against the world," a very different notion from the one expressed by the Palestinian community, where belonging to the family or the group takes precedence over the individual. Here, loneliness is created by the Arabs' defeat. Pamela and the world she and Ramzy create bring hope in the midst of tragedy because of their love. Yet what Pamela represents symbolically as an American negates this hope. This is why Ramzy feels so torn. Pamela does not find a place in Ramzy's religious universe of good and evil, of sin and punishment. For Pamela, war and defeat are events that belong to a secular world, and history is a "trial." For Ramzy, defeat is the result of the Arabs' sins and of the hyena's spell; the curse that weighs on the Arab world is brought by the contact with the hyena.[5] This section gives us the first image of the hyena endowed with a magical power.

The chapter covering the first day, "Thunder in the Voices of Children," describes the war starting between the Arabs and Israelis and the feelings and questions it evokes in Ramzy. "Hope and despair were engaged in relentless battle for control of his inner most feelings" (p. 39). His life appears in new light and intensity. He cannot teach his classes as he had before. He discusses with his students the events taking place and cannot understand the reaction of one of his colleagues, who tells him that "War is a passing phenomenon. My concern is with teaching and doing research" (p. 29). He believes war brings about deep changes and different consciousness in people and that "Arabs were establishing once again that they did have some will and courage to demand their rights, to refuse submission to the will of others who ignored their rights and feelings. They rejected, and therefore they existed" (p. 14). This awareness leads him to want to change his life. He breaks off his relationship with Fatina, a married woman, and her crowd, and no longer spends evenings with them "discussing sex, drinking and eating . . . their lives unbelievably empty" (p. 14). Fatina does not understand anything about politics. She does not even know that a war has started. And even when she learns about it, she is more preoccupied with her own pleasure. Daily living and marriage routines predominate in her life.

Ramzy has a critical view of Arab society, its decomposition, its isolation, the absence of institutions capable of using individual competence. While his colleagues and students chew on words and dream of the past, Ramzy is pessimistic. He believes the war to be lost before it even starts. He is very conscious of Israel's military power and organization and of the Arabs' naïve optimism. This optimism—ignorance—is one of the sins described in the first part.

Here also, Pamela appears when the hero is sunk in his dark thoughts. She rescues Ramzy from despair. We don't yet know her nationality. The word *hippy* is used to describe her. She is characterized as someone whose living logic is pleasure, happiness—eating, playing tennis, swimming on a deserted beach.

Ramzy is very worried about the outcome of the war. He sees the Arab world as terribly underdeveloped, and, what is worse, "there are no bridges between the Arab countries. There are no bridges between individuals and groups. . . . We are living in the past. We sail through swamps. We eat mud. We seek sanctity from stones and graves" (p. 18). He is convinced that a revolution only in politics is not enough; the revolution must also occur within society: "There's not one of us in revolt against our customs" (p. 19). This is an important statement, but how his premise is developed in relationships between men and women in the novel is a different story and worth analyzing.

The central story, which takes place in Beirut, is intermixed with stories about the daily life and conjugal conflicts of the Palestinians in Jordan and the territories occupied by Israel. Palestinian society is torn between two norms: the community, with its arranged marriages and constrictions, and individualism, with its love and freedom of choice.

The Palestinian people are described as being full of hope and naïveté; their daily living before the uprising seems happy; the flute they play is as old as Palestine. It is in this context that the tale of the hyena is narrated. The hyena is a disgusting animal that wants to eat up the bride. The groom tries to get to his bride but is prevented by the hyena, which pisses on its tail. Finally, he is able to kill the hyena, and through blood flowing, he can get back to the bride. The tale is significant on the sexual and political levels and illustrates my topic. Men in Arab society view women's virginity as the only warranty for fidelity, and it is only through fidelity that they can recapture their lost land and end exile. Their notion of women and country is one of exclusive ownership.[6] Virginity of a woman is the honor of her husband and of her family. As long as this virginity is not checked, fear and anxiety remain present. At a very deep level, the war with Israel is like marriage, a trial of virginity.

The myth of the wandering ship is associated to the popular Arab myth of the hyena. There can be no salvation, no hope in this life except through the woman, but one cannot trust women. The ship is Palestine and the woman is the deceptive leader. Ramzy wants a democratic leader. The woman is also the earth/Palestine, which Ramzy wants to penetrate. The ship is the Palestinian people, and Palestine, as a country or as a people, as a collective body, is woman. Throughout, these interwoven images of political and sexual relations occur. There is an obsession with relationships between men and women, as if the political world were permeated with an impossible dream of love. This impossibility and the fact that one cannot be oneself lead to a search for other dreams, other values that one can find outside of oneself, in violence, destruction, and war. Individuals are unable to discover themselves as *one* without a leader, as man cannot discover himself as man without the honor of a woman.

In the chapter of the second day, "The Sailor Returns to the Sea," the Arabs start to lose the battle, and Ramzy is about to initiate a relationship with Pamela, who has decided to remain in Beirut, despite the fact that other Americans have been evacuated by their embassy the preceding day and her husband is already gone. Ramzy feels he has no control over a world that totally dominates him. "He could not believe what had happened to his country. Jerusalem was burning. Palestine was turning into ruin, like Sodom . . . he looked back at his country, back at the past. He did not care if he were to turn into a pillar of salt" (p. 57). The image of Sodom evokes sexual sin, and his stating that he does not care if he were to turn into a pillar of salt expresses a sense of guilt. He feels despair and disappointment.

The discussions he has with his colleagues and students only add to his gloom. One of his colleagues thinks that the problem with the Arabs remains that they "have lost both their identity and their sense of manhood. Each one of us is suffering from a split personality, especially in Lebanon. We are Arab, and yet our education is in some cases French, in some cases Anglo-Saxon, and in others Eastern-Mystic. A very strange mixture. We're all schizophrenic. We need to go back and search out our roots" (p. 60). This search for roots is in contradiction with his previous expression of the need to go forward towards modernity and technology in order to defeat the Israelis. The character expresses here guilt of an intellectual who has lost his relations with the people and wants to find his roots, even though they belong to a world of fantasy. People are what they are, just as an intellectual is who he is. The incapacity to accept oneself constitutes the first handicap to action.

Unlike Andrée Chedid, who explores this theme in many of her works, particularly in *La maison sans racines,* and sees such a mixture of varied backgrounds as positive, a way to broaden one's horizon, one of the characters in Barakat's novel despairs at this multiplicity and sees it as one of the causes of the war. It is also interesting to notice that identity is associated with manhood. Throughout the novel, victory is associated with a sense of manliness, while defeat is connected with a loss of power.[7]

In his study of the students' prelude to the Lebanese civil war, Barakat makes a distinction between a *pluralistic* and *mosaic* society. A pluralistic society holds consensus on fundamental principles and provides balanced participation of its different groups, so that not one of them can dominate the others, while in a mosaic society, the various groups interact without consensus and with an imbalanced distribution of rewards and powers (*Lebanon in Strife,* p. 25). According to Barakat, Lebanon is a mosaic society, and it is this precarious arrangement that led to the civil war.[8]

In both his novel and his study, Barakat blames the educational system for the conditions prevailing in the country. In *Lebanon in Strife,* Barakat says that the educational system in Lebanon reproduces the existing religious and ethnic communities in the society. "Education does not constitute a liberating force—it provides an environment for perpetuating tradition. Such patterns of socialization prevail throughout Lebanon's institutions— home, school, church, government, and university. . . . They reinforce each other, maintain the status quo, and preserve the culture of silence" (p. 5). Ramzy, in *Days of Dust,* despairs at seeing the isolation of Arab universities: "He could not see culture in isolation but only in participation. Yet the universities, both in their own view and in that of most Arabs and

Arab governments, were an ideal place, divorced from life itself" (p. 47). As a professor at the American University in Beirut, he tries to be different from the institution and to lead his students into thinking and taking active parts in the events.

But he feels completely powerless over what is happening. "His country was a mass of wounds within his heart. His country was piles of rubble . . . earthquakes were occurring deep inside himself; the rocks were crumbling, falling, and scattering. . . . He had no control over his destiny" (p. 53). War and defeat, collective events, are at the same time interior events. It is a very modern notion. And it is at this point that he decides to invite Pamela to stay in his apartment. He wonders why it has to happen now, in the middle of the war. But if he turns towards Pamela, it is because his emotional world has turned upside down. His adventure with Pamela is a tentative way to be himself or to find himself, to let go of his need for love. War becomes a liberation of his inner self.

The beginning of his relationship with Pamela appears like a conquest game in which he sees her as "my prey which calmly looks at me in the eyes and I feel like a hunter without a gun" (p. 55). He does not want her to notice yet that he desires her. On the other hand, Pamela is at a loss for what she should do. She decides to join a demonstration against the American Embassy. Ramzy does not understand the logic of demonstrations. But aren't these demonstrations the prefiguration of "the stone war," the *intifada*, an effective way the Palestinian people have discovered in asserting their rights within Israel? I will discuss these implications further in the chapter. For now, it is worth noting that Ramzy seems outside of the people's logic. He reasons as an intellectual.

Ramzy also worries about what people might say, especially the women he had previously known. But his real objection to inviting Pamela to stay with him is that his country is in a state of war. It doesn't feel right. The theme of the Flying Dutchman comes back. Ramzy is sure the Flying Dutchman will never return to his country unless he gives of himself and is true to his ideal till death. This is why Ramzy feels so torn about starting such a precarious relationship with Pamela. It does not hold the notion of an absolute love, which the Flying Dutchman/allegory implies he needs.

Is Ramzy also the captain of the wandering ship? He wants to drop his anchor. He feels split between Arab honor and an American woman. It is a conflict between a sense of community and honor towards the community, and individualism or self-realization. Is Ramzy searching for love with a woman? He seems to desire and need it. He would like to find real love and break down his society's taboos; this is why Pamela attracts him. The fact that Pamela cannot stay in Lebanon makes her even more attractive in Ramzy's eyes. He can throw himself in the adventure without fear of the consequences. The affair emphasizes his schizophrenia. It is both real—in the sense that Pamela is the person he is searching for—and impossible— she is bound to leave.

Because of his ambivalence, he directs his greatest admiration toward the guerrilla, "a person who could resist any temptation and remain true to something till death" (p. 69). This is an image of a guilty fighter who is unable to fulfill his desire but who sacrifices it to an aim located outside of himself. This image of the guerrilla as the only hope in the midst of utter despair I already noted at the end of Awwad's novel. In *Death in Beirut,* Tamima decided to join the guerrillas in an act of defiance, revolt, and vengeance. In *Days of Dust,* Ramzy sees the guerrilla as someone able to resist temptation, remaining true to his aim till death. "It occurred to Ramzy that the guerrillas were the only bridge that would take the Arabs to the future. And the tragedy was not that they had lost the war but that they had lost it without heroism" (p. 179). But heroism is a problematic notion often associated with violence, war, and domination. In the name of a "just" cause, some of the most horrible deeds have been committed and wounds inflicted. One could argue that the Palestinians, being the down- trodden and the oppressed, are justified in returning the knife plunged unjustly into their body and soul, a concept developed by Fanon, who in *Les damnés de la terre* advocates the use of violence as the only cure for the oppressed.[9] But is it not precisely such argument that gave birth to Zionism? And doesn't heroism feed on such ideologies? How does one break off the chain of repetitious horrors and historical errors, except through nonviolent active resistance?

Barakat does make a connection between the oppression of the Jew during World War II and the oppression of the Palestinian now, through one of his characters, Sister Marie Thérèse. She works with the wounded in one of the Jordanian hospitals and sees in the eyes of the people she treats the same despair she witnessed when she worked in a hospital on the Swiss border during World War II (p. 59). On the fifth day, she tells one of the Israeli officers what she thinks of him: "I'll tell you that I began my adult life in a monastery in Switzerland caring for people who had survived Nazi concentration camps. . . . I used to watch over them just as I try to care for these Arabs. And you are no different from the Nazi officers who worked in the concentration centers. I see in your face the same insensitivity that I used to see in theirs" (p. 132). Sister Marie Thérèse is very courageous and daring in what she says and in the way she behaves during the day. At night, she breaks down in tears and cannot sleep because she is thinking of the wounded and the dying she had to take care of during the day. She figures in direct contrast to the Israeli women soldiers she watches, "carrying revolvers, gurgling with laughter, obviously intoxicated with victory" (p. 134).

The concept of revolution comes out here as a myth that could save, but is not effective because it is unreachable. Revolution at one level supposes saving the honor of the one who believes his or her honor to be lost—that is, revolution is a projection, outside of oneself, of an internal revolution one is incapable of accomplishing. Both the psychological and political revolutions must work together to bring about real change.

The night of the second day, while Pamela is sleeping in one room, Ramzy, in another room, cannot sleep thinking of the war and of the tragedy of his people. When he finally falls asleep, he dreams of the hyena. His country is a bride abducted and hidden away in an inaccessible cave. The angry bridegroom fires his gun, missing the target; he runs and climbs a tree named Revolution, which offers no protection. A hyena casts a spell on him by relieving itself on its tail (p. 77). The visions of the cave, the gun, the tree, and the tail are explicitly sexual. Ramzy is frustrated at his country's defeat and at sleeping in a different room from Pamela, as the sexual metaphors and symbols reveal. His masculinity is threatened by both. The woman/land has been carried within a cave, symbol of the uterus and at the same time symbol of the underground, savage forces; the man, or Palestinian, cannot get to her, his masculinity is of no use to him. Someone else's masculinity is stronger and has overpowered him, stealing his bride.

Why does this myth of the hyena come back over and over again? Here, the hyena is also "the other"—evil projected onto the other. It is the projection of oneself, of one's fears, of one's feelings of impurity onto the other. It is the id, its feeling of impurity, which has to be overcome to meet the woman, to meet the other, and finally to fulfill oneself. Only the purity of woman revealed through blood, or the purity of the people demonstrated by the flowing of blood, delivers from fear and allows such renewal. The hyena in that sense is the incapacity to be oneself, to realize one's desires. It is the feeling of powerlessness, of having been castrated (the gun being deviated). Neither revolution nor the tree can protect against such a spell. The image of Israel as an essential evil haunts the Palestinians. Only blood can purify and bring some relief.[10]

The chapter for the third day, "Death is a Field," reveals the horrors of napalm and of the war. The relationship between Pamela and Ramzy becomes more intense, and the sexual act is associated with war. Death images of seared bodies are mixed with visions of sexual conquests.

The morning of that day, after Ramzy's dream, he and Pamela discuss the war, the American biases directed against Arabs, and their other affairs. He tells her what he had liked in Najla, his previous lover: the virtue in her lack of independence and her reliance on her family.[11] He used to think that if they married, she would be primarily a housewife, that she would obey him and take care of the children and the house. "Second, there was no other woman around at that time to offer her any competition" (p. 90). He is not really honest with Pamela in telling her the relationship lasted only six months. Actually it had lasted for two years and had never been terminated, even though they had not seen each other in a long time. Here is a deceptive rapport between a man and a woman similar to that in Khoury's *La petite montagne*. How can there be trust at the social and political level when it does not exist at the personal one? In contrast to the woman in *La petite montagne*, Pamela appears a little more sincere. She couldn't stand her husband being dependent on her and clearly verbalizes the fact, therefore justifying their separation, her stay in Beirut, and starting an affair with Ramzy, even though it fills her with remorse.

War appears as a release of tension caused by relationships that have become insurmountable—between Ramzy and himself. War is expected to bring a rebirth, a liberation from feeling powerless, a liberation from oneself and from one's ego. When this liberation does not take place, it is war that is accused of not fulfilling one's expectations. The desire and need for liberation are incapable of investing themselves in reality.[12]

Ramzy is always worried about what people might say. Now he worries about what his male friends will think of him, having a woman in his house without having sexual relations with her. They will say: "Do we have to lose the war on *all* fronts?" (p. 88). Here sex is clearly associated with conquest and domination. The fact that the woman is American reinforces the link and makes sex appear even more like a battlefield, the colonized overcoming the colonizer.[13] Ramzy worries that Pamela might think he is impotent. But most of all, he is upset at flirting with a married woman while his country is aflame with napalm. It strikes him as "the height of both tragedy and foolishness" (p. 88). As he finally makes love to her, images of the war overcome him: "Pamela was swooping down on Ramzy. Napalm was burning his body. He was on fire. He let himself burn, like a Buddhist monk in Viet Nam. At the climax he was thinking that death was indeed a field from which his country sprouted like a flower in bloom" (p. 101). The sexual act could not be more explicitly war-like, but in this image, the American woman is the aggressor of the Arab male. She is on top, inflicting wounds on the man, who, powerless, is being consumed.[14] What bothers Ramzy is that even in the sexual act, he is being humiliated. It is the opposite of Fanon's notion in which the black man gets "whitened" by the white woman. The image of the hyena comes back. The waters of the Jordan River are not able to wash away evil. The war planes are associated with the hyena. The notion of good and evil is once more naïvely connected with the Arabs and Israel.[15]

In still another passage, Ramzy compares his country to his body, and even though he does not use the word *rape,* he describes it symbolically:

Ramzy felt hot tears in his eyes. The Israeli army was occupying ever more of his country. It was as though they were occupying his body. The boots of Israeli soldiers were stamping on his chest. Their planes were dropping napalm bombs on his face. Their artillery was aimed at his eyes, piercing his heart. Israel was occupying all of his being. He had no being left. He was crumbling like the ancient buildings of Jerusalem. He was being filled with holes like the streets of Bethlehem, being smashed to pieces like the glass in Hebron. He was weeping like the children of Jericho. (Pp. 94–95)

In both passages, Ramzy is identified with a woman, used as an object, invaded, dominated, destroyed, and left with nothing but tears. In the first one, his body is able to engender life because of love, while in the second, the end result is only the wounds of napalm and death. This identification with women, the body being raped or giving life, is an interesting aspect of Barakat's writing.[16] It shows that at certain moments of his writing, he assumes the feminine role. It also could be an expression of men's envy of women's procreative power and a projection of male fantasies: men like to imagine that women desire to be raped. It also suggests that defeat represents womanization/feminization, while only victory is masculine. Ramzy identifies with Palestine under napalm. When women are in control of sexuality, it becomes associated with war. Male honor is at stake. Ramzy talks about the thousand years of sexual frustration for which Arabs must compensate.

The chapter of the fourth day, "Jacob Circumcises the Palestinians," is about history repeating itself. The biblical story of Jacob is compared to the present. Pamela begins to fall in love with Ramzy. He likes to see her strong, brave, independent, and adventurous (p. 119), even though these characteristics are the opposite of what he had described as desirable in a woman. In both his politics and his personal life, Ramzy feels torn between tradition and modernity, between East and West. In the end, he lets go of Pamela and what she symbolizes and he admires—the West—because he feels more secure and comfortable with tradition—the East.

Pamela and Ramzy analyze chapter 34 of Genesis, comparing the naïveté of the Canaanites with the shrewdness of the Israelis, a contrast that recurs in the present war: "The Palestinians of the modern era thought the original Zionist immigrants were a peace-loving people and so gave them a friendly reception and let them settle on their land. They did not realize the Zionists had a plan to circumcise them and slaughter them and plunder their land" (p. 107) (circumcision here symbolizes castration). But their analysis is not complete or honest, because they fail to acknowledge the Canaanites had raped one of Jacob's daughters and that the Israelis' action was one of revenge. Even if revenge is not justifiable, it does put the story in a different perspective and shows the Canaanites not as naïve and peace-loving as the two would like to believe.[17] Ramzy says Judaism is no different from any other religion and that "all religions are anti-sex" (p. 116); unlike what some people claim about Islam, "repression is a way of life in this country, its roots run deep into our lives" (p. 116).

In the Bible, the problem is the violation of Jacob's honor of the tribe. Women are invested with honor; they are merchandise, goods to be exchanged. Why does Ramzy use this example from a biblical past—he, who claims Arabs must live in the present and not look back into their past?[18]

The fifth day, described in the chapter entitled "Death Shall Have No Dominion," is again a mixture of war scenes, feelings of despair at what is happening, and political, religious, and other discussions mixed with love scenes between Pamela and Ramzy. Most of the chapter is a kind of love-hate dialogue Ramzy has with his country. Again, he becomes his country, burnt, murdered, and occupied. He blames the Arabs and their preference for words over action. He feels the Arabs have been deceiving him, hiding the truth from him. He would like his country to be protected against invasion, impregnable. He wishes there were marches in which he could participate, like the ones he joined with the blacks in the United States. But no such marches are taking place in any of the Arab countries for the Palestinians. Has he forgotten the march against the American Embassy Pamela joined at the beginning?

Pamela tells Ramzy he suffers from a split personality, a key for understanding Ramzy. In a dialogue, Pamela says she is convinced that Arab men scorn foreign women, whom they see as "easy prey." Ramzy denies it, telling Pamela he likes to see her strong. Has his image of women changed from when he described to her what he wanted in a woman: dependence and a sense of the family? Ramzy fundamentally misunderstands Pamela; for him a free woman can only be a "frivolous" one (p. 118). Ramzy, who is quite Westernized, especially when he describes the Arab people—he sees them as an outsider—does not understand Pamela. The sexual relationship is the point of limit, the stumbling block of his Westernization. Ramzy's lack of understanding for Pamela grows. He attributes to her his own feelings and strategies; he projects onto her his own petty ideas about love and sexual expectations.

The topic of roots comes up once more, and Ramzy wishes to pluck out his country "by its roots, to provide it other roots, branches, fruits, air and skies. He wanted to destroy its institutions and organizations, its fable-filled, otherworldly constitutions imported without modification from days gone by" (p. 127). He is in such a state of despair that he wishes an air raid on Beirut would take place "to tighten up those flaccid nerves. The Arabs were dying from excessive complacence" (p. 127). The same wish appears in *La petite montagne*—the desire to see Beirut destroyed—except that here it is not in the same proportions and is the result of utter frustration. Ramzy would like to be able to cut out his roots, have someone take them, burn them, cast them into the sea. He wants the Arabs to be able to change their leadership by themselves and not have Israel do so for them. "The Arabs had already lost their lands; they must not now lose their own will" (p. 141). Once more, destruction is associated with liberation. Ramzy reasons like someone outside of his culture, an intellectual who is not in touch with the people. It is precisely from his culture that the Palestinians have invented the war of stones, the *intifada,* one of the most effective ways of struggling for their rights within Israel.

All this is happening along with his growing relationship to Pamela, her frustration about being married, her wondering what she should do. She is described as the one always preparing the food and asking Ramzy if he wants to eat. She is shown pulling off his shoes, at which point he tells her she could easily pass for a woman of the East. She worries about being stoned for adultery if she were to pass for one. In these half-serious, half-joking remarks, it comes out that they both feel quite uneasy about their relationship. They decide to go to Amman and help with the refugees and the wounded. In a way, it is an immediate solution to their dilemma: to submerge themselves in a larger humanitarian issue and avoid facing their relationship.

Some of Ramzy's students have also decided to go to Amman, among them many women "who had not stopped to consider what their families might think" (p. 125). Ramzy sees it as a sign that "Arab women were beginning to feel genuinely independent, to view themselves as full citizens and individual human beings rather than as women who were somehow complementary to men, mere machines or pleasure objects. They were searching for new capacities and roles" (p. 125). As with Awwad, we see in Barakat a real awareness and sensitivity to women's issues. Why then, is living with them on a daily basis, in a one-to-one relationship with another, so difficult? Voicing beautiful statements about women's liberation comes out with strength and conviction, but when these ideas have to be put into practice, not just into actions the world can see, but in the privacy of the home, it is a totally different story. Women's issues defined publicly are to be defended, but in privacy, men ask to keep their domination. Women always get trapped: what they win publicly must be given back privately, and what they acquire privately must be paid for publicly.

In the chapter for the sixth day, "Floods in the Streets and Ants Creeping Through the Arteries of the Heart," the turmoil begins to spread to the streets of Beirut, and Ramzy begins to feel more for Pamela than he would like to: "Until he met Pamela, he had always believed himself free. Now he felt more like a slave" (p. 143). Is he also beginning to feel she is conquering him, as Israel conquered the Arabs? The main event is that the war is over and the Arabs have been defeated. Ramzy feels all that in his body: the wounded, the corpses, the houses blown up. "Tears welled in his eyes. His enemies were really in occupation of his whole life. They were burning his face with napalm. They were cutting out a piece of his chest and throwing it to the hungry. His enemies were in occupation of all of Jerusalem. They were moving through its narrow streets, throwing the Arabs out of their homes. They had occupied Ramzy's heart and were creeping like ants through his arteries" (p. 153).

The sexual act is compared to two worlds longing to meet: "They do meet. Suppressed cries rise up from a river in a deep valley to the heights of towering mountains. The voices merge together. They surge and arrive at the summit together. Calm covers the world" (p. 145). Sexuality is here described as fulfilling, bringing peace and transcendence from daily worries, not only for the two persons involved, but to the world in general. Unlike the other love scenes portrayed negatively, this one is serene and positive. Is it because Ramzy is beginning to feel he loves Pamela? He compares her to the other women he has known: "In his relationship with Pamela he did feel he could move freely and in directions not drawn in the past" (p. 146). This statement contradicts the one he had made that morning about feeling like a slave, and this contradiction shows how split he is deep inside. Dialectics enter his most intimate wishes: "He wanted to be like a wave, to be independent and yet attached, to be free and yet part of something big" (p. 146).

The last pages take up where the novel begins. Ramzy and Pamela, along with some students, are in Jordan helping the refugees. Tears are flowing from all of them when they witness the devastation that has occurred. The biblical story of the creation taking place in six days, is reversed: "All the Arabs had created in the first six days was dust, and now the tempests were revealing the nature of his creations. There was nothing but the future left for him now, but he still reached back for the past" (p. 163).

Ramzy thinks exile is the worst thing that can befall people, and the loss of the war means sure exile. He compares the guerrilla to a wounded bird trying to fly. He sees oppression throughout the world, and sees that it is similar everywhere: "The cries of slaves beneath the whip of the Pharaohs mingled with the screams coming from a village burning in Viet Nam, from Baghdad and Damascus occupied by Tamerlane. The wailing of European Jews in concentration camps mixed with the cries of the Arab refugees. The face of Anne Frank became the face of Adla Kanaan in the Jordanian lowlands" (p. 172). He pronounces once more the idea that the guerrilla is the only hope: "It brought a sense of pride to him and affirmed his convictions as an Arab. For him the word had become a symbol of someone able to reject all those worldly temptations for which we strain and compete and sell our lives. The guerrilla, the *fedaï*, fulfills his life by means of his own death. He rejects all temptations of the world and carves out his future with his own hands" (p. 174). Would Ramzy's notions—and through him Barakat's—be the same today? Would Ramzy still feel the Palestinian guerrilla to be the only hope today? Even so, Ramzy had not chosen that path for himself, because he loved life too much: "He had a passion for movements and for growth. He liked to plunge into the streams. He loved rain, clouds, the sea, mountains, and valleys. Ideas stimulated him" (p. 174). But is it fair to assume that the guerrilla does not have such desires?

Ramzy hopes for an Arab world that is united, growing, moving, inventing, "propelled toward the future. He eagerly awaits the time when the institutions of religion, politics, education, the family, and all the rest will have given up their attempts to mold man, to break him down, to pressure him, and to obstruct his natural desires" (p. 175). The worst thing that has happened to the Palestinians is that they have been exiled and uprooted. And just as the Palestinians want roots, Pamela also decides she needs roots and will return to New York. She tells Ramzy: "I'm bored with casual relationships. I too want to have roots" (p. 178). Pamela's notion of roots is not like Ramzy's. For her, it means being anchored in life, having stability; for him, it is connected with identity and authenticity. Ramzy does not try to keep her. Even though he has discovered he loves her, he doesn't think he wants to marry her.

Is Pamela putting her finger on his true feelings when she tells him, "You don't really want an independent woman like me, someone you couldn't control. . . . I believe you will marry a girl like Najla, one who will obey you, who will listen to you, who will put up with anything from you?" (pp. 177–78). Ramzy seems confused about what he wants in life. The loss of the war had made him even more unhappy and puzzled by himself and the world. A sense of hopelessness and helplessness has taken hold of him, and he seems unable to see anything else or to decide what to do with his life. Had Pamela stayed, could they have given more meaning to their personal life than what was happening around them? Why does he not ask her to stay? Was she only a pastime diverting him from the anxiety of war? Pamela is not always identified as an enemy of the Arabs, even though she is American. In fact, she is portrayed as participating in demonstrations on the Arab side. But her identity is ambiguous. In Ramzy's dreams, she sometimes appears as an aggressor and oppressor. Thus, there is a conflict in Ramzy between his solidarity and identification with the Arabs and his love for Pamela.[19]

In this novel, Barakat has painted the Arabs, most specifically the

Palestinians, as condemned into exile. They keep hoping from generation to generation to find their roots through war. They wish to win the war, to find a land/woman that has remained faithful so they will be able to stay anchored in its harbor. Ramzy's criticism of the Arabs is from the point of view of someone who puts his trust in technology, therefore in the West. In order to be victorious, the Arabs must identify with the West. But the Palestinian people have discovered that they cannot trust any state or government. They have invented the war of stones, a reversal of the myth of Goliath.

Barakat implies criticism in his use of the myth of the hyena. Through Ramzy, he criticizes Arab behavior—moving from total despair to stupid hope, mouthing words—similar to the bridegroom's attitude when he sees blood on the sheet and is suddenly delivered from an immeasurable fear. But he does not explicitly criticize the myth itself either by deconstructing it, by showing that the political attitudes are directly linked to the relationship with women, or by opposing another myth. The relationship of Ramzy to Pamela is another implied criticism. Ramzy never questions Pamela about her virginity (how many men she has known); on the contrary, Barakat places such questions in her mouth, which is not consistent with Pamela's character and could mean that the male protagonist, once more, projects his own views (like rape) on her.

On the other hand, the hero criticizes the Arabs' behavior, therefore placing himself outside of them. He wants an organization that more or less copies the enemy's (army, guerrillas); but the Palestinians have invented something else: the revolt with stones, the affirmation of themselves and the recognition of Israel. For the young Palestinians of the stone war, Israel is no longer the filthy beast, unnameable, from which one moves from utter despair to excessive hope, but a real enemy against which one can fight with the most powerful weapons one possesses, the symbolic ones. With the stone war, there has been a real move beyond the myth of the hyena. But the hero, citing the Bible, remains locked into the myth of an enemy as "absolute evil."

Barakat seems to want to imply that the war could bring out values the Arab world lacks. War could have revolutionized it and made it move into the twentieth century, if only it had been victorious. In that sense, war appears as a necessary evil. The guerrilla, in particular the Palestinian one, is glorified. His vocation is romanticized. His sense of heroism and martyrdom is praised. Ramzy is constantly depressed and gloomy because he sees that the dreams he has for the Arab world are not being fulfilled. Israel has been victorious, and the Arab world is plunged into lethargy. Never once does he question his beliefs in heroism or in the Palestinian cause. In that sense, he merely reproduces notions held within history's mainstream—namely, that change takes place through violence, and that revolutions are won through blood. His depression does not lead him into new paths of resistance or into nonviolent actions. He can only propose what the world has seen repeated over and over again.

This traditional way of looking at history is reproduced in his personal life. He is also depressed about it because he feels split between tradition and modernity, between the East and the West. That he does not ask Pamela to stay in the end and knows she is not the one he wants to marry leads me to believe he might opt for tradition, even if this is not clearly shown in the story. In that sense, this novel is a good illustration of how the political reflects the personal.

Even if Pamela appears a little freer than the other women described by the male authors discussed in this section, she is nonetheless trapped in men's views of her, not just as a woman but also as a blond Western one. She inspires both attraction and rejection, fascination and repulsion. Pamela is also confused about what she should do in her life. She represents the "good" aspect of the Western world: she has rejected capitalist values, is engaged in assisting the oppressed, and would like to help the developing countries. She does all this in a rather naïve way, though. Her romantic notions about the East are similar to those Ramzy has about the Palestinians. She comes to the Middle East with a husband; they are hippy-artists. She wants freedom; she feels trapped in marriage because her husband is too dependent on her. She manages to send him away, although she feels guilty about it. She participates in the anti-American, anti-imperialist marches in Lebanon without thinking about the effectiveness or the dangers of such acts. She leaves to go back to the States as she came without precise direction. Why does Barakat seem unable to imagine and portray a "liberated" Lebanese woman?[20]

In Barakat's novel, a male protagonist integrates into his personality not only masculinity but also femininity. He often identifies his body with a woman's, for example, when he feels it being raped by the Israeli soldiers, or in making love with Pamela when she takes the leading role. His idea of rape could be a wish-fulfillment of his own male fantasies.[21] Barakat's view of the "feminine" is quite conventional—passive, victimized, shameful. He admits femininity only in defeat. Why can't he imagine a resistant, assertive feminism?[22] The feminine side is constantly depressed and ill at ease. It has not found a harmonizing balance within the central hero. It is a reflection of the mosaic rather than pluralistic culture Barakat criticizes in his study on the war. In other words, Ramzy's schizophrenia is mosaic—unable to integrate the various sides of his personality—rather than pluralistic—finding harmony and balance within variety. In that sense, too, the personal is once more the political.

NOTES

1. I will be quoting throughout from the English edition by permission of Three Continents Press, Washington, D.C. © Halim Barakat, 1983.
2. I will be including in the notes, remarks, and reactions Halim Barakat sent me after reading two versions of this chapter, seeking thereby to show that what the author intends and what he writes are two different things and that writing betrays one's secret thinking, one's fantasies. It also illustrates how a text lends itself to many interpretations.
3. After reading a first draft of my chapter, Halim Barakat made these observations in a letter dated January 16, 1989: "I feel your statement about 'the symbolism of the woman . . .' is not accurate. Woman is not found unfaithful and incapable of providing love. On the contrary, it is man who fails to discover love. The legend tells us that the Flying Dutchman was a victim of his own doubts as a result of previous bad experiences. When he did discover the right woman, he could not believe it. Upon returning to my novel to present you with evidence, I discovered to my amazement that the English translation skipped over a scene that exposes the blindness of the Flying Dutchman (the last few pages of the Sixth Day)."

    I read all three versions of the novel: Arabic, English and French, and I fail to see that Barakat's point makes a big difference in the interpretation of the story. The search is for the ideal woman. Reality can never correspond to fantasy. Bad experiences and the incapability to recognize the "right" woman are one and the same thing. The story is about relationships between men and women. In other words, if the Flying Dutchman does not find the ideal woman, it is because women do not correspond to his ideal. The problem lies in the ideal being a fantasy.
4. The reading of my second draft led Halim Barakat to the following observations in a letter dated February 13, 1989: "There is a misinterpretation of the myth of the hyena. Simply, I used this myth to mean two things: force and spell, the need to regain consciousness. Arabs before the 1967 war, I suggested, were under a spell, i.e., had little control over their destiny and direction. According to the myth, the person under spell can regain his or her consciousness when

his or her forehead hits something solid (mainly rock) and receives a shock (as when wounded). It is through a shock that the one under spell regains consciousness. So the hyena is not meant to represent evil, not at all, though it implies force, nor is it associated with death (p. 145). It does not piss on the bridegroom's tail (p. 145); it pisses on its own tail and sprays it. If a drop falls on a person, that person goes under a spell and follows the hyena aimlessly. It is also not true that the spell can only be broken through blood; it is broken through a shock. The wound only on the forehead is an effective shock. So the stone is not the bride's virginity or the pledge of fidelity. And most certainly, it is not accurate nor does it represent my intentions to say: 'only blood, war, can prove that Palestine has remained faithful.' "

My observations are that the myth of the hyena is repeated in several passages of the novel with different variations, showing the importance it has in the novel and in the subconscious of the author. The fact that it is a popular tale would incline me to say that, at some level, it must have a sexual significance, even if the author did not intend it this way. The hyena—any dictionary on symbolism would confirm this—is almost always associated with death and dirt because, among other things, it eats cadavers.

5. In his response, dated February 13, 1989, Barakat writes that it is not accurate to say that 'defeat is the result of Arab's sins and of the hyena's spell,' especially if sins are given religious meanings. Ramzy is secular and does not argue issues in religious terms such as evil versus good. "The defeat is a result of a complex number of external and internal conditions, such as a combination of external domination and internal fragmentation and false consciousness. It is also not fair to bring the question of virginity into the picture in this context. So the last paragraph is most unfair and damaging. Even when you talk about this problem in a different context, it is *not* accurate to say that 'men in Arab society view women's virginity as the only warranty for fidelity.' This is not accurate, even of the traditional Arab, let alone Ramzy who is struggling to liberate himself. Virginity does not mean a thing to him." One can, however, be secular and at the same time function in a universe of good and evil created by one's cultural inheritance. On the topic of virginity, Barakat's reaction really surprises me: Did he read Awwad's *Death in Beirut,* to cite only one example in the hundreds, dealing with the importance of virginity in Arab society and how it is connected with all the other problems of our society? Even if Barakat is referring to sociological studies, there is not a single study that negates the importance of virginity in Arab society.

6. As a continuation to the previous remarks, Barakat writes that it is also unfair to say that their 'notion of women and country is one of ownership, possession, and exclusive property.' Nevertheless, the use of the symbol of the Flying Dutchman looking for this faithful, absolute love and the use of the myth of the hyena over and over again indicate the importance it holds in the author's subconscious. The implications of these symbols to the collective imagination of the people are obvious and further analyzed in this chapter.

7. In his letter dated February 13, 1989, Barakat writes that the conclusions about Ramzy's views on sexuality and feminism connected to his own are troublesome. "Woman is not seen as the deceptive leader who must give love. Victory is not associated with manliness nor identity with manhood." I am glad that Barakat finds some of the implications of my analysis of his novel troublesome, especially if this leads him to seek changes in the private and political domains. Only to deny the conclusions I have reached through a careful association of the various symbols, themes, and meanings interwoven within his text does not seem to me sufficient.

8. In his letter dated February 13, 1989, Barakat writes that multiplicity is not seen as a cause of war, but of defeat. In the context of Lebanon, the mosaic structure and not pluralism has contributed to the civil war. I don't see the contradiction of his statement with what I wrote. The defeat is *before* Israel and not against Israel. It is different from the civil war.

9. In his letter dated February 13, 1989, Barakat writes: "I use the concept of *Fidaʾi* in Arabic. This is not the same as army, guerrilla. Christ in the Christian understanding of the area represents *Fidaʾi*, the one who sacrifices himself for others and not the one who kills. There are different conceptions of resistance and revolution. To understand my concept of *Fidaʾi*, you need to see it against Arab defects. Because of selfishness, one is willing to sacrifice or pay a price for public good. Heroism in the present context is not associated with violence, war, and domination. It is resisting invasion and occupation of the country. Because of prevailing conditions, Palestinians did not resist in Jerusalem, Nablus, and so on in 1967, and Israel easily occupied the area. How do you describe that? It is lack of heroism. Arabs retreated when they should have stood up, as they do at the present time in the West Bank and Gaza. So heroism is not what you assumed. Hence the unfairness of thinking that the novel implies that 'Palestinians . . . are justified in returning the knife.' "

10. In his letter dated February 13, 1989, Barakat writes that I make too much of the hyena myth and misinterpret it, that the whole novel is more a criticism of the self rather than the other. Furthermore, it is self-sacrifice (in Arabic *al-fidaʾ*, which also describes Christ) and not blood that makes for renewal. Every time I discuss the myth of the hyena, it is because it reoccurs in the novel, indicating its importance. The notion of *fidaʾ* also describing Christ reinforces the symbol of blood, which is connected to the notion of sacrifice and of purification. The story of Christ in the Gospels and its interpretation by the apostles in the New Testament shows that Christ died for people's sins by sheding his blood on the cross so that whoever believed in Him could gain eternal life. But why use this example and symbolism if one is trying to get away from religion?

11. In his letter dated January 16, 1989, Barakat writes that Ramzy does not see a virtue in Najla's and his own lack of independence. On this issue, there is a lot of self-criticism and self-exposure.

12. In his letter dated February 13, 1989, Barakat writes that there is even greater

oversimplification or misstatement when you say: 'war appears as a release of tension' and that 'it is war that is accused of not fulfilling one's expectations!'

13. For an important analysis of this aspect of sexual relations, see Frantz Fanon's *Peau noire, masques blancs* and Eldridge Cleaver's *Soul on Ice.* Fanon explains the attraction white women exert on black men who marry them to "whiten" themselves. Cleaver describes his desire to rape white women as revenge for white domination.

14. In his letter dated January 16, 1989, Barakat writes: "The sexual act is associated with boiling coffee (see p. 89) and with fire and fields (p. 100). Woman is not seen as inflicting wounds—never. What Ramzy experiences is a sort of self-criticism as a result of guilt feelings for the great enjoyment at a time of war."

15. In his letter dated February 13, 1989, Barakat writes that to bring back the image of the hyena—and link it to notions of good and evil is wrong. I make this connection because the image of the hyena comes back at this point in the novel with these associations.

16. In his letter dated January 16, 1989, Barakat writes that the question is not one of rape. The idea is Ramzy's total identification with the country. The reader should be able to reach his or her conclusions through an analysis of the quotation.

17. In his letter dated Feburary 13, 1989, Barakat writes that the analysis of the circumcision in the Bible is not about rape but refusing intermarriage and integration. The story in the Bible shows that the son first raped Dina, then she liked him, and then the king asked Jacob to give her in marriage to his son. The Bible story seems also to be a misogynistic wish-fulfillment of male fantasies. How can a woman fall in love with a man who has raped her?

18. In the same letter, Barakat claims that "using examples from the biblical past is not a question of living in the past or the present—it is about repeated patterns of behavior."

19. In his letter dated February 13, 1989, Barakat writes: "The sexual act is not associated with war, as you often imply. There happened to be a war, and Ramzy feels guilty about not doing much to help. Instead, he is making love. Ramzy does not see dependency, loyalty, and passivity as desirable in woman. That is why he discontinues his relationship with Najla. As to why he discontinues his relationship with Pamela, there are at least two reasons. One, she herself is not sure. Second, beside the reality of Pamela, she is supposed to symbolize Western temptation for the Arab. In other words, though based on real experience, the relationship is intended to depict some basic contradictions between the West and the Arab world. Both Pamela and Ramzy feel these contradictions. In spite of attraction, both are not sure. What Ramzy admires in Pamela is her independence, adventurism, and rebelliousness. It is what he wants to be. He never wants dependence and sense of family, as you put it. He never sees Pamela as conquering him, nor is he engaged in an act of conquest. It is not true that he opts for tradition."

The connection between sexuality and war is made clear through a close reading of the text. Psychoanalysis has taught us that things happen in our subconscious that we might not be aware of. The same applies to the reading of a literary text: the association of ideas, symbols, images make us discover in-depth layers of meanings not obvious otherwise, not even to the author. The story shows that Ramzy feels split and does not really know what he wants. It is not clear from the story that he discontinues his relationship with Najla. In that domain, the choices remain vague and ambiguous. Of course, my own reading and interpretation of a text can also be seen as my own construct.

20. In his response to my second draft, Barakat writes that showing a liberated Arab woman was not the basic theme of the novel, and that he did portray some liberated Arab women in his novel *Al-rahil bayna al-sahm wal-watar* (Letter dated February 13, 1989.)

21. In the same letter, Barakat continues: "One of the most unfair conclusions is saying that 'his idea of rape could be a wish-fulfillment of his own male fantasies."

22. In the same letter, Barakat concludes: "More unfair are the last few lines. To me, this is a shocking accusation. I just cannot see how you could have reached such a conclusion. . . . The misunderstanding is so deep. It can perhaps be resolved through greater communication."

I am sorry if my reading has caused deep misunderstanding; I hope it can be bridged through better communication. It proves to me how deep and important these issues are and how great the gaps between women and men they can create. And it therefore demonstrates the need to speak about them more often and more forcefully.

NINE

Elias Khoury: Ambivalence, Fear of Women, and Fascination with Death and Destruction

We live near the sea shore in a sunken ship; when we reach the sea, the ship will sink and our story will end.

When war starts spreading, it holds only surprises. . . . The war has become a surprise. . . . War is implicitly within us. Now we are doing it for real.

Death is the last possibility. . . . Whom should we reproach for not dying? If we don't die now with all that's happening, we will perhaps be able to fight other wars, which might be better than this one.

Elias Khoury, La petite montagne

Elias Khoury, a Christian Lebanese, was born in Beirut in 1948. Student and professor of history and sociology, he has taught these subjects at the Lebanese University in Beirut and at Columbia University in the United States. He participated in the creation of several literary reviews and has contributed to the daily Lebanese Arab newspaper *Al Safir* (The Ambassador). He has written three novels on the Lebanese war which have had quite an impact in the Arab world. Among his publications are three novels —*Fima yata'alak rawabit al-nitak* (Concerning the relations of the Circle, 1975), *Abwab al-madinat* (The City Gates, 1981), and *Wujuh bayda'* (White Faces, 1981)—a collection of short stories—*Al-tasbit wal mawdu'* (The Predicate and the Subject, 1984)—and essays on the Arabic novel, poetry, the "lost memory," and the time of occupation. The novel I am going to analyze, *La petite montagne*, first published in Arabic as *Al-Jabal al-saghir* in 1977, is particularly significant in terms of this study. It illuminates many of the aspects of the war in terms of sexuality and women. It should be noted that Elias Khoury is the only one of the writers discussed here who actively participated in the fighting at the beginning of the war. This direct experience with war has given him insights the others do not have and

135

seems to have reinforced a fascination with death and destruction I do not find in the other novels.

La petite montagne is structured into five parts, each one with a symbolic significance, not always clear. Like the war itself, the narrative is often disconnected and absurd, expressing a hopelessness and meaninglessness spreading to the rest of the world through phrases, sentences, and descriptions that recur with the monotony of despair. In this bleak tale, some positive elements occur at the beginning, in the hero's memories of his childhood, and in the middle, in his experience with an androgynous-looking woman, who is somewhat "liberated" compared to the other female characters in the novel and who laughs, argues, moves freely, captivates the hero, runs towards the sea, and is unattainable because the man is too busy fighting "the revolution."

The sections are: "The Small Mountain," or one's childhood; "The Church," or the battles; "The Last Possibility," or nostalgia for life and freedom, "The Stairs," or the horror of relationships between men and women, the family, the daily routines, the marital sexual rites that kill pleasure, modernity, and all the other ugly things war destroys; and "The Place of the King," or the spreading of the war to other cities, the perpetual revolution, the unending destruction of cities and of women connected to decadent modernity, compared to whores.

In the first part, the central character—obviously the author himself because like him he is a Christian who belonged to the Communist party, fought for the Palestinians at the beginning of the war, and worked for a major newspaper—mixes memories of his childhood with his political inclinations at the beginning of the war: the Left, Nasser, international communism, the Palestinians. Members of the right-wing Kataëb party come to search him and his house, but only his mother is there, sad and trembling, refusing to answer their questions. This image comes back several times like a leitmotif. Women stay at home silent, afraid, and trembling, while the men fight it out. The protagonist goes into the city, towards the sea, looking for the small mountain. What could be the meaning of this "small mountain"? At the beginning, the central character tells us it is the popular name given to Achrafieh, the Christian district east of Beirut, but it becomes obvious, as the novel unfolds, that it has a symbolic meaning connected with the message of the novel. In this first part, it is the place of his childhood, opposed to Beirut, far away with its cement and high buildings encroaching on the fields and trees. If it sounds strange for wild fields to be part of Beirut, remember that the narrator sees it with his child's eyes, and in those days, some forty years ago, most of Beirut was full of fields and gardens. It is the place of quest and of the poor. The child learns that his country has had a history of colonialism, occupied by the French, who came with barefooted Indochinese they used as servants. He also learns that theft started with the arrival of industry, and that everything deteriorated when a factory was established, bringing capitalism, profit, and theft. The mountain is being penetrated, with holes dug into all its sides (p. 31).[1] The invasion of cement and modernity kills the memories of his childhood, of his dreams. The smell of the sea—of dreams and freedom—is replaced by the smell of concrete (p. 32). The right-wing militias who penetrate his home and rip the pages of his books are also destroying the world of his childhood, the world of peace he knew on the small mountain. The victory of the Christians means the death of the poor (p. 39). His quest is the small mountain: "I was searching for the small mountain confounded with the bodies of these men in whose eyes the sea was rising" (p. 47). The small mountain, the place of childhood, is mirrored within the sea, the place of dreams. Between the two stand the city, the war, and the fury.

In the second section, the leftist militia to which the hero belongs wages battles, the meaning of which is not very clear. It emerges that they are fighting for and with the Palestinians, because they believe "Palestine is everyone's dream. . . . Palestine is a state of mind, every Arab is a Palestinian, every poor person with a gun is a Palestinian" (p. 88). As in Etel Adnan's *Sitt Marie-Rose*, what seems like the "just" cause at the beginning of the war is the Palestinian one. Unlike Marie-Rose, however, who struggles for it with love, devotion, self-sacrifice, and mercy, the hero of *La petite montagne*, along with his comrades, fights for it with their weapons, with the destruction of Beirut, its streets, walls, churches, buildings, stores, and most of all its civilians. " 'This is the true Beirut,' says Talal [one of the comrades], covered with dust from head to toe. Full of pride, he laughs, 'We learned to make war and we invented new laws' " (p. 60). His words recall Ahmad's, in *The Story of Zahra*, who also says that the war brings new laws considered immoral in normal times and who looks at Beirut with contempt and the pride of ownership. Like Ahmad, Samir (another comrade) in *La petite montagne* says: "We are the masters of the streets. . . . Dreams are in the middle of the street. Shells come smashing the small low constructions" (p. 52). Fighting is in the middle of the street. It is not clear why, but the weapons of the war are dreams, and its objective the sea, also a kind of dream. One is already tempted to say: what irresponsibility. To kill, destroy, maim, torture, mutilate for that! But I will leave such judgment—if called for—till the end, after having analyzed the book as completely as possible—after having tried to understand what the dreams are all about. Adam Farrar's discussion of how war is closely connected to male desire comes to mind: "Masculinity is not an essence, an attitude, or an undifferentiated kind of subject, but rather a *potential* way of assembling the world which can at any time be invoked or retreated from. We can only capture 'masculinity' in those few moments of unalloyed male desire— pornography, rape, science and . . . war" (p. 68). By analyzing war, how the battles are fought in this section, what makes men fight should become clearer.

This section takes place in five scenes. In the first one, the hero has joined a militia advancing in the Bab Idris district. They are moving towards the famous hotels of Beirut located near the sea (where one of the biggest battles between the Palestinian and pro-Palestinian forces against the Christian ones took place at the beginning of the war). They hide in a church where they try to raise the statue of a half-broken Christ, fallen on the ground. All their attempts are in vain, indicating how hopeless their lives have become. "Even if he stands now, He will fall tomorrow. Tomorrow is the battle" (p. 57). How could Christ help them? They are not searching for the spiritual Christ, but trying to raise a statue of stone; rather than praying with faith, they go against His message of love and peace as expressed in the gospel: "But I tell you who hear me: Love your enemies, do good to those who hate you, bless those who curse you, and pray for those who ill-treat you. If anyone hits you on one cheek, let him hit the other one too" (Luke 6:27). It is no wonder the church is empty, destroyed, broken, when the people come to it with their weapons and hate, far, far away from the true Christian message, and when the priests sitting in it preach a colonialist message, having first come to Lebanon as French soldiers. War is compared to a mass, to new laws, to making a movie, to flying, to reaching the sea, to organizing disorder, to fear, to a feast with wine, to chaos, to an aimless struggle.

In the second scene, the quest about the meaning of the war continues. It is not clear why the war is taking place. Many questions are raised without answer.

He said that an answer was not important. All answers are equal. The important thing is to raise questions. . . .

—What does war want?

—War wants nothing. But it says that the asphalt leads this street to the next one facing it. (Pp. 58–59)

Questions about the war are useless. Even having the war ask itself what it's all about leads nowhere. The only objective is the sea.

The deflagration of shells shake one's body. To the right, fires; to the left, a building gets dislocated like an old man disarticulated by the bombs. Between the sea and us: walls, stones, and metal. . . . Between the other extremity of the street and our positions, the noise of steps, the screams, the laughter of fighters. . . . Between the hand that pulls the trigger and the feet that jump, the body bends, straightens up, crawls. And, at the end of the road, his hand grasps the sea. (P. 59)

The sea is often a symbol of woman, and Khoury also uses it as such, as becomes evident in the fifth scene of this second section, where Talal plunges into it "as one makes love to a woman," a scene we will analyze later. The sea, woman, or dreams—is it not precisely one of the problems about this war, and war in general, that those who got involved in it do so with aimless, romantic notions? To use Farrar's words again:

War lends experiences of great intensity. It eliminates most of the background decisions, simplifying everything, existing only in the moment. Comradeship and trust are matters of basic survival not utopian dreams, and are constantly reinforced by the ever present utter loneliness of death. In all these ways it is an enactment of 'mythic' oppositions. It is, for men, at some terrible level the closest thing to what childbirth is for women: the initiation into the power of life and death. (P. 61)

The sea is also a symbol of renewal, of life and death, but why does it have to be reached through destruction? "Fire can make a hole in the net [meaning the city, oppression] and the fish [symbol of the people, of life and of rebirth] can invade the sea [the place of dreams]" (p. 60). It is through the destruction of the city (the woman) that the people can plunge into their dreams.

They fight, advancing, reaching Bab Idris, and when three of their comrades are wounded, they don't even feel sadness. One of the comrades, Talal, feels he is acting in a movie. Dreams of conquest enacted in Western films become reality. Then as they sit resting after the battle, a crowd of looters invades the space: men, women, and children, later joined by men in uniforms, rush to steal in the stores and ruins. The hero screams that they must be stopped, but it is impossible to stop them, and one of the comrades remarks that they steal in order to live. The hero philosophizes, "this is not theft, it is folklore. A feast. This is the revolution, all revolutions are like that. Beautiful and terrifying" (p. 63). Another group of fighters breaks into a music store. They steal the trumpets, cymbals, and drums and march in the street—named France!—playing music in the midst of screams and gun shots. One of them falls, victim of a bullet. This is war, with the face of feast, and feast with the mask of war!

In *Beyrouth ou la fascination de la mort,* Issa Makhlouf explains how war takes on aspects of great amusement. Destroying Beirut is like lighting a fire of joy.

The true feast is, by essence, animal-like, pagan, and for the most part orgiastic. One can understand why killers often associate with it music, alcohol, drugs, or dance; so many things to make war a feast, the supreme feast because bloody. Blood is charged with complex symbolism . . . it links the members of a clan, a family, or a people; it carries the memory of collective history or is seen as such. It is therefore an object of reverence and jealousy, the two being often closely associated. . . . The Lebanese war is a collective delirium reinforced by the fighters' emulation. . . . War, like feast, is the outburst of all vital, sexual, and death-leading pulsations. . . . The libido seems to get fixed on all the objects close to it. Economically, like the feast, war is an immense waste. (Pp. 75–77)

And for Farrar: "Combat involves a *gestalt* shift in which one's relation to people and things changes utterly. All the norms and mores which determined our attitude to others are changed. If we are to avoid the view that without the humanising constraint of civilisation the natural beast emerges, we must ask what underpins this new life form. After all, considerable work is required to effect this *gestalt* shift" (p. 66). He goes even further, claiming there is a *jouissance,* an intensity of pleasure men reach in war that transforms reality into a kind of magic, the manifestation of a wish. Farrar believes that nowadays, this experience is most strongly manifested in the world of super-science and nuclear technology. Easlea and others explain this phenomenon through the rejection and jealousy men feel towards women's childbearing capacity, which they aim at overcoming with their "magic."

For the crowd in Khoury's book, war is also a class struggle: a revenge the poor are taking over the wealthy. The people who invaded the plush hotel districts of Beirut, come from camps, ghettos, and the poor areas of Lebanon. Khoury ironically names the street "France" to show it is also a revenge of the colonized against the colonizers. In his very interesting article on "Working Class Boys and 'Crime': Theorising the Class/Gender Mix," Chris Cunneen shows how class and sex are closely linked:

Working class male resistance is irrational, it is simply a sign of overly exaggerated masculinity which is caused by inappropriate family relations in the first place, in particular a family structure that is mother-dominated. According to Parsons this was exacerbated by a 'strong tendency to instability of marriage' among the 'lower-class'. The point is simple: aggression in working class males is irrational, and it is a *woman's* fault. (P. 82)

Even if this statement does not totally apply to the Lebanese situation, which cannot be explained only in Marxist terms, it shows the connections among class, family, economic relations, and the war, and how domineering mothers trigger violence in their sons—a notion that applies to Lebanon, as Etel Adnan's novel suggests. In Lebanon, the poor—usually Muslims— want to take revenge and steal what the rich—usually Christians—have accumulated, often at the expense of the poor.

In the third scene of this second section, the quest takes the form of a confrontation between East and West. A dialogue starts between the hero and one of the priests in the church, a Capuchin. Father Marcel says that the church is a ship that navigates in the world (the sea) but is not part of it. It is indestructible, but the war is attempting to destroy it. The West is rationalist and the East mystic. For Father Marcel, this is the fundamental difference between the two forms of Christianity. Locked into his Western "good conscience," he does not seem to realize that his religion is also part of war, that the clash between East and West is one of the components of the Lebanese war. Having first come to Lebanon with French soldiers after World War I, believing they were bringing "civilization to the enslaved people of the East," he "finally understood that the only means of conquering the heart of this country's inhabitants was not the sword but culture" (p. 72). Even the words he uses connote war. The comrades answer and ask questions, but they are not really present. While for the priest, the object of religion seems to lie mainly in its institution—the church—the young Christians from the Orient are searching for the sea—their mystic dream.

In the fourth scene, other descriptions of the war and death appear: "Here death is a distance, a split second of love or of spite. Death is an instant we penetrate, that we wait for. . . . What connection is there between death and big eyes?" (p. 78). One of the comrades sees war as a victory, the poor and the colored becoming masters while the old masters stay on, but without domestics—a Marxist revolution? They will carry victory to the Jordan River and John will speak to this victory—in an allusion to John in the Gospel who baptised Christ in the Jordan River? But why this association? Christ as the ultimate victory? It does not make sense in terms of the rest of the book. One fighter wants to write about the most beautiful and the longest of wars, while another asks "to take life as it is, to fight, and to die on top of the mountain" (p. 82). It all sounds like a big confusion, even when they say that the prisoner—it is not clear who he is or where he came from—must be killed. The main character feels "the bird trembling on his shoulder, blood flowing on his face and his body . . . the bird moaning for the last time" (p. 79), and he carries him through the shelling, talks to his warm body, reaches the hospital where he is told the prisoner is dead, does not understand, rejoins his comrades, continues to pull the trigger, moving on and joking. We are never sure whether the prisoner is real, if it is he or someone else who gets killed. The writing and images are as disconnected as the absurdity of the war they reflect. The sole objective, the sea, is repeated; so is the image of the sunken ship, into which both the priests and the militias are put together this time (p. 83). When the ship reaches the sea, it will sink for good, and history will end. Here the sea appears as the ultimate death. Through death, one attains absolute peace. Ross Poole, in "Structures of Identity: Gender and Nationalism," argues that death renders life meaningless, while nationalism, like religion, provides, through the self-sacrifice of an individual's life, a meaning that transcends the isolation and separation characteristic of market existence. Could that be why men fight war, to make their lives more meaningful? If so, why don't they search for constructive, creative ways, rather than the destructive ones of war?

The fifth and last scene is about the objective reached—the sea. It is the hardest battle (p. 85). How can one know what one is fighting for when everything is so entangled? Snow is confounded with the sea, and the rain is mixed with salt spat through the gun's muzzles. One of their comrades, Jaber, dies, falling like an arrow from the top of the mountain. The men shoot movements and glimmers. They reach the sea, and one of the comrades, Talal, undresses and plunges naked in the waves. The others scream at him that the fight is not over with yet, to which he replies that the fight is precisely what he is doing: "He swims like one loves a woman, he floats, plunges. In his hands, in his mouth, he takes water, he sprinkles the sky. He holds in his arms the cold, the drizzle and the salt. He comes out trembling like a bird" (p. 86). The implications could not be more clearly sexual. For Talal, fighting is like making love to a woman or plunging into the sea. It is frightening and cold. He may get sick from it, but "he will continue to fight. He will carry the struggle on his shoulders, from sunken ship to sunken ship, and, after having carried the pledged treasure to the sea, he will die on the summit of the mountain" (p. 87). If one carries the metaphor further, his words signify that for him, love will continue to be sex in the form of a battle, never being fulfilled, never happy, moving from one unfulfilling experience to the next until he learns to sublimate, or dies for a higher ideal. It is the same idea expressed in Barakat's myth of the Flying Dutchman: Women cause men's unhappiness and lack of fulfillment.

Isn't this the core of the problem of war and sexuality? To explain further, using Dworkin's words: "Men become advocates of that which they most fear. In advocacy they experience mastery of fear. In mastery of fear they experience freedom. Men transform their fear of male violence into a metaphysical commitment to male violence. Violence itself becomes the central definition of any experience that is profound and significant" (*Pornography: Men Possessing Women,* pp. 50–51). Man goes to the sea for appeasement after battle, as he makes love to calm his innermost fears of life and death. Unfortunately, he does so through a cycle of violence and destruction, and violence only begets violence. The cycle is repeated infinitely. Only a nonviolent act could break it. Only a rapport of mutual love, tenderness, equal sharing could break the battle of the sexes.

The result of such attitudes and behavior can only be death. And this is what happens in this scene. One of the comrades, Jaber, dies from a bullet in his head. "Because he knew he would die, he was laughing harder as he aimed. He knew how to aim a gun; he would pull and pull the trigger as a child who played" (p. 88). What more pathetic image of the war could be given than this manchild who laughs as he pulls the trigger knowing he will die, while the others mumble over the signficance of a meaningless war? His coffin is described as a ship. While previously the image of a ship appears in relation to the church and the country, it is also a symbol of the mother. Thus, Jaber goes back to his mother's womb and to the earth— both symbols of life and death. "Jaber, inside of it, is captain for the last time. It is his last cruise. . . . Death is a bird, says Jaber. . . . We stop in front of the big hole. We entrust the ship to the sand and the earth. . . . The ship, in the depth of the grave, finds peace amidst the fire shots and the slogans" (pp. 89–91). It is one of the practices in Lebanon to mark any celebration—birth, marriage, death, feasts—with gun shots and the shouting of slogans. This rite has been reinforced by the war and by the use and availability of all kinds of weapons. Even in death, Jaber is accompanied by war and violence. How else could it be, given the context and circumstances of his death?

Salem asks how the war will end, to which Samir replies that this war will never end: "Death has started, the war settles in" (p. 90). In *Les larmes d'Eros,* Georges Bataille explains how historically the curse of war has led to degrading sexuality. The beginning of war marks the regression of material civilization. According to Bataille, by choosing war, humanity also chose slavery in all its forms, including prostitution.

The third part, entitled "The Last Possibility" is about death as the last possibility. This phrase comes back many times; it refers to the protagonist —and he repeats it several times—to his relationship to a woman, strangely androgynous in appearance, and to the fighting he is engaged in with his comrades. Introduced by a poem of Chbarou, its first lines "What were you doing three hundred years ago in the old gardens?" which recur several times throughout this part, give the section a sense of nostalgia and immo- bility, involving, in a cyclical notion of time, memories of an expected death, memories of a moment, of a woman condemned to death. This woman, who could she be? A projection of the fighter's fantasies? How he imagines Arab society, freed from gender confines and able to accept love and pleasure? The last possibility is also about the possibility of love and life contrasted to death, a choice the hero seems unable to make, being too entangled with "revolution."

His relationship to the "young negro, androgynous-looking woman" is interesting, especially when contrasted to the one with his wife in the following section. Who is this woman with a dark skin who wears pants? Why is her name Maryam—Arabic for Mary, mother of Jesus in both Christianity and Islam? Is she the free woman, come to liberate Arab society and the hero? Why is their union impossible? She makes fun of the *fedayeen* (Palestinian guerrillas), their dreams and the revolution. She makes fun of the hero's shoes (fedaï, fighter's shoes) and of his romantic notions. She wants to live, and when the hero tries to reach her, her neck stretches and she becomes unattainable. She plunges into the sea and calls out for him, but he is not able to follow her. The sea and swimming are sexually pleasurable, but the *fedaï* (guerrilla, fighter) remains frustrated. They don't understand each other. She asks him why he is a *fedaï*, and he tells her it is because he loves her. It is the old notion of men fighting the war to win their women's love, to prove their masculinity. She rejects that notion; she calls it romantic.

The two of them discuss truth and lies (pp. 107–9). For the *fedaï*, truth is in dreams, in projecting and making a movie. Reality is a lie. For the androgynous negro woman, lying is the incapacity to see reality, to grasp it. For the *fedaï*, it is the invented color that transforms reality, gives it meaning, creates the possible. The androgynous woman also creates a reality through speech, with her story of the apple. She claims an apple is still on her head, when it has fallen in the sand and water. Two ways of inventing, seeing reality are clashing here: one has to do with dreams, the projection of dreams through revolution," the other one is about speech, a way of naming reality. The author does not tell us which one is better. He notices the clash between the two of them, the impossibility of union, therefore also of marriage between the *fedaï* and the androgynous woman. The first one has chosen death, the second life. She tells him she won't marry a *fedaï* because fighters die; besides, she does not want to be his prisoner. He tells her that "consciousness negates death," but she reverses his words by saying that "it is death that negates consciousness." Always this play on irreducible oppositions. He accuses her of being a "petite-bourgeoise"; she runs away from him shouting she "will not be shut off in a box" (pp. 148–49). He knows she is right and that if he imprisons her, he will be like a dictator afraid of truth (p. 136). It's almost as if he were having an unresolvable dialogue with himself. The "jeune nègre" becomes his double.

For the *fedaï*, colors gain their real colors only when they sink (p. 110). It is death that gives meaning to life. Each death transforms the sea, the promise, creates the bigger—national?—identity, the promise of a millenium, the reign of justice and peace on earth. Ross Poole argues that war and masculinity are closely connected to different concepts of morality between men and women. Public (masculine) and private (feminine) moralities often oppose each others. "The state embodies the power of death; and death is, from the perspective of that individual, both the ultimate sacrifice of self-interest and the ultimate irrationality" (p. 74). In *La petite montagne* the state can be replaced by the revolution the *fedayeen* are fighting for and talking about. They both require self-sacrifice, even in death, while reversing that concept by promising immortality through the coming of a new age.

The women do not participate in the war. They are its victims. They think of practical things, like getting bread. The mother feeds her son who is fighting. She regrets his not making money; he had a talent for it in his childhood (p. 106). She would prefer for him to be in business rather than politics. In war, women usually contemplate, wait. Women are both nostalgia and expectation—the line about three hundred years in the old gardens is repeated here (p. 128). The mountain and the war have become sisters. The mountain is pierced. At the top, a hole strangles the stretched neck of a woman—the tomb, death of his childhood, end of his dreams. At the center, a hole from before birth—the demarcation line, irreconcilable no-man's land, the impossibility of communication between East and West, between man and woman. The war had been implicit for fifty years, now they are fighting it for good (p. 129). The mountain is connected to war and to love. War is waited for like an appeasement, like death and love.

The rapport between man and woman seems impossible, the separation irremediable. Sexuality is a curse (p. 132). Nazih, a peasant, being practical, has decided that sex is not worth the trouble. Since all women are alike, why bother making love to one? Man dies but it doesn't matter. If he dies, his wife will cry. All women cry—it is in the nature of things. He does not believe in victory, it is a coat full of holes, impossible to reach even when one is close to it (pp. 133–34). He is desperate and resigned in his notions about war, women, and victory. In such bleakness, some lines of hope—where the problem may lie and how to solve it—are called for. As Farrar argues:

As the desperate and intractable situation produced by society's military obsession has forced many people to look for new political strategies, women's actions have offered such a new hope. A corollary of these activities is the focus on war as a *male* problem. War, on such accounts, is a paradigm of masculinist practices because its pre-eminent valuation of violence and destruction resonates throughout other male relationships: relationships to other cultures, to the environment and, particularly, to women. If the 'masculinism' of war is the explanation for its intractability, then we must follow this path to its conclusion, wherever that may be. (P. 59)

Could Nazih, the peasant of *La petite montagne* be convinced with such an explanation, he, who looks at women with such contempt and scorn? Could one ask him to look at the roots of his despair, precisely in the relationship he has with his wife, a rapport he presents as so "natural" and "in the order of things"?

Sexual images are mixed with the concept of war and with the notion of love. The *fedaï* tells the androgynous woman he has become a fighter because he loves her. "She laughs. She vibrates like an arch. Man took his arch and he threw it. The arrow went nowhere. It fell into the sea where it slowly started to sink" (p. 98). The arch or love bow is thrown. The arrow of love does not know where to go. War has no real aim except the sea, place of dreams, pretense for love. The woman is the instigator of his desire for destruction; therefore, she will have to be destroyed, as we shall see in the following sections. Intermixed with the scenes of "love" are scenes of war and reflections about the revolution. The main character has been pulling the trigger of his gun and throwing a grenade without seeing his target because it is pouring rain, shells, and bullets. Someone—we are unsure whether it is the chief—has been telling them they must resist for the honor of revolution. One of the comrades, Salim, says: "You do not understand anything about revolution. This is revolution, revolutions are like that. Do you know why bread is round? Because it is bread. Bread cannot be different. Likewise for the cemetery. The cemetery is round, but one does not notice it from the inside. Everything is like that, the tiniest thing. We only see the surface of things" (pp. 124–25). Bread—symbol of life—is linked to the roundness of a cemetery—symbol of death. But a cemetery is not necessarily round. Could he be describing returning to the earth, back to the womb, origin of life and death? This revolution is said to be better than the previous ones because it takes into account the martyrs (p. 119). It is the hope of the poor. It brings the destruction of prisons (p. 145). A fascist prisoner is taken, and Nazih wants him killed, but the others are opposed. Talal says that he is poor like them. "Since when do the poor have a war? A war only for the poor does not exist. . . . The war of the poor will be born from destruction" (p. 152). It is an old Leninist theme: that in the breaches of order, people can express themselves. This theme of destruction is repeated later, applied to Beirut and other cities in all its frightening horror: "Buildings must destroy each other, slums must destroy buildings, and cities must destroy cities" (p. 152). Why this obsession with destruction? And why the connection with women? It becomes clearer in the last two sections. Already I can say, along with Bob Connell in "Masculinity, Violence and War," that:

In contemporary society, hegemonic masculinity is strongly associated with aggressiveness and the capacity for violence. Modern feminism has shown us one of the bases for this: the assertion of men's power over women. This relationship itself has a strong component of violence. Wife-bashing, intimidation of women in the street, rape, jealousy-murder, and other patterns of violence against women are not accidental or incidental. They are widespread and systematic, arising from the tension of a power struggle. . . . There are many complexities and contradictions. The main axis, however, remains the social subordination of women, and men's general interest in maintaining it. (P. 8)

In this context, Talal's words acquire a meaning one might not have seen otherwise: "I love women. Tonight, we are going to move from the honor of the revolution to the honor of death. Death is an appeasement. You zigzag in the midst of bullets, in the uproar, you jump, then you dip into calmness, the perfect serenity" (pp. 129–30). Does this not describe a kind of sensual sensation, a release of tension brought by the fear of combat? With revolution no longer having a real aim, isn't the attraction of death made even stronger because of its connection with women and sex? Love is reduced, like war, like revolution, like death to the release of tension. It is not communication with the other, but narcissistic withdrawal of oneself. Nazih asks: "Why always this connection between war and women?" To which Talal replies: "Why talk of death and women? One must talk of victory" (p. 133). The views expressed in these sentences come out even more strongly with the fear of death mixed with the fear of war and of women:

—We are all afraid. . . . We are always afraid, before or after. . . . we are afraid of death before dying. After the combat, we are afraid of the war. We are afraid of women before getting married.
—No, we are afraid of women after. (P. 147)

Here a group of fighters has lost the meaning of life; it is a fraternity of men always afraid, attracted and repulsed by women and by war, who know only destruction in which they loose themselves.

It is no wonder that in such a context of hate and fear of women, destruction becomes the ultimate motivation for war. Destruction, result of the fear and hate of women, is epitomized by the relationship of the central character to his wife, the topic of the following section. On the other hand, there is the androgynous negro woman who thinks of life, who refuses death. But her meeting with the *fedaï* is a failure. Why does the author use an androgynous-looking woman to represent freedom? Is he saying that given genders are doomed to destructive tropes that only the androgynous can evade? This whole section is a debate on the significance of fighting, what it leads to: revolution or death, revolution or life, dreams or reality, *fedayeen* or women. There are no answers to this dilemma: the war-revolution is the hope/despair of the poor.

The fourth section, "The Stairs," is very revealing in terms of the hero's relationship to women, his wife in particular, his mother, sexuality, the war, the city, life, and death. He feels he has known his wife for a million years. When he married her, he told his father that the first and last woman are alike. His father, "who used to beat his mother to have pleasure after making love" (p. 161), laughs. The main character talks about his notion of sex, how it was perverted by his parents' relationship, about his wife "who loves him like she loves pastries" (p. 161), about the women in the pornographic magazines he used to buy in secret, and about death mixed with how one holds the stick or the penis. "No matter how we hold the stick, we will all die, it is the only thing I retain. And we cannot hold everything by the same end. If so, how could we make love to a woman? We must hold her by the middle, hold her firmly, to make love to her. In the middle there is the sex, and sex is life. Who is right? Who is wrong? Where is life?" (p. 164). Holding the stick or holding the gun is like making love to a woman. The image is rendered even more violent through the adverb *firmly (ferme)* and making love *to her (lui)*. In this image, the woman is subdued, made passive to be penetrated. The sexual act is not one of exchange, mutual love, respect, and admiration of the other, but one in which the man inserts his penis while holding the woman down, the same way he makes war. And he calls that life! And he dares raise the issue of who is right and who is wrong!

The protagonist's scorn of women comes out in how he views his wife, "who is becoming worse than his mother. . . . She does what she wants. She chatters the whole day long and she cries the whole night. And she is afraid" (p. 167). He describes a death ritual that women perform and he considers absurd. Women gather around the corpse of a dead man. They sprinkle him with perfumed water and cry over his death. His father used to consider it a sexual rite and found it ridiculous women would wait for a man's death to perform it. The son couldn't agree more. At his father's death bed, he cannot help but laugh, and his mother is shaken with shame in front of her female friends. But is it not significant that women get together, give each other support, to exorcise their life's pain and suffering, symbolized in the death of their man or of a man, through a rite of purification with tears and perfumed water? Doesn't the solidarity of women come out strongly in such an act? And isn't the desire of the man to see such ritual performed sexually in his lifetime a perverted desire to recuperate women's solidarity by reenslaving them through orgy? There is also in such ritual a power women wish to reclaim from men—perhaps even a vengeance in death. The magicoreligious rite is used to get over their miserable life.

The protagonist's wife manages to buy a car by saving on his "ridiculous" salary. He is very happy to own a car, which he compares to his wife. Etel Adnan, in *Sitt Marie-Rose,* also makes the connection between how the *chabab* (young men) gang treat their cars and women, although her treatment differs from Khoury's. The protagonist feels that the car has made him a real man. In it, he drives through Beirut, which he compares to "a whore one has the right to get close to, only with filled up pockets, otherwise one gets stepped on, humiliated" (p. 180). Chris Cunneen shows how cars and machines in general are connected with masculinity:

The relationship of males to cars involves a particular practice which defines masculinity, while class relations are integral to that practice. . . . The male relationship to the car or motorbike is one of power. Power over objects, power over the 'world,' power over women. . . . Machines, like the penis, are seen as supremely powerful. Technological domination and sexual domination go hand in hand. . . . There is a necessity in seeing the ways cars and motorbikes are symbolic objects of masculine power. Advertisers have long recognised the link between [*sic*] fantasy, masculinity, domination and 'success' under capitalism. Motorbikes and cars have been associated with women and racehorses. . . . Probably the most obvious is the naked woman stretched over the long extended forks of the motorbike. Here the images of machine and penis, with the fantasies of domination, exploitation and power, are complete. Women are treated as objects of desire while men are desiring subjects. One is possessed, the other the possessor. The ideology of male domination cannot be separated from capitalist social and economic relations. (Pp. 85–86)

In Lebanese society, women also get seduced by the prestige a car brings. The central character shows his wife as someone petty who imposes rules as to how the car ought to be used. He says that "to lead a woman to renounce her advice is a victory worthy of the first steps on the moon" (p. 181). His descriptions of the car, Beirut, and his wife emphasize heavily macho attitudes of the man who wants objects, women, and cities to serve his needs. The car is a necessity. Its acquisition leads to many sacrifices, but rewards one with prestige and the envy of others. He has to work very hard at a job he hates in order to own a car. Everyday monotony is emphasized in the poisoned atmosphere of the office, described as a funeral. In this unbearable progression of days reducing man to a rat, the only way out is death.

The husband's behavior is epitomized by his desire to rape an old woman who cleans the toilets where he and his friend Ahmed have gone. They are drunk. He is bullied into attacking the woman he describes as old, ugly, and orange. She disappears before they are able to complete their act. The sexual act is here associated with waste through the toilet, an image one finds in pop representations. But here also, as with the "jeune nègre," desire is unattainable because the woman disappears. The only thing he worries about as he drives back home is how he will get there safely, being as drunk as he is! His relationship to his male friends is a sick one in which each one reinforces the other's ego by boasting, drinking, getting ready for screwing, and ultimately for combat.

He describes having sex with his wife. He gets into bed and is sure she pretends to be asleep. He has to think of her "not as *his* wife, but as *a* woman" (p. 193) in order to make love to her. Thanks to the alcohol he has absorbed, he is able to kiss her "like a young boy kissing a woman for the first time" (p. 193); he lies on top of her and penetrates her. She tells him she does not want babies anymore, to which he replies she is more beautiful than a baby. He falls asleep. She is utterly frustrated, tries to wake him up to make love again. He believes she is using her old strategies of telling him she is scared when she really wants more. But he is too tired, having drunk too much to look after her needs.

The scene is significant for many reasons: the man has to think of *a* woman and not *his* wife to get aroused; he has to be drunk to get excited. He seeks the release only of his own tension; only his pleasure counts. The woman is afraid of getting pregnant one more time. She tries to convey to him her fears, but he reacts to them casually. It is clear he lays the whole responsibility for contraception on her. She cannot reach orgasm as quickly as he. She would like to be caressed but doesn't dare ask him to satisfy her. She is economically and psychologically dependent on him. Neither one of them is honest with the other. They both play games. They haven't learned to talk to each other, to love and respect each other, to seek one another's happiness and pleasure, knowing it would be returned through mutual sharing and giving. Here is the core of the problem. How can a society based on such immature individuals, who seek their immediate needs and pleasure without concern for the other, make a nation strong and stable enough to stand against forces linked to destroy it? Personal relationships based on lies and deceit can only give birth to corrupted political forces that lead the country evermore to its downfall.

Through his characters the author describes boredom and weariness over the absence of change, thereby trying to justify the need for war. Both man and woman are unhappy in their situation and relationship with one another. Such a realization could be positive if it were followed with the desire for change other than through destruction. The problem in this novel is that a "solution" to life's miseries seems to lie only in death, violence, destruction, and war.

The car has been destroyed by a bomb. His wife accuses him of having parked it in the wrong place. He says, "This woman detests me. She despises me, I am certain" (p. 198). Her attitude toward him changes. She says she is nervous because of the war, but he is convinced it is because of the car. His father's words come back to him: "He would repeat that women are monstrous. If you fall, they climb on your back. You must remain upright, strong, in front of them. Everything is falling. The car is destroyed, work has dissipated, and the goat has won over the he-goat. I was all alone, with my days, my arak [anise-tasting alcohol] and my dark thoughts" (p. 200). His words are pathetic! His pride hurt because the war has destroyed his material possessions, his reaction is to accept his wife's humiliating attitude and lose all self-respect. He views his relationship to his wife as a battlefield and feels vanquished. The destroyed car signifies the loss of his social status. The car, like his wife, means prestige, which the war attacks and destroys.

The relationship between men and women is a battlefield, a kind of war. It is the battle of the sexes in which sexuality provides the occasion for one to *win* over another. Jean Libis makes some interesting remarks concerning war between the sexes. He notices that if one's love life is a "war" where one risks losing oneself, so, metaphorically, one must say that man—who assumes war functions in society—has a favorable strategic position. Some frightening images connected with this notion are that war carries its load of sexual violence and that the warrior settles his accounts with the archaic femininity which threatens him (p. 250).

Again Beirut is compared to a prostitute: "And this city, what is it? A whore. Who could imagine a whore sleeping with a thousand men and continuing to live? The city receives a thousand bombs and continues its existence nonetheless" (p. 204). These lines are very significant. It is man who drops the bombs, and it is he who inflicts his sex onto a prostitute. Yet he is incapable of feeling her wounds, her despair, and her destruction. He thinks she continues her existence, in spite of his violence, when she is already dead. He does not want to see this because it would force him to change his ways. He scorns that which he himself prostitutes, thus denying his own responsibility. In her study on prostitution, Kathleen Barry argues:

Sex-is-power can be cast into may forms including denying or demanding female response. Both replace mutuality with domination. Sexual domination acted out in one-to-one relationships is the basis for the cultural domination of women and female sexual slavery. Because such domination is expressed in separate, personal, private sexual experiences, and because on that level there is no visibility of collective action, the generalized abuse of women from the sex-is-power ethic has been seen only as individual acts. (P. 259)

In the last section, "The Place of the King," war spreads to other cities, leading to the total destruction of the planet. The action takes place in Paris, where the central character has two major encounters. The first is with a Lebanese businessman who has had to start his life all over again three times, in Latin America, Vietnam, and Algeria. Now in Paris, he is afraid the socialists will win and he will lose again. The second encounter is with a woman who embodies some positive elements like the "jeune nègre" and unlike his wife; their relationship ends in failure because he runs away from her. This section is also about dialectics, as the key to everything, revolution as a state of constant discovery, as nothingness, as being always at the beginning "like love, like death, like the woman" (p. 232). The connection between women and cities is made again. In the end, the central character runs away from both of them, wondering if either one is still waiting for him. These are his last lines; "I left her/it and I ran towards the metro. I did not look back. I was running like the wind. She might still be waiting for me" (p. 260). He tries to destroy what he feared and disliked most. Unable to create new ways of dealing either with modernity or with women, he reacts by eradicating the two objects of his hate, bringing about his own downfall. Unable to face the consequences of his acts, he can only escape underground.

The protagonist's discussion of revolution takes place with a woman who, like most women in the novel, tells him she does not like politics. Like the "jeune nègre," she is his double, a kind of "transparency . . . where one sees behind things as in dreams" (p. 232). Through her, he discovers life and marvels (p. 231). She puts him in a trance-like dream that frightens him (p. 230). Libis underlines the ambivalence of erotic life and the state of being in love: lovers feel ambivalence because hatred and aggression are the counterpoint of erotic attachment. The discovery of dependence through love provokes, often unconsciously, a feeling of insecurity and anxiety. In a lovelife where the feeling of dependency is connected with a fragile sense of self, aggression finds a fertile soil. The loved/hated object appears as the source of unhappiness and must be abolished (pp. 245–46). This is why the main character in this section, repeats several times that *the woman is the problem*, a problem that must be gotten rid of, like the city, a symbol of modernity. Why doesn't this woman understand that civilization is the source of decadence and microbes, he wonders? (p. 249). Talking to her is an impossibility (p. 231). It is not even a dialogue of irreducible contradictions, as with the "jeune nègre." She doesn't see that he is at the center of the city, like the king, and that his forehead is crowned with blood, like a Christ figure. She has to be thrown into the water, made to disappear (p. 232).

The key symbol in this chapter is a triangle within a circle. Each side of the triangle represents a male figure who has had an impact in the hero's life. The first, a psychology professor, a Marxist-Christian, Marxist-humanist, talks of dialectics as the key to everything—a key that emerges strongly throughout the novel. The second, a comrade, philosopher, admirer of Aristotle, leaves Lebanon before the war. The third, also a professor, is an instigator of revolutionary ideas in 1969 Beirut. "The triangle flew in pieces and blood never ceased flowing. Blood covered everything and the whole circle fell. Every circle is bound to collapse. It is the rule" (p. 239). The triangle is a masculine symbol, and when contained within a circle, it connotes a sexual image—the male sex within the female womb. Both are inevitably destroyed.

In *La petite montagne*, the main character has an obvious fascination with death and destruction closely related to his sense of pleasure. Listen to his frightening words as he is about to end the narrative:

I could become convinced that all cities are alike and that all squares are alike. But I couldn't believe that all women are alike. The problem seemed more complicated; it needed reexamination. When we had destroyed Beirut, we thought we had destroyed it. We ran through its devastated squares, its buildings in ruins and those that soon would be too, and we were convinced we had destroyed Beirut. *We had destroyed this city at last.* But, when the war was declared finished and the pictures of the incredible desolation of Beirut were broadcast, we discovered we had not destroyed it. We had only opened a few breaches in its walls, without destroying it. For that, other wars would be necessary. (Pp. 251–52; my emphasis)

It was not enough for the hero to have destroyed Beirut once; he wants to destroy it many more times. Why this stubborn need to destroy, this obsession with destruction? This novel was written at the beginning of the war, in 1975. More than fourteen years of war have accumulated now, and Beirut has been subjected to much more destruction coming from inside, outside, and all possible directions. Is this one of the messages Elias Khoury was trying to convey? Why not even a word of mourning or sadness at the horror of such destruction? If the author criticizes the actions of his characters, why not introduce through a narrative device some lines of sorrow, some cries of despair that would make it clear to the reader that he is not celebrating the destruction of Beirut? As it appears now, both character and author seem to delight in destroying the city and the woman it symbolizes.

The responsibility of Elias Khoury and of other Lebanese intellectuals is great. They should face the consequences of how they might be molding and influencing their readers and the youth in Lebanon. The implications are very serious and grave. If it is hard for the reader to understand why such lines make me so upset, it is probably because he or she has never experienced such devastation, the anguish and the despair at seeing one's beautiful country, the streets of one's childhood, destroyed senselessly, and then have someone write or talk about it in such light and sarcastic terms.

What Vieille says about Iran also applies to Lebanon: "The intellectuals have been incapable of proposing concrete solutions to meet popular expectations. They did not aim at their actualization; they missed it for the most part. They did not even plan it because they were after old dreams, the old dreams of proletarian revolution . . . in reality, behind these old dreams, they were seeking their own power" ("Le chaos du monde," p. 20).

The hero tells the businessman, Borgès, that the destruction will spread to other cities: "Paris will be destroyed, like all cities . . . a world war to reach that" (p. 240). And Borgès muses: "When I see what has happened to Lebanon, I have a strange premonition that the devastation will spread to the whole world" (p. 241). The need to destroy does not stop. It is so great and so strong that it must spread and conquer the whole planet! Revenge, cruelty, and sadism are reflected in these lines in which not a parcel of regret or sadness for the miseries caused by the war and its destruction are expressed.

The destruction of the city also means getting rid of injustices. At the center of the square, in the heart of the city, a man has been hanged. The condemned man had been tortured and judged illegally (p. 258); this is why there had to be another time to destroy the city, and with it the rope that hanged that man (p. 259). In the face of such misery, Borgès claims that the Foreign Legion is the only solution. And the hero, shaken by what he has just witnessed, disappears into the underground (p. 260). The "solutions" the last lines of this novel seem to imply, are destruction, joining an army, or running underground. Are these really the only alternatives to human problems? Couldn't we search for a "different peace" with nonviolent acts that would break the patterns of wars, violence, and destruction, along with the injustices and miseries they bring?

In his fascinating *L'aggressivité détournée*, Henri Laborit has important remarks to make concerning these problems. He wonders how a society can be talking about more social justice when the fundamental motivation of its individuals is aggression and domination. In such a society, the passive ones, the nonaggressive, will always be losers. Social justice becomes a farce. The best thing to wish adults is that they remain like children, willing to explore and constantly look for new ideas. The exploitation of people by one another is a sociological reality that has its roots in aggressiveness. For Laborit, the only solutions are either drugs, which will subdue aggression, or sublimation, which will channel it toward new creations, new discoveries. If the world is to survive, aggression as we know it will have to change.

La petite montagne is a complex novel with several interlaced layers of meanings that are not always clear. On many themes—women, sexuality, violence, war—it gives dialectical visions. Women, for example, are portrayed, on the one hand, as diabolical bitches, decadent whores who must be destroyed like the protagonist's wife, or, on the other, as free spirits like the androgynous "jeune nègre" or the woman in the last chapter who teaches the hero about life. He is chained to his wife through habits he can destroy only through war. And he runs away from the other two, unable to accept life, which he destroys everyday. In fact, he wants to destroy the last one and in a gesture of despair throws her in the water knowing she cannot swim (p. 232). Sexuality for the men is portrayed as a chore, a release of tension, connected to waste, not worth the trouble, on the one hand, while the free women seem to live it with a *jouissance* the men don't possess, being too busy fighting the revolution. Violence and war are also shown with these two faces. On the one hand, people fight injustice, oppression, the ugliness of modernity and industrialization, the boredom and hypocrisies of routine and tradition, and, on the other, they bring about their own desolation, a loss of *jouissance*, of freedom, the destruction of life, the coming of the end of the world.

Tahar Ben Jelloun's introduction to the French version is worth noting for several reasons. He makes the connection among "the fear of the war, the fear of death, and the fear of woman" (p. 10). He says that in Beirut, one waits for death like one waits for a woman on a summer night. Some of his introductory lines—quite in tune with part of Elias Khoury's message —are especially revolting in view of the thousands of innocent corpses, victims of a senseless war: "How many faces, lands in mourning, wounded memories will recognize themselves in the evocation of the small mountain! Stairs reaching childhood, the meadows of loving women, death that is not ugly but simply optimistic, in a hurry, mad, panic-stricken in front of such congestion" (p. 12). The lightness of the tone, the sexual connotation of "meadows of women" juxtaposed to death, seen as something positive, the inevitable face of life, make me want to scream: "Do you really understand what war is about? Can't you see what your interpretation perpetuates? When will you go deep down in yourself and change the deadly mortuary images that feed your sexuality?"

Ben Jelloun's reading of *La petite montagne* and of the war is heavily marked by romanticization. It is to be expected, coming from someone who superficially seems to advocate women's liberation, while deeply perpetuating all the stereotypes that feed the male fantasy of women, thus reinforcing their oppression. In Jelloun's own most recent novel, *La nuit sacrée* (which won the Goncourt, one of the most prestigious French prizes), the central female character frees herself by asking to be raped. She leads a blind man to a brothel—his favorite place of relaxation when he is tense—because she wants to engage in sexual activity with him and cannot ask him directly. She is pornographically excised in the end (the genital mutilation operation is described as an erotic performance), by her own sisters, who take revenge on her for having been their father's favorite—he had hidden her female identity, disguising her as a boy, giving her all the attention and freedom he would deny them. And the sister of the blind man is also very possessive and castrating, playing the role of wife-mother to her brother. What more explicit scenes and images could one use to titillate male's fantasy of women, reinforcing the wife/whore dichotomy? And how revealing of men's subtle way of breaching women's solidarity by turning them against each other?

Jelloun's images of the war conjuring women and the city of Beirut bring to mind Andrea Dworkin's analysis of why men fear women:

The boy keeps the distance between himself and women unbridgeable, transforms women into the dreaded She. . . . He learns to be a man—poet man, gangster man, professional religious man, rapist man, any kind of man—and the first rule of masculinity is that whatever he is, women are not. . . . Women must be kept out because wherever there are women, there is one haunting, vivid memory with numberless smothering tentacles: he is that child, powerless against the adult male, afraid of him, humiliated by him. (*Pornography: Men Possessing Women*, pp. 50–51)

Elias Khoury's novel shows war as a solution to cultural and personal schizophrenia. Men's self-division arises from the way they see women. They compartmentalize them in the old, traditional way: the wife and the liberated woman; the madonna/whore syndrome. The essentialization of women, existing in themselves—the wife and the whore being the bad, evil ones—or in the narrator's dreams, his creation—the young negro woman who never becomes real, or when she does, like the third woman in the last part, is thrown into the water by the narrator who knows she cannot swim —illustrates the split, the malaise the protagonist lives with. This ambivalence also comes out in the images of the city; the whore, decadent bitch who must be gotten rid of, but also the utopia, full of childhood memories, open to the sea, an arch, a garden.

In such an unresolved duality, malaise and unhappiness are the natural outcomes. Uneasiness does not lead the narrator to questions or answers that might help solve the conflicts. War appears as *the solution* to people's miseries. But how can war be a good solution? War only leads to more wars, more violence, and more destruction—therefore, to more malaise and sorrows. The choice for life and freedom is never made because it would mean a change of life and values, which the narrator seems unwilling to make. Why is the fascination with death, destruction, and war so strong that it annihilates the other possibilities? As Khoury poses the *duality*, death and destruction triumph over life and freedom.

NOTE

1. Throughout I will be quoting from the French edition by permission of Arléa, Paris. © Elias Khoury, 1987. All translations are my own.

TEN

War/Masculinity Versus Life/Freedom

The observation that there is a special connection between men and warfare is a commonplace. Recently this commonplace has been given political teeth with the development of a critique of 'masculinist' values, practices and cultures. There are, it is claimed, a wide range of practices which are not only in the interest of men—securing patriarchal relations of power—but which also function in the construction and maintenance of male identity. These practices with their associated values and systems of belief constitute a hegemonic culture of masculinity, from under whose sedimentations a feminine culture is only now being excavated. As the desperate and intractable situation produced by society's military obsession has forced many people to look for new political strategies, women's actions have offered such a new hope.

Adam Farrar, "War, Machining Male Desire"

In a country doomed to inside and outside destruction "death pulsation is the only alternative." To avoid what is terrifying in violent death, the only way is to go towards death itself. Death becomes its own defiance.

Issa Makhlouf, *Beyrouth ou la fascination de la mort*

The future cannot be created on tyranny, be it traditional or modern, but on the freedom to conceive and to preach, even naïvely, a future different from the present, with no horizon, and the past with its mythological perception feeding violence and barbarism.

Georges Corm, *Géopolitique du conflit libanais*

In the war novels written by men, war reveals man's nature as marked by what has typically been considered masculinity. Male authors construct images of war inscribed by codes of masculinity learned from their culture. Masculinity involves aggressiveness and violence, which are directly linked with political and personal exploitation of nature and women. Exploitation takes on various forms, from exhausting and misusing the world's resources, to oppressing other races, sexes or ages, to invading and/or dominating other countries or continents, to running the arms race. The consequences of such values are death, destruction, and more violence and death. It is a vicious circle that keeps repeating itself, as if human beings were incapable of breaking it: war creates valorizing codes of heroism and masculinity, and masculinity creates war. Only a different vision of the world can break this cycle. Only different values, only a change in the social construction of identities and relationships, such that they are grounded no longer in dominance/submission but in harmonized acceptance of differences, can bring about harmony and a future of life and hope.

In all three of the novels I have discussed, war is one of the major components of people's destiny. It has a life of its own, and it shapes the characters' lives and choices. None of the authors questions the existence of this force or asks how it could be eliminated, except through a repetition of war and violence—as with the Palestinians fighting Israel. There is even a fascination with it and a belief that it is cathartic and can bring salvation and/or solution to the dilemma of relationships—as with the narrator in *La petite montagne* or Tamima in *Death in Beirut.*

None of the major male characters directly suffers from the war, as do the female protagonists in the women's novels. Male writers also portray the female characters as the ones getting most hurt by war. In this, they concur with the women writers, although the purpose of showing harm is different. In both male and female writers men are victimized only once by the enemy and by death, while women are victimized by a number of factors: patriarchy, society, families, bodies, and religion. In *Days of Dust* the male protagonist is deeply hurt in his pride, and he exists in a constant state of depression because of the defeat of the Arabs in the war. But his wounds are not like those of Zahra in *The Story of Zahra* or of Marie-Rose in *Sitt Marie-Rose*, both of whom die in the end because of mental and physical violence inflicted directly on them. In *La petite montagne,* the male protagonist seems to enjoy the excitement the war brings, even if he becomes frightened at times; it releases some of his tensions and solves the conflicts of daily living, boredom, and frustrations.

Minor male characters like some of the guerrillas in *Death in Beirut* or the napalm victims in *Days of Dust* or comrades like Jaber in *La petite montagne,* do die in the war, but their deaths are not questioned as something evil or the direct result of a violence that must be dealt with as such.

They appear more as heroes or the victims of imperialism or Zionism, or as destined to return to the womb (like Jaber's death portrayed as returning to the ship), and thus their deaths reinforce masculine values.

On the other hand, the female characters find themselves trapped in dead-end situations caused by both tradition and the war, the two being closely linked. Awwad makes the most obvious connection between the two: violence is the product of the male protagonists, and the women are the direct victims of it. They get used, raped, beaten, and killed by the customs that circumscribe their lives. That in the end the major female character joins male violence, in the form of guerrilla resistance, hoping no longer to be its victim, could be explained—if not justified—through Fanon's understanding of violence. Khoury shows the protagonist wanting to destroy women through war and violence because he feels they, like the City, are destroying him. The young negro woman is portrayed as free and alive, but the major male character is unable to join her because he has chosen war/masculinity instead of life/freedom. And Barakat's female protagonist, the only one not subjected to Arab customs, thanks to her Western identity, is also trapped by the war and by her relationships to the men in her life, from both East and West. Interestingly in this novel, it is the female side of the male narrator that appears when he fantasizes his body being raped by the Israeli army and thus as more vulnerable to war and violence.

The male protagonists are portrayed as quite advanced and open when it comes to voicing ideas about relationships between men and women, or women's liberation and their freedom to choose and live their lives as they see fit, but when it comes to actualizing their revolutionary vision on a daily basis, it is a completely different story. Their beautiful notions suddenly seem to disappear in the face of reality. Neither major male character in *Death in Beirut* can accept Tamima's desire to be herself and live her life, even though both claim that reform is one of the avenues for Lebanon's survival. Ramzy, in *Days of Dust,* who also sees women's liberation as central to revolutionizing the Arab world, is unable to accept it totally in his personal life, feeling more secure with tradition. Perhaps these contradictions are part of the authors' conscious constructions of a society that has a built-in double-standard, like a time-bomb.

In *L'échange symbolique et la mort,* Jean Baudrillard explains how the fascination with death is closely connected with violence and sexuality through symbolic rites of sacrifice, the most obvious ones today being the automobile accidents and the taking of hostages.

Unanimously condemned, the taking of hostages is becoming a first-class political ritual, at a time when the political is falling into general indifference. Hostage-taking holds a symbolic benefit a hundred times superior to the car accident, itself already a hundred times superior to natural death. We find here a kind of sacrificial time, an execution ritual, the imminence of collectively waiting for death, completely undeserved, therefore totally artificial. Perfect from a sacrificial point of view, the "criminal" generally accepts death as an exchange value. We all adhere to the rules of symbolic exchange, much deeper than to the economic order. (P. 252)

We are all hostages; this is where the secret of hostage-taking lies. And we all dream of *receiving* and *giving* death, instead of stupidly dying from wear and tear. Because to give and to receive are symbolic acts (they are the symbolic acts par excellence). They take away from death its indifferent negativity in the "natural" order of the capital. (P. 246)

Unlike what Baudrillard is claiming, we are not all dreaming of receiving and giving death. But his lines illustrate what the male authors have been saying in their novels. They all seem to concur in finding war a necessary event in the present state of things and even better than the daily boredom of routines and uneventful existence. While Baudrillard refers to a kind of *ennui,* a numbness that has befallen modern societies due to the frequency and mundane quality of death, my study addresses turmoil, political unrest, societies in transition searching for their identity, resorting to violence and hostage-taking to affirm themselves and make their voices heard by precisely the indifferent societies Baudrillard talks about. These societies are subjected to hostage-taking, while the ones studied here inflict it—but perhaps this would not make a great difference in Baudrillard's notion of symbolic exchange.

The male authors and their male characters all seem to concur that death and destruction are an expression of or a substitute for sexuality and a fear of women. They live a schizophrenia, torn between East and West, tradition and modernity. War comes as a liberation from this tension, a cure to the sickness they are in. The male authors discussed in this section try to understand violence and seem to be aware of the link between war and sexuality. Their difference from the female authors is that they are unable to imagine alternatives.[1]

NOTE

1. The male authors may be different from their characters, but they might also be closely related. To which extent one expresses the other will not alter the conclusions of this study. If, however, an author feels I have unfairly projected on him what he was criticizing in his or her character, I apologize for the misunderstanding. On the other hand, if I was able to successfully show an author what he or she was not only writing but also living, I hope my criticism was helpful in making them move forward.

ELEVEN

Personal and Political Action for the Transformation of Society

Women's nonviolent direct action has a more extensive history and has been more influential in the history of political action for social change than is generally recognized.
For centuries women have shared this vision of the power and danger of the word and the duty to speak and write the truth.

Berenice Carroll, "Women Take Action!"

Where the trend in Lebanon among male writers became rejection or passivity or frustration, among the Beirut Decentrists [female writers] it was activism. There could be no resting, because rest brings in its wake numbness. This discursive activism led to a challenge directed at men. It was not an attempt to exclude them but to draw on feminine resources in women as well as men whose patriotism has earned them the right to be Lebanese in thought as in action.

Miriam Cooke, *War's Other Voices*

This book is a result of my emotional and intellectual commitment and history of the last twenty years. It has grown out of my condition as an Arab woman, which made me leave my country of birth, Lebanon, at the age of twenty-two, in order to free and assert myself as an autonomous human being. It has come out of my anguish and pain at seeing my beautiful country destroyed senselessly over the last fourteen years. It is also the development of previous studies I did on the role of women in North Africa and the Middle East through sociological and anthropological research as well as an analysis of the literature of these countries.

What Miriam Cooke writes about the Lebanese women writers' vision of Lebanon as a sick child in need of care became for me a reality. It was the Lebanese war that made me want to go back and try to help. I would not have felt the same concern for Lebanon had it not been for the war and for what I perceived as real suffering in my friends and many of the people I

165

came in contact with. I shared their pain and desire to remedy. It led me to apply for grants to go and teach there. And this is what I did in 1978, 1981, 1984, 1985, and 1988, during sabbaticals or when I received teaching and research grants. My experiences in living the war, talking with students, teaching, conducting research, traveling in Lebanon, crossing the demarcation line dividing the city, participating in nonviolent peace initiatives, spending time in the shelter when shelling became too violent, sharing the anguish and suffering of friends and relatives gave me insights I might not have had otherwise. It led to a conviction that only peaceful means can bring about a solution to Lebanon and reunite the country. It also showed me the importance of activism for the transformation of society: peace marches, hunger strikes, consciousness-raising groups, solidarity among women, singing, writing, crossing the divided city, and most of all, changing the system of rapport between men and women, the values connected with these relations, and the confessional structures tied to the concepts of honor, virginity, exclusive property, and oppression.

It also became very clear to me that women's solidarity and an international feminism, uniting women all over the world, are vital in bringing about such changes. In the first two chapters, I have described how the feminist movements in the Arab world and in the United States allow themselves to be split up and how these divisions often prevent them from challenging male hegemony. I would like to stress here again the importance of achieving unity in the midst of our cultural differences, if we want to provide some hope in ending the war culture that exists all over the world. When in Lebanon, I became very aware of the strength the peace initiative started by two women from enemy communities had, first on women, and then on the population as a whole, in uniting people in the goal of peace. It is one of the rare times in my life I witnessed the tremendous impact that values of love and tolerance can have on people.

The activities undertaken as a result of my concern and suffering over the destruction of my country are directly involved in the transformation of society. Changing the system and the values behind it requires more time and a long process of in-depth political, economical, psychological, religious, sexual, familial, and social transformations established on an understanding of the different factors, causes and links between these various fields. My concern over long-range plans to bring about social transformations necessary to end the war and reunify the country made me undertake this study and analyze the relationship among sexuality, war, and literature.

When I started establishing a bibliography and reading what had been written about the Lebanese war, I was struck by the quantity of works of all kinds: political, economical, and journalistic reports, testimonies, novels, poems, songs, and literary studies. But it surprised me to find hardly any analysis of the connections I had come to believe were major in bringing about the tragedy: namely violence and war taking their roots in badly lived sexuality, conceived within a tribal system based on honor, virginity, possession, jealousy, and the exclusive propriety of women. This book is an attempt at bridging the gap and hopes to inspire more studies and works in this direction.

What was lacking in the studies could be found clearly and forcefully in the novels. The connection between sexuality and war is pervasive in the novels. It demonstrates how strongly at work it is in the collective "imaginary" or culture of the people and how central it is to an understanding of the situation and the causes of the war. The similarities and differences in the ways women and men express and deal with violence and sexuality can lead to a greater comprehension of the complexities in the relationship between the two and bring us closer to a solution. As I have described throughout this book, there is a need for a new rapport between men and women, women and women, and men and men; there is a need for relationships based on trust, recognition of the other, tenderness, equal sharing, and love void of jealousy and possession. Since the personal is the political, changes in relationships traditionally based on domination, oppression, and power games will inevitably rebound in other spheres of life.

In this study, my hypothesis has been that although both female and male novelists make the connection between sexuality and war, their ways of expressing it and most of all the solutions implied are quite different. Women writers paint the war and the relationships of women, men, and their families in the darkest terms: sexuality is tied to women's oppression and the restrictions put on their lives; the war brings destruction, death, and despair. The female protagonists look for alternatives in nonviolent active struggles such as peace marches and other forms of engagement in causes to help the oppressed and the dispossessed. At the same time, they seek changes in their lives and in their relationships with the men and families around them. Men writers also paint the war and relationships among men and women in the bleakest terms, and they emphasize the connection between the two. But their depression does not lead them to search for alternatives different from the historically accepted ones: heroism, revenge, and violence as catharsis.

In both women's and men's writing, the war is used to break down the patriarchal system and the traditional order. The female protagonists do it through masochism, while the male ones use cruelty and sadism. But such actions and reactions lead nowhere because the use of war to free oneself from domination and oppression only reinforces the authoritarian order by reproducing the power structure with different colors.

Both women and men writers question God and the use of religion in war. Institutionalized religion is blamed explicitly, while faith and personal belief are praised implicitly and constitute—more specifically in women writers—a strength and a way of overcoming war. While male protagonists justify their fighting through religion or to show how religion is used for imperialist purposes, the female ones draw their strength in helping the oppressed, sacrificing themselves for others' welfare and in active nonviolent struggles.

Both women and men writers seem to concur in showing female protagonists whose political outlook and actions are reflected in their personal lives, while male protagonists live double standards. In male authors, the female protagonists who are concerned and active politically also reject the traditional passive roles and refuse the taboos surrounding virginity and sexuality. They find themselves in situations where they are unable to live this conscious desire to be free because the men around them cannot cope with it. The irony is that these men voice beautiful statements concerning the need to achieve revolution in both domains, the private and the political, but when it comes to actualizing these theories in interpersonal relationships, it is as if they are paralyzed. It leads me to really doubt the effectiveness of what they advocate. Both male and female authors agree in portraying this difference between their male and female protagonists. To this characterization, women authors add an element not found in the men: their female protagonists often affirm themselves and live different lives, even if doing so means being marginalized, having to live in exile, or being put to death.

Another major preoccupation of female and male writers is their outlook on multiculturality and the question of roots, exile, and pluralism mixed with violence and war, and how these are reflected in interpersonal relationships. Female authors tend to see multiplicity as something positive. Exile often means freedom. The search for roots can be an expression of nostalgia for one's childhood or a need for security and love. Male authors tend to depict multiplicity as confrontation. They search for purity, multiplicity meaning dishonor. Multiculturality increases their schizophrenia and makes them uneasy and depressed. Roots are a search for identity, and exile is a terrible fate.

Intercultural and interconfessional marriages reflect the same outlook. Women authors depict female protagonists who live them harmoniously and with a great sense of achievement and commitment, and they represent such marriages as possible solution to the war (even when they get killed because of it, as Marie-Rose is). Men authors show male protagonists split between a desire to achieve plurality on the political level and their inability to live it in their personal lives, even when they have voiced the importance of breaking down tradition on that level. Men authors also depict female protagonists better able to harmonize the personal with the political. Their failure to achieve true liberation stems not from their lack of action, but from the males' inability to realize it with them.

In her study on civil war novels, "Civil Wars and Sexual Territories," Margaret Higonnet reaches similar conclusions:

Among the male authors, the realm of the feminine remains emblematic of withdrawal from politics, whether into anarchy or into a protected idyll. By contrast, the women authors expose sexual politics as a truly political issue. They raise the problem of women's access to political discourse—can words without acts have any authority? And, finally, they show that the difficulties of literary representation are also difficulties of political representation.(P. 23)

Another notion implied by both female and male novels is androgyny. In this domain, there is less contrast between the two genders. Both women and men authors depict the negative and positive aspects of androgyny. Adnan refers to an androgynous mythical past to confront the male protagonists with their corrupted values. Chedid shows women characters who assume traits traditionally viewed as masculine. And Awwad also portrays women who, in order to free themselves, take on a masculine discourse and decide to engage in guerrilla warfare. In these last two authors, however, the outcome is not positive. It does not engender life; nor is it a solution to war. Barakat's male protagonist, who assumes both the female and male sides of his personality, is not portrayed as having harmoniously integrated the two. He is constantly ill at ease and torn between aggressiveness and masochism, the male side being associated with victory and the female with defeat. The most positive portrayal of an androgynous character is in Khoury. She is obviously a projection of who the central male character would like to be, how he imagines freedom and a way to reject war. Why does the author use an androgynous-looking woman to represent freedom? Is he saying that woman and man are doomed to destroy each other and that only the androgynous can escape such fate? The novel as a whole does not seem to imply such a solution. Freedom is never chosen as the answer to men's and women's miseries. Instead, destruction appears as the ultimate response to human condition.

The question of poverty and class consciousness related to war and women's condition emphasizes women writers' awareness of these issues. This awareness leads them to search for positive alternatives, while men writers use their recognition of the problems to justify violence. Both male and female authors show the links in the fate of the dispossessed, their struggle to overcome it, women's oppression, and war. Awwad makes a direct connection between the classes his female protagonists belong to and the degrees of abuse and violence they are subjected to. Chedid shows women characters whose private and political consciousness and commitment give them real awareness and sensitivity to the condition of the poor and vice versa: watching the lives of the poor leads them to become socially committed and active in seeking change in their personal and political lives. Similarly, Adnan portrays a female protagonist who is socially, politically, and personally committed to women's issues and to the fate of the poor, the dispossessed, and the oppressed in general. Khoury often talks about "the war of the poor" to describe the link between oppression and war and to justify a revenge of the dispossessed.

Both male and female authors portray the disastrous consequences of virginity rites connected with the notions of honor, ownership of women, and sexual relationships. It is these customs that lead al-Shaykh's female protagonist to despair, madness, and final death. She rejects them from the beginning and is revolted by male's views of her body and sexuality. She would like to be freed from them and in control of her body and of her life. She uses the war to break down the taboos and to assert herself sexually. She finds out that the war is much stronger and more destructive than anything she has known before and that the customs she hoped to get rid of through it are only temporarily altered. They come back with greater strength and more destructive violence. Adnan uses the narrator's voice to comment on the frighteningly dangerous outcome of the codes of honor related to virginity and how they reinforce tribal confessional sectarianship. Barakat, through the interwoven stories of the hyena and the Flying Dutchman, demonstrates the importance of the concept of virginity and the codes of honor in relation to women's roles in society. Awwad shows the way in which the customs of virginity and the exclusive possession of women, at the foundation of a society built on divisions and an exclusive sense of propriety, lead to violence and crime. In such a system, women are dominated, raped, led to suicide, or killed by men, who are themselves manipulated by political power they seek to wield. It is a vicious circle of power struggles in which women are the ultimate victims.

In most of the novels under study, the codes of honor—related to virginity and to crimes meant to wash the family's or tribe's honor and pride in blood—are connected to rape, itself associated with death. Rape is the absolute forbidden action (especially of women of one's tribe); it therefore also involves the absolute temptation of death (when inflicted on women of another tribe). Men prove their masculinity through sexual acts of violence against women of the other clans, and such action also reinforces the system of the clan by making women vulnerable and in need of the men's protection. In al-Shaykh, the major female protagonist is subjected to rapes throughout her life; her death is the ultimate rape. In Awwad, the sexual act, in most of the men's imagination and in their practice, is associated with rape. They seem unable to conceive of it differently; it is part of the system of power whereby they prove their masculinity and domination. Their way of conceiving sexuality often results in the death, suicide, or annihilation of the female protagonist. And in Khoury, the wish of the central male protagonist is for the city/woman to be raped because she is like a prostitute and incarnates all the decadent moral values of industrial and modern life. But rape is not enough; the devastation has to spread to other cities/women in the world, leading to annihilation and oblivion. While Adnan also compares the city to a woman, she sees her rape/destruction as men's ultimate cruelty, sadism, and violence. She feels sorry for this woman/city and seeks for solutions in peaceful nonviolent alternatives, even in the notion of self-sacrifice if that could help aleviate the hate and destruction. As for Barakat, the images used for the Arabs' being defeated by Israel are of invasion, destruction, and rape taking place on the male protagonist's body who is utterly frustrated and depressed because he is rendered powerless.

Sexual relations conceived in a system of power struggles and a structure of submission and domination will obviously result in rapes and in the abuse of women. Rapes are associated with unwanted pregnancies and abortions. In none of the war novels are conception, pregnancy, and giving birth positive and happy. Both female and male authors seem to view life conception and creation as impossible and repulsive in the context of the war. The female protagonists are the ones who pay the price, because the male protagonists view women as having to assume the whole responsibility of contraception and pregnancy. The sexual act being, in most instances, one of rape and domination, women appear as mere objects of possession, vessels into which the men pour their anger and frustration, extenuations of the feelings and acts of war. Abortion is the direct result of rape, as destruction is the direct result of war. Life cannot be engendered in such a context.

The novels by both male and female authors end with the brutal death of some of the female protagonists. Their death is the direct result of the male protagonists' violence. Zahra and the child in her womb die from a bullet from the sniper—and father of the child. Marie-Rose is executed by a gang of young Christian militiamen. Young Sybil also dies from a sniper's bullet. Zennoub is cruelly gang-raped, and, as a result, she commits suicide. Miss Mary, who shows real solidarity for her female friends, tries to protect Tamima and dies herself, shielding Tamima from her brother's cruel hand. In only one novel by the male authors discussed does one of the male protagonists die. But his death is from fighting, and one does not feel as sorry for him as for the female protagonists who die. His death is the result of his own violence and not a cruelty inflicted from the outside, as is the case with the women. Even if violence coming from the oppressed holds a certain justification, the death of its victims does not stir our sympathy as does the death of innocent victims who do not engage in violence. In all of the novels studied, female and male authors concur in portraying their female protagonists as the ultimate victims. Where they disagree is in showing their responsibility and/or innocence. Khoury is the one who portrays characters who hold women responsible for their own victimization. Their rage against the victims is so great that they call for their total destruction. It is as if they were blaming the oppressed for being oppressed and calling for more oppression to get rid of oppression. Fanon's view of violence as catharsis can be compared to Khoury's call for total annihilation. Both call on negative, destructive means for the transformation of society. There is a similar element in al-Shaykh's novel where a homeopathic cure against the war is sought by Zahra who goes to the sniper. The difference between Khoury and al-Shaykh is that Zahra seeks a cure through masochism, thereby emphasizing her own victimization, while Khoury's protagonist inflicts a cure through sadism, thereby increasing the cruelty and expressing a total lack of compassion for victims.

The style and language shape the various expressed messages. The sensual lace-like quality of al-Shaykh's writing give it poignancy, strength, tenderness, and anxiety. Khoury's broken, absurd, and surrealist sentences, images, and symbols add to the torment and brutality of his representations. Adnan's social realism and dogmatic appeals simplify the tragedy while emphasizing the dimension of a woman and the people she defends, and the rigourous construction of her story in time and place delineates the urgency of her appeal. Barakat's symbolism, recurrent images, stories, and myths, and the poetry of his prose add to the overall melancholy and sadness brought about by defeat, and his careful division of time and space sharpens and strengthens his plea. Awwad's realism, psychological dimension, the thorough depiction of his characters, and the meticulous narrations of the interwoven plots contribute to the sense of commitment at showing the degradation of his society brought about by violence and the oppression of women. And Andrée Chedid's innovative structural device, her experimentation with a cinematographic technique, her masterful construction, and the placement of each movement carefully chosen endow her message for peace and justice with vigor and intensity.

Finally, an obvious conclusion to this study is that the fear men have of women leads them to domination and war, while the fear women have of men's violence leads them to masochistic submission and/or rejection of men and commitment to political, humanist, and feminist causes. Both the female and male authors agree on this. For example, the sniper's first reaction to Zahra is to rape her, as a way of proving his masculinity through control and domination. Fear is one of his primary motivations: fear of life, fear of women's capacity to reproduce, to give birth, fascination with death and destruction. He does not want to assume the responsibility for the life he has engendered in Zahra's womb when he daily kills innocent victims and destroys life. In order to reestablish the chaos, daily drug, and only meaning of his existence, he must kill her. And for Talal in *La petite montagne* fighting is like making love to a woman: it is frightning and never fulfilling. The author describes a group of fighters who have lost the meaning of life, a fraternity of men always afraid, attracted, and repulsed by women and by war, who know only destruction in which they loose themselves. The hate and fear they feel for women becomes their ultimate motivation for war. Destruction becomes pleasure.

On the other hand, the central women characters in *La maison sans racines* live their lives independant from men and with a commitment to bring about the transformation of society through peaceful means. Marie-Rose stands in front of the fascist young men of her country, confronting them with their perverted values, in an act that defies their violence and rejects them all together. This *chabab* gang is afraid of Marie-Rose who epitomizes feminine/feminist values and who dares confront them with words, showing them their corruption while asserting her femihumanism and her commitment to the oppressed and the down-trodden. They have to get rid of her, just like the sniper has to get rid of Zahra.

Thus, while women writers are finding a way out, a circle of hell is being perpetuated, each sex fearing the other, the male one starting the chain through violence and domination. Only a different vision, new actions, and altered relationships based on trust, recognition, and acceptance of the other can help heal the wounds and bring about the cure necessary to project a new future for Lebanon and for the world. Such a change has already started taking place with personal and political actions aimed at solving the problems rooted in oppression, domination, and the victimization of women. Writing this book has been one of these actions.

Bibliography

Aba, Noureddine. *L'Aube à Jérusalem*. Algiers: SNED, 1978.
———. *Montjoie Palestine! or Last Year in Jerusalem*. Paris: L'Harmattan, 1980.
———. *Tell El Zaatar s'est tu à la tombée du soir*. Paris: L'Harmattan, 1981.
———. *C'était hier Sabra et Chatila*. Paris: L'Harmattan, 1984.
Abd al Satir, Hasib. *Minal ramad ya Bayrut*. Beirut: Matabi Khalifa, 1977.
Abdo, Leila. "Iman Khalifeh Receives 'Right to Livelihood Alternative Nobel Prize for Peace.'" *Alumni Bulletin*. Beirut University College, 1985.
Abi Fadil, Rabi'a. *Wadi' fil Day'a*. Zuq Mikhaïl: Al-Maktaba Al-Ahliya, 1984.
Abou, Sélim. *Le bilinguisme arabe et français au Liban*. Paris: PUF, 1962.
———. *Béchir Gemayel ou l'esprit d'un peuple*. Paris: Anthropos, 1984.
———, and C. Hernandez and M. Micolis, collabs. *Liban déraciné, immigrés dans l'autre Amérique*. Paris: Plon, 1978.
Abraham, Antoine. *Lebanon: A State of Siege (1975–1984)*. New York: New York Institute of Technology, 1984.
Abu Chawar, Rachad. *Al-'uchchaq*. Beirut, 1977.
———. *Muhr al-Barari*. Beirut, 1977.
———. *Ah . . . Ya Bayrut*. Tunis: Salammbo, 1983.
Abu-Khalil, A. "Druze, Sunni and Shi'ite Political Leadership in Present-Day Lebanon." *Arab Studies Quaterly*, 7, 4 (1985): 28–58.
Abul Faraj, Ghalib. *Wahtaraqat Bayrut*. Beirut: Dar al Afaq al Jadida, 1983.
Abul Hayja', Nawwaf. *Al-istichhad difa'an 'anil watun*. Baghdad, 1984.
Abunasr, Julinda. *The Development of Three- to Six-Year-Old Lebanese Children and their Environment*. Beirut: Institute for Women's Studies in the Arab World, 1980.
Abu Nasr, Julinda, and Irini Lorfing, eds. *Women and Economic Development in the Arab World*. Beirut: Institute for Women's Studies in the Arab World, 1988.
Accad, Evelyne. *Veil of Shame: The Role of Women in the Contemporary Fiction of North Africa and the Arab World*. Sherbrooke, Canada: Naaman, 1978.
———. *L'Excisée*. Paris, L'Harmattan, 1982.
———. "Mashreq and Maghreb Women Writers of Arabic Expression." *Celfan Review* 7, 1–2 (November 1987–February 1988): 43–46.
———. "Salammbô Femmes." *Celfan Review* 7, 1–2 (November 1987–February 1988): 30–37.
———. *Coquelicot du massacre*. Paris: L'Harmattan, 1988.
———. "Feminist Perspective on the War in Lebanon." *Women's Studies International Forum* 12, 1 (1989): 91–95.

Accad, Evelyne, with Rose Ghurayyib. *Contemporary Arab Women and Poets*. Beirut: Institute for Women's Studies in the Arab World, 1985.

Accaoui, Sélim, and Magida Salman. *Comprendre le Liban*. Rome: Savelli, 1976.

Adam, Azir. *Un homme de parole*. Paris: Editions Papyrus, 1984.

Adib, Auguste. *Le Liban après la guerre*. Paris: Lerousc, 1918.

Adnan, Etel. *Five Senses for One Death*. New York: Smith, 1971.

―――. *Jebu and Beirut-Hell Express*. Paris: Oswald, 1973.

―――. *Sitt Mari-Rose*. Paris: Des Femmes, 1977. Translated in English as *Sitt Marie-Rose*. Sausalito, Calif.: Post-Apollo Press, 1982.

―――. *L'Apocalypse arabe*. Paris: Papyrus, 1980.

―――. *From A to Z*. Sausalito, Calif.: Post-Apollo Press, 1982.

―――. *Pablo Neruda Is a Banana Tree*. Lisbon: Da Almeda, 1982.

―――. *The Indian Never Had a Horse and Other Poems*. Sausalito, Calif.: Post-Apollo Press, 1986.

―――. "To Write in a Foreign Language." *Connexions* 22 (Fall 1986–Winter 1987).

Ahdab, Abdel Hamid. *A Joumana, pour un Liban nouveau*. Beirut, 1978.

Ajami, Fouad. "The Shadows of Hell." *Foreign Policy*, 48 (Fall 1982): 94–110.

―――. *The Vanished Imam: Musa Al Sadr and the Shiʿa of Lebanon*. Ithaca: Cornell University Press, 1986.

―――. "The Silence in Arab Culture." *New Republic*, April 6, 1987.

Alamiyya, Naʿim. *Sahira*. Beirut, 1983.

Al-Banna, Sami. "The Defense of Beirut." *Arab Studies Quarterly* 5 (Spring 1983): 105–15.

Alem, Jean Pierre. *Le Liban*. Paris: PUF, 1963.

Alroy, Gil Carl. *The Kissinger Experience: American Policy in the Middle East*. New York: Horizon Press, 1975.

Alternatives non-violentes. Special issues: *Armée et non violence: Mariage ou union libre?* no. 55; *Christianisme et violences (René Girard et débat)*, no. 36; *Défense nucléaire, non-sens militaire*, no. 50; *Femmes et violences*, no. 40; *Guerres saintes, guerres justes*, no. 48; *L'agressivité en question*, no. 51; *La politique de la peur*, no. 35; *Religions et violence*, no. 64; *Violences banales*, no. 38.

Amri, Nelly. *Le dernier carré du vert*. Tusson, Charente: Du Lérot, 1987.

Anhoury, Sami. *Enfer familier*. Beirut: Nawfal, 1985.

Antonius, Soraya. "Fighting on Two Fronts: Conversations with Palestinian Women." In *Third World—Second Sex: Women's Struggles and National Liberation*, *Third World Women Speak Out*, Miranda Davies, ed. London: Zed, 1983.

Arbid, Marie Thérèse. *Ma guerre, pourquoi faire?* Beirut: An-Nahar, 1980.

Atallah, Daad Bou Malhab. *Le Liban, guerre civile ou conflit international?* Beirut: Al-Hurriyat, 1980.

Audouard, Antoine. *Le voyage au Liban*. Paris: Gallimard, 1979.

Awwad, Tawfiq Yusuf. *Al-sabi al-aʿraj*. Beirut, 1936.

―――. *Al-raghif*. Beirut, 1939.

―――. *Tawaheen Beirut*. Beirut: Dar al-Adab, 1972. Translated as *Death in Beirut*. London: Heineman, 1976.

Azar, Antoine. *Le Liban face à demain*. Beirut: Librairie Orientale, 1978.

————. *Le Liban à l'épreuve: Ambivalence d'un régime, remodelage d'un pouvoir*. Beirut: Naufal, 1982.

Azar, Edward. *International Conflict Resolution: Theory and Practice*. Boulder Colo.: Lynne Rienner, 1986.

————. *The Emergence of a New Lebanon; Fantasy or Reality?* New York: Praeger, 1984.

Badinter, Elisabeth. *L'un est l'autre: Des relations entre hommes et femmes*. Paris: Odile Jacob, 1986.

Baghdadi, Maroun, and Nayla De Freige. "The Kalashnikov Generation." *L'Orient/ LeJour* (1979).

Baguet, Georges. *Café amers au Liban*. Paris: Cerf, 1985.

Bakhtin, M. M. *The Dialogic Imagination*. Austin: University of Texas Press, 1986.

Ball, George W. *Error and Betrayal in Lebanon: An Analysis of Israel's Invasion of Lebanon and Implications for U.S.–Israeli Relations*. Washington, D.C.: Foundation for Middle East Peace, 1984.

Bannerman. Graeme. *Lebanon in Crisis*. New York: Syracuse University Press, 1979.

Bar, Luc Henri de. *Les communautés confessionnelles du Liban*. Paris: Edition de Recherche sur les Civilisations, 1983.

Barakat, Halim. *Al-qimam al-khadraʾ*. Beirut: Al-Muʾassassat Al-Ahlyyat, 1956.

————. *Al-samt wal-matar*. Beirut: Dar Majalat Shiʿir, 1958.

————. *Sittat ayyam*. Beirut: Al-Muʾassassat Al-ʿArabiya, 1961.

————. *ʿAwdat altaʾir ilal bahr*. Beirut: Al-Muʾassassat Al-ʿArabiya, 1969. Translated in French as *Le vaisseau reprend le large*. Sherbrooke, Canada: Naaman, 1977. Translated in English as *Days of Dust*. Washington, D.C.: Three Continents Press, 1983.

————. *Lebanon in Strife: Student Preludes to the Civil War*. Austin: University of Texas Press, 1977.

————. *Visions of Social Reality in the Contemporary Arab Novel*. Washington, D.C.: Georgetown University Press, 1977.

————. *Al-rahil bayn al-sahm wal-watar*. Beirut: Al-Muʾassassat Al-ʿArabiyya, 1979.

————. *Al-mujtamaʿ al-ʿarabi al-muʿasir*. Beirut: Markaz Dirasat Al-Wahda Al-ʾArabiyya, 1984.

————. *Taʾir al-hown*. Casablanca: Toubkal, 1988.

Barker, Francis, Peter Hulme, Margaret Iverson, and Diana Loxley. *Literature, Politics, and Theory*. New York: Methuen, 1986.

Barrat, Denise. *Liban, escale du temps*. Paris: Centurion, 1976.

Barril, Capitaine. *Missions très spéciales*. Paris: Presses de la Cité, 1984.

Barry, Kathleen. *Female Sexual Slavery*. New York and London: New York University Press, 1984.

Barthes, Roland. *Sade, Fourier, Loyola*. Paris: Seuil, 1971.

Bataille, Georges. *Les larmes d'Eros*. Paris: Pauvert, 1971.

Bauderot, J., et al. *Palestine et Liban: Promesses et mensonges de l'Occident*. Paris: L'Harmattan, 1977.

Baudis, Dominique. *La passion des Chrétiens du Liban*. Paris: France-Empire, 1979.

Baudrillard, Jean. *L'échange symbolique et la mort*. Paris: Gallimard, 1976.

Bavly, Dan. *Fire in Beirut: Israel's War in Lebanon with the PLO*. New York: Stein and Day, 1984.

de Beauvoir, Simone. *La force des choses*. 2 vols. Paris: Gallimard, 1963.

———. *La force de l'âge*. Paris: Gallimard, 1966.

———. *Le deuxième sexe*. 2 vols. Paris: Idées, 1969.

Becker, Jilian. *The PLO: The Rise and Fall of the Palestinian Liberation Organization*. New York: St. Martin's Press, 1984.

Beji, Hele. "La métamorphose nationale: De l'indépendance à l'aliénation." *Peuples méditerranéens* 35–36 (April–September 1986).

Benassar, Menassa Béchara. *Anatomie d'une guerre et d'une occupation*. Paris: Galilée, 1978.

———. *Dimitrov et les roses d'Arabie*. Paris: Galilée, 1980.

———. *Paix d'Israël au Liban*. Beirut: L'Orient–Le Jour, 1983.

Benaudis, Jacques. *Tsahal, les légions d'Israël des milices paysanes à la puissance nucléaire*. Paris: Ramsay, 1984.

Ben Ghadifa, Ilham. "Interview in Tunis." Manuscript, 1985.

Ben Jelloun. *La nuit sacrée*. Paris: Seuil, 1987.

Bettelheim, Bruno. *Les blessures symboliques*. Paris: Gallimard, 1971.

Beyrouth, souvenirs, réalités. Preface by Ghassan Tuéni. Paris: Hachette, 1983.

Biqaʿi-Juha, Iman. *Waminnil Wafaʾ*. Beirut: 1984.

Bolling, Landrum R., *Reporters under Fire: U.S. Media Coverage of Conflicts in Lebanon and Central America*. Boulder, Colo.: Westview Press, 1985.

Boons, Marie-Clarie. "A propos de l'orgasme." *Revue française de psychanalyse*. 4, 77: 620–26.

Bou Malhab Atallah, Daad. *Le Liban: Guerre civile ou conflit international?* Beirut: Al-Hurriyat, 1980.

Boukhedenna, Sakinna. *Journal "Nationalité: Immigré(e)"*. Paris: L'Harmattan, 1987.

Bourgi, Albert, and Pierre Weiss. *Les complots libanais*. Paris: Berger-Levrault, 1978.

———. *Liban: La cinquième guerre du Proche-Orient*. Paris: Publisud, 1983.

Boustani, Fouad. *La crise libanaise et les évènements des quatre années*. Beirut, 1979.

———. *Le problème du Liban*. Jounieh: University of Saint-Esprit, 1979.

Bouzar, Wadi. *Les fleuves ont toujours deux rives*. Algiers: Entreprise Nationale du Livre, 1986.

Boyer, Evelyne. *La poudrière libanaise*. Paris: La Pensée Universelle, 1977.

Brière, Claire. *Liban guerres ouvertes, 1920–1985*. Paris: Ramsay, 1985.

Brogan, Patrick, and Albert Zarca. *Deadly Business: Sam Cummings, Interams, and the Arms Trade*. New York: Norton, 1984.

Brown, William. *The Last Crusade: A Negotiator's Middle East Handbook*. Chicago: Nelson Hall, 1980.

Browne, Walter. *Death of a Country: The Civil War in Lebanon*. London: Weidenfeld and Nicolson, 1977.

————. *Lebanon's Struggle for Independence.* Vols. 3–4. Salisbury, N.C.: Documentary Publications, 1980.

————, and William Snyder. *The Regionalization of Warfare.* New Brunswick, N.J.: Transaction Books, 1985.

Brownmiller, Susan. *Against Our Will: Men, Women, and Rape.* New York: Bantam, 1976.

Bruss, Elizabeth W. *Beautiful Theories: The Spectacle of Discourse in Contemporary Criticism.* Baltimore and London: John Hopkins University Press, 1982.

Bryson, Thomas. *U.S.–Middle East Diplomatic Relations, 1784–1978.* New York: Scarecrow Press, 1979.

Bulloch, John. *Death of a Country: The Civil War in Lebanon.* London: Weidenfeld and Nicolson, 1977.

————. *Final Conflict: The War in Lebanon.* London: Century, 1983.

Bustros, Nicolas. *Je me souviens.* Beirut: Librairie Antoine, 1983.

Camhi, Leslie. "War and Remembrance." *Afterimage* (March 1989): 20–22.

Canetti, Elias. *Crowds and Power.* New York: Seabury Press, 1978.

Carré, Olivier, and Claire Brière. *Islam: Guerre à l'Occident.* Paris: Autrement, 1983.

Carroll, Berenice. "Women Take Action." *Women's Studies International* 12, 1 (January 1989).

Cerf, Muriel. *Une passion.* Paris: Lattès, 1981.

Césaire, Aimé. *Cahier d'un retour au pays natal/Return to My Native Land.* (Bilingual edition. Trans. Emile Snyder. Preface André Breton) Paris: Présence Africaine, 1971.

Chabry, Laurent and Annie. *Politique et minorités au Proche-Orient.* Paris: Maisonneuve, 1984.

Chaktoura, Maria. *La guerre des graffiti, Liban 1975–78.* Beirut: An-Nahar, 1978.

Chalouhi, Robert. "The Crisis in Lebanon: A Test of Consociational Theory." Ph. D. dissertation. University of Florida, 1978.

de Chalvron, Alain. *Le piège de Beyrouth.* Paris: Le Sycomore, 1982.

Chami, Georges. *Watan bila jazibiyya.* Beirut: Dar ʿAchtarut, 1979.

————. *Abʿad bila watan.* Beirut: Dar ʿAchtarut, 1977.

Chami, Joseph. *Religion and Fertility: Arab Christian-Muslim Differentials.* New York: Cambridge University Press, 1981.

————. *Days of Wrath: Lebanon 1977–82.* New Brunswick, N.J.: Transaction, 1984.

Chamoun, Camille. *Crise au Moyen-Orient.* Paris: Gallimard, 1963.

————. *Crise au Liban.* Beirut, 1977.

————. *Mémoires et souvenirs: Du 17 juillet 1977 au 24 décembre 1978.* Beirut: Imprimerie Catholique, 1979.

————. *A soixante ans d'intervalles.* Beirut: Cèdre, 1980.

Chamussy, René. *Chronique d'une guerre: Le Liban 1975–1977.* Paris: Desclée, 1978.

————. "Le Liban dans l'étau." *Etudes* (March 1979).

Charaf, Georges. *Communautés et pouvoir au Liban.* Beirut: Cèdre, 1981.

Charaf, Rafiq. *Kitab Rafiq Charaf,* Beirut: Dar Al-Taliʿa, 1980.

Charara, Yolla Polity. "Women and Politics in Lebanon." In *Third World—Second Sex: Women's Struggles and National Liberation, Third World Women Speak Out,* Miranda Davies, ed. London: Zed, 1983.

Chatelier, J.–P. "Entretien avec Béchir Gemayel: Libérer le Liban." *Politique internationale* 16 (Paris, 1983).

Chauvel, Geneviève. *Les émeraudes de Beyrouth.* Paris: Presses de la Cité, 1979.

Chawaf, Chantal. *Retable-rêverie.* Paris: Des Femmes, 1974.

———. *Cercoeur.* Paris: Mercure de France, 1975.

———. *Blé de semences.* Paris: Mercure de France, 1976.

———. *Le soleil et la terre.* Paris: Pauvert, 1977.

———. *Rougeâtre.* Paris: Pauvert, 1977.

———. *Maternité.* Paris: Stock, 1979.

Chedid, Andrée. *Liban.* Paris: Seuil (Petite Planète), 1974.

———. *Cérémonial de la violence.* Paris: Flammarion, 1976.

———. *Epreuve du vivant.* Paris: Flammarion, 1983.

———. *La maison sans racines.* Paris: Flammarion, 1985. Translated as *House Without Roots.* London: Serpent's Tail, 1989.

———. *Textes pour une poème (1949–1970).* Paris: Flammarion, 1987.

———. *The Sixth Day.* London: Serpent's Tail, 1987.

———. *Mondes miroirs magies.* Paris:: Flammarion, 1988.

Chehdan Khalifé, Michel. *Les relations entre la France et le Liban, 1958–1978.* Paris: PUF, 1983.

Chevalier, Dominique. *La société du Mont-Liban à l'époque de la révolution industrielle en Europe.* Paris: Geuthner, 1971.

———. "Proche-Orient: Les états de la paix." *Politique internationale* 19 (Paris, 1983).

Chiha, Michel. *Propos d'économie libanaise.* Beirut: Trident, 1965.

Cleaver, Eldridge, *Soul on Ice.* New York: Delta, 1968.

Clifton, Tony, and Catherine Leroy. *God Cried.* New York: Quartet Books, 1983.

Cloudsley, Anne. *Women of Omdurman: Life, Love, and the Cult of Virginity.* New York: St. Martin's Press, 1984.

Cobban, Helena. *The Palestinian Liberation Organization: People, Power, and Politics.* Cambridge: Cambridge University Press, 1984.

———. *The Making of Modern Lebanon.* Boulder, Colo.: Westview, 1985.

———. *The Shiʿa Community and the Future of Lebanon.* Washington, D.C.; American Institute for Islamic Affairs, 1985.

Collin, Françoise. *Le jour fabuleux.* Paris: Seuil, 1959.

———. *Rose qui peut.* Paris: Seuil, 1962.

———. *Le rendez-vous.* Paris: Tierce, 1988.

———, ed. "Jouir." *Les cahiers du grif* 26 (March 1983).

———, ed. "L'Indépendance amoureuse." *Les cahiers du grif* 32 (Winter 1985).

"Communist Parties in the Middle East." *Khamsin* 7 (Great Britain, 1980): 7–12.

"Conflicts in the Middle East." *Social Praxis* 4, 3–4 (Pays-Bas 1976–1977): 191–364.

Connell, Bob. "Masculinity, Violence, and War. In *War/Masculinity*, Paul Patton and Ross Poole, eds. Sydney: Intervention, 1985.

Cooke, Miriam. *Women Write War: The Centring of the Beirut Decentrists.* Oxford: Center for Lebanese Studies, 1987.

————. *War's Other Voices: Women Writers on the Lebanese Civil War, 1975–82.* Cambridge: Cambridge University Press, 1988.

Corm, Charles. *La montagne inspirée.* Beirut: La Revue Phénicienne, 1964.

Corm, Georges. *Politique économique et planification au Liban 1953–1963.* Paris: Médicis, 1964.

————. *Géopolitique du conflit libanais.* Paris: La Découverte, 1986.

————. *Le Proche-Orient éclaté, 1956–1982: De Suez à l'invasion du Liban.* Paris: Maspero, 1983.

Cramer, Pat. "Responses to World War in the Writings of Virginia Woolf and Hilda Doolittle." Ph. D. dissertation. University of Illinois, 1989.

Cunneen, Chris. "Working Class Boys and 'Crime': Theorising the Class/Gender Mix." In *War/Masculinity*, Paul Patton and Ross Poole, eds. Sydney: Intervention, 1985.

Dahdah, Nagib. *Evolution historique du Liban.* Beirut: Librairie du Liban, 1968.

al-Daʿif, Rachid. *Al-Mustabidd.* Beirut: Dar Abʿad Liltibaʿa Wal Nashr Wal Tawzih, 1983.

————. *Fushat mustahdafat bayna al-naʿs wal al-nawm.* Beirut: Mukhtarat, 1986.

————. *Ahl Al-Zull.* Beirut: Mukhtarat, 1987.

el Dareer, Asma. *Woman, Why Do You Weep?* London: Zed, 1982.

David, Astor, and Valérie Yorke. *Peace in the Middle East.* London, 1977.

Davies, Miranda, ed. *Third World—Second Sex: Women's Struggles and National Liberation, Third World Women Speak Out.* London: Zed, 1983.

————. ed. *Third World—Second Sex 2.* London: Zed, 1987.

Davis, Angela. *Women, Race, and Class.* New York: Vintage Books, 1983.

Davis, Lennard J. *Resisting Novels.* New York: Methuen, 1987.

Dawisha, Adeeb. *Syria and the Lebanese Crisis.* New York: St. Martin's Press, 1980.

DeBar, Luc-Henri. *Les communautés confessionnelles au Liban.* Paris: Recherche sur les Civilisations, 1983.

Deeb, Marius. *The Lebanese Civil War.* New York: Praeger, 1980.

Dekmejian, R. H. "Consociational Democracy in Crisis: The Crisis of Lebanon." *Comparative Politics* 10, 2 (1978): 251–65.

Delburgo, Alberto Sidi. *Avic un L comme Liban, avec deux ailes comme liberté.* Sherbrooke, Canada: Naaman, 1982.

Depardon, Raymond. *Notes: Guerre civile 1976.* Paris: Arfuyen, 1979.

Deschodt, Eric. *La gloire au Liban.* Paris: Lattès, 1982.

Desjardins, Thierry. *Le martyre du Liban.* Paris: Plon, 1976.

"Droit à la mémoire." Special issue of *Esprit* (Paris, April 1984).

Dualeh, Abdalla, and Raqiya Haji. *Sisters in Affliction: Circumcision and Infibulation of Women in Africa.* London: Zed, 1982.

Dubar, Claude and Salim Nasr. *Les classes sociales au Liban*. Paris: PFNSP, 1976.

Dupont, Pascal. *Vous avez remarqué, les nuits sont de plus en plus courtes*. Paris: Hachette, 1979.

Dupuy, Trevor Nevitt, and Paul Martell. *Flawed Victory: The Arab-Israeli Conflict and the 1982 War in Lebanon*. Fairfax: Hero Books, 1986.

Durtal, Jean. *Trottoir des veuves*. Paris: Editions Latines, 1984.

Duvignaud, Jean. "Violence et société." *Violences et non-violence: Raison présente 54*, (1980).

Dworkin, Andrea. *Marx and Gandhi Were Liberals: Feminism and the "Radical" Left*. Los Angeles, Calif.: Frog in the Well, 1980.

———. *Pornography: Men Possessing Women*. New York: Perigee Books, 1981.

Easlea. *Science and Sexual Oppression: Patriarchy's Confrontation with Women and Nature*. London: Weidenfeld and Nicholson, 1981.

———. *Fathering the Unthinkable: Masculinity, Scientists and the Nuclear Arms Race*. London: Pluto, 1983.

Eddé, Raymond. *Save Lebanon*. Beirut: n.p., 1980.

El-Amine, A. "Systèmes d'éducation, changement social et dépendance (Un cas: le Liban)." *Congrès mondial de sociologie* 9 (1978).

El-Khatib, N. "Nation libanaise?" 2 vols. Ph. D. dissertation. University of Bordeaux, 1978.

Elshtain, Jean Bethke. *Women and War*. New York: Basic Books, 1987.

Enloe, Cynthia. *Does Khaki Become You?: The Militarisation of Women's Lives*. London: Pluto Press, 1983.

Entelis, John P. *Pluralism and Party Transformation in Lebanon: Al-Kata'ib 1936– 1970*. Leiden: Brill, 1974.

Erlich, Michel. *La femme blessée: Essai sur les mutilations sexuelles féminines*. Paris L'Harmattan, 1986.

Eshel, David. *The Lebanon War: 1982*. Hod Hasharon: Eshel-Dramit, 1983.

Faith, Hanna M. *An American Mission: The Role of the American University of Beirut*. Boston: Boswork Printing, 1979.

Fakhuri, Riyad. *Lubnan tahtal ramad*. Beirut: Dar Al-Waqa'i, 1978.

Fanon, Frantz. *Les damnés de la terre*. Paris: Maspero, 1961. Translated as *The Wretched of the Earth*. Constance Farrington, trans. Harmondsworth, Middlesex, England: Penguin, 1982.

———. *Peau noire, masques blancs*. Paris: Seuil, 1952.

Farrar, Adam. "War, Machining Male Desire." In *War/Masculinity*, Paul Patton and Ross Poole, eds. Sydney: Intervention, 1985.

Favret, Rémi. *La ville du dernier jour*. Paris: Lattès, 1987.

Fayyad, Tawfiq. *Habibati milichiya*. Beirut: Al-Mu'assassa Al-'Arabiyya Lil Dirasat Wal Nachr, 1976.

———. *Al-Bahlul*. Beirut: Al-Mu'assasa Al-'Arabiyya Lil Dirasat Wal Nachr, 1978.

Feldmann, Shai. *Israeli Nuclear Deterrence*. New York: Columbia University Press, 1983.

———. and Heda Rechnitz-Kijner. *Deception, Consensus and War: Israel in Lebanon*. Tel Aviv: Jaffee Center for Strategic Studies, 1984.

Fernea, Elizabeth, and Basima Qattan Bezirgan. *Middle Eastern Muslim Women Speak*. Austin: University of Texas Press, 1976.

Fine, Jim. *The Tragedy of Lebanon*. Ann Arbor: University of Michigan Press, 1981.

Finkelkraut, Alain. *La réprobation d'Israel*. Paris: Denoël Gonthier, 1983.

Fitzgerald, Lawrence. *Lebanon to Labuan*. Melbourne, 1980.

Focke, Harold. *The Lebanese War, Its Origin and Political Dimensions*. London: Horst, 1978.

Fontaine, André. *Le dernier quart du siècle*. Paris: Fayard, 1976.

Foucault, Michel. *Histoire de la sexualité: La volonté de savoir*. Paris: Gallimard, 1976.

———. "Tales of Murder." In *I, Pierre Rivière*. London: Penguin, 1978.

———. *Discipline and Punish: The Birth of Prison*. Alan Sheridan, trans. New York: Vintage, 1979.

Freedman, Robert. *The Middle East Since Camp David*. Boulder, Colo.: Westview, 1984.

Freiha, Adel A. *L'armée et l'état au Liban, 1945–80*. Paris: LGDJ, 1980.

Freud, Sigmund, and Albert Einstein. *Why War?* Paris, 1933.

Frugier, Jean-Raymond. *Liban, terre éternelle*. Paris: La Pensée Universelle, 1979.

Gabriel, Philip. *In the Ashes: The Story of Lebanon*. Ardmore: Whitmore, 1978.

Gabriel, Richard A. *Operation Peace for Galilee: The Israeli-PLO War in Lebanon*. New York: Hill and Wang, 1984.

Gadant, Monique, ed. "Femmes de la Méditerranée." *Peuples méditerranéens* 22–23 (January–June 1983). Translated as *Women of the Mediterranean*. London: Zed, 1986.

Gale, Jack. *Lebanon Time-Bomb*. England: New Park, 1982.

Gallissot, René. "Transnationalisation et renforcement de l'ordre étatique." *Peuples méditerranéens* 35–36 (April–September 1986).

Gauthier, Xavière. *Surréalisme et sexualité*. Paris: Gallimard, Idées, 1971.

Gavron, Daniel. *Israel After Begin: Israel's Options in the Aftermath of the Lebanon War*. Boston: Houghton Mifflin, 1984.

Gebeyli, Claire. *Mémorial d'exil*. Paris: St.-Germain-des-Prés, 1975.

———. *La mise à jour*. Paris: St.-Germain-des-Prés, 1982.

———. *Dialogue avec le feu: Carnets du Liban*. Caen: Le Pavé, 1985.

Gebrane, May. "La situation conflictuelle de la femme libanaise." Ph. D. dissertation. University of Paris VII, 1981.

Gemayel, Amine. *Peace and Unity, Major Speeches 1982–1984*. England: Colin Smythe, 1984.

———. *L'offence et le pardon*. Paris: Gallimard, 1988.

Gemayel, Bachir. *Libération et unification*. Beirut: Editions de la Résistance Libanaise, 1982.

Gennaoui, Josette. *Le Liban-Sud*. Paris: Pylone, 1978.

Germanos Ghazaly, L. *Le paysan, la terre, et la femme: Organisation sociale d'un village de Mont-Liban*. Paris: Maisonneuve, 1978.

Gervasi, Frank Henry. *Media Coverage: The War in Lebanon*. Washington D.C., 1983.

Ghali, Ilham. "Le thème de la guerre dans l'oeuvre de Ghada Samman." Ph. D. dissertation. University of Paris VII, 1984.

Ghanem, Hanna. *Liban: Guerre ou génocide?* Sherbrooke, Canada: Naaman, 1979.

———. *Liban: Finissons-en.* Canada: Didon, 1979.

———. *Une solution pour le Liban: Système vital intégré et valorisation personnelle.* Sherbrooke, Canada: Naaman, 1980.

Ghanem, Khayrallah. *Le système électoral et la vie politique au Liban.* Kaslik: Saint-Esprit University, 1983.

Gharib, Sidi. *A'assir al-neel.* Beirut: Dar el-Mashrek wal-Maghreb, 1983.

———. *Aghani Beirut.* Beirut: Dar el-Mashrek wal-Maghreb, 1986.

Ghousoub, Mai. "Feminism—or the Eternal Masculine—in the Arab World." *New Left Review* 161.

Gilbert, Martin. *The Arab-Israeli Conflict: Its History in Maps.* London; Weidenfeld and Nicolson, 1984.

Gilmour, David. *Lebanon: The Fractured Country.* London: Sphere, 1984.

Giniewsky, Paul. "Le Liban dans la stratégie globale de la Lybie." *Politique internationale,* 13 (Paris 1981).

Girard, René. *La violence et le sacré.* Paris: Grasset, 1972.

Golan, Matti. *Négotiations secrètes de Henry Kissinger au Proche-Orient.* Paris: Laffont, 1976.

Gorce, Jean-Marie de la. *La guerre et l'atome.* Paris: Plon, 1985.

Gordon, David. *Lebanon, the Fragmented Nation.* Stanford: Hoover Institute Press, 1980.

———. *The Republic of Lebanon: Nation in Jeopardy.* Boulder, Colo.: Westview, 1983.

Granotier, Bernard. *Israël, cause de la 3ème guerre mondiale?* Paris: L'Harmattan, 1982.

Graves, Robert. *The White Goddess.* New York: Noonday Press, 1966.

Gresh, Alain, and Dominique Vidal. *Proche-Orient: Une guerre de cent ans.* Paris: Editions Sociales, 1984.

Guillebaud, Jean-Claude. *Un voyage vers l'Asie.* Paris: Le Seuil, 1970.

Haddad, Jean-Pierre. *Le combat du Liban: Pour qui, pour quoi?* Meaux: Henri Conchon, 1976.

———. *Liban, le courage d'exister.* Paris: Maisonneuve, 1978.

Haddad, Wadi. *Lebanon: The Politics of Revolving Doors.* New York: Praeger, 1985.

Hage-Chahin, Samir. *Suluq al-madina.* Beirut: Al-mu'assasa al-'arabiyya lil dirasat wal nachr, 1983.

Haidar, Nabil. *Le déserteur.* Dakar: Nouvelles Editions Africaines, 1983.

Haig, Alexander. *Caveat: Realism, Reagan, and Foreign Policy.* New York: Macmillan, 1984.

Haïk, Farjallah. *La croix et le croissant.* Paris: Fayard, 1959.

Haley, Edward, and Lewis Snider, eds. *Lebanon in Crisis: Participants and Issues.* New York: Syracuse University Press, 1979.

Hammel, Eric. *The Root: The Marines in Beirut.* San Diego: Harrout, 1985.

Hanf, T. "The 'Political Secularization' Issue in Lebanon." *Annual Review of Sciences and Religion* 5 (1981): 225–53.

Harding, Esther. *Les mystères de la femme.* Preface by C. G. Jung. Paris: Payot, 1976.

Harik, Iliya F. *Politics and Change in a Traditional Society: Lebanon. 1711–1845.* Princeton: Princeton University Press, 1968.

———. *Lebanon: Anatomy of Conflict.* Hanover: American University Field Staff, 1981.

Harlow, Barbara. *Resistance Literature.* New York: Methuen, 1987.

Haykal, Muhammad Husayn. *Zaynab.* Cairo: Al-Nahda, 1914.

Held, Jean-François. *La déchirure: Voyage au coeur d'Israël.* Paris: Ramsay, 1983.

Helou, Charles. *Mémoires.* 2 vols. Jounieh, Lebanon: Saint-Paul, 1983.

Henry, Paul-Marc. *Les jardiniers de l'enfer.* Paris: Olivier Orban, 1984.

Higonnet, Margaret. "The Double Helix." In *Behind the Lines: Gender and the Two World Wars,* Margaret Randolph Higonnet, Jane Jenson, Sonya Michel, and Margaret Collins Weitz, eds. New Haven and London: Yale University Press, 1987.

———. "Civil Wars and Sexual Territories." In *Arms and the Woman,* Helen Cooper, Adrienne Munich, and Susan Squier, eds. Chapel Hill: University of North Carolina Press, 1989.

Hitti, Philip Khuri. *Lebanon in History from the Earliest Times to the Present.* London: Macmillan, 1967.

Hof, Frederick. *Galilee Divided: The Israeli-Lebanon Frontier 1916–1984.* Boulder, Colo.: Westview, 1985.

Hosken, Fran P. "Female Genital Mutilation and Human Rights." *Feminist Issues,* 1, 3 (Summer 1981); 1–23.

Hoss, Salim. *Lebanon: Agony and Peace.* Beirut: Islamic Center for Information and Development, 1984.

Hourani, Albert. *Syria and Lebanon: A Political Essay.* London: Oxford University Press, 1954.

Hudson, Michael. *The Precarious Republic: Political Modernization in Lebanon.* Boulder, Colo.: Westview Press, 1985.

Hunt, James. *Gandhi in London.* New Delhi: Promilla, 1978.

Ilyas, Ilyas Maqdisi. *Al-Safaqa al-akhira.* Beirut: Al-Usbuᶜ Al-Arabi, 1983.

———. *Malak al-mawt yaᶜud thaniyatan.* Beirut: Al-Usbuᶜ Al-Arabi, 1984.

Irani, George. *The Papacy and the Middle East: The Role of the Holy See in the Arab-Israeli Conflict, 1962–1984.* South Bend, Ind.: Notre Dame University Press, 1985.

Ismaᶜil, Ismaᶜil. *Al-Chiyah.* Beirut: Dar al-Adab, 1977.

Jabbra, N. W. "Sex Roles and Language in Lebanon." *Ethnology* 19, 4 (1980): 459–74.

Jabre, Antoine. *La guerre du Liban: Moscou et la crise du Proche-Orient.* Paris: Belfond, 1980.

Jabre, Jamil. *L'éclair et la foudre: Le défi libanais.* Beirut: Horizons Nouveaux, 1979.

Jameson, Fredric. *The Political Unconscious: Narrative as a Socially Symbolic Act.* Ithaca: Cornell University Press, 1981.

———. "Postmodernism, or the Cultural Logic of Late Capitalism." *New Left Review* 146 (1984).

Jan Mohamed, Abdul, and David Lloyd, eds. "The Nature and Context of Minority Discourse." Special issue of *Cultural Critique,* 6 (Spring 1987).

Jansen, Michael. *The Battle of Beirut: Why Israel Invaded Lebanon.* Boston: South End Press, 1983.

Joseph, Suad. "Women and the Neighborhood Street in Borj Hammoud, Lebanon." In *Women in the Muslim World.* Cambridge: Harvard University Press, 1978.

Joumblatt, Kamal. *Pour le Liban.* Paris: Stock, 1978. Translated as *I Speak for Lebanon.* London: Zed Press 1982.

Juha, Mustafa. *Habibati ma zalat tughalibul fajr.* Beirut, 1984

Jundi al, Asim. *Bayni wabaynaki al-yasamin.* Beirut: Dar Al-Nidal, 1984.

Jureidini, Paul and William Hazen. *The Palestinian Movement in Politics.* Lexington, Ky.: Lexington, 1976.

Kaafarani, S. "Classes sociales et confessionalisme au Liban." Ph. D. dissertation. University of Tours, n.d.

Kapeliouk, Ammon. *Enquête sur un massacre: Sabra et Chatila.* Paris: Seuil, 1982.

Kass, Ilana. *The Lebanon Civil War 1975–76: A Case of Crisis Mismanagement.* Jerusalem: Hebrew University of Jerusalem, 1979.

Kauffman, Linda S. *Discourses of Desire: Gender, Genre, and Epistolary Fictions.* Ithaca: Cornell University Press, 1986.

Kenyon, Susan, ed. *The Sudanese Woman.* Khartoum: Graduate College Publications, 1987.

Khaïrallah, Shereen. *Lebanon: A Bibliography.* Santa Barbara: Clio Press, 1979.

Khaïr-Badawi. *Le désir amputé: Vécu sexuel des femmes libanaises.* Paris: L'Harmattan, 1986.

Khaled, Leïla. *Mon peuple vivra.* Paris: Gallimard, 1973.

Khalidi, Walid. *Conflict and Violence in Lebanon: Confrontation in the Middle East.* Cambridge: Center for International Affairs, Harvard University, 1979.

Khalife, Michel. *Les relations entre la France et le Liban, 1958–1978.* Paris: PUF, 1983.

El Khayat-Bennaï, Ghita. *Le monde arabe au féminin.* Paris: L'Harmattan, 1985.

al-Khazin, William. *Al-wilada al-jadida wa qisas ukhra.* Beirut: Dar Jukar Lil Nachr, 1979.

———. *Al-Zujaj al-maksur.* Beirut: Dar Marun ʿAbbud, 1985.

Khleif, B. B. "The Ethnic Crisis in Lebanon: Towards a Socio-Cultural Analysis." *Sociologus* 34, 2 (1984); 121–39.

Khoury, Elias. *Fima yataʿalak rawabit al-nitak.* Beirut: dar Al-Adab, 1975.

———. *Al-Jabal al-saghir.* Beirut: Muʾassassat Al-Abhath Al-ʿArabiyya, 1977. Translated as *La petite montagne.* Paris: Arléa, 1987.

———. *Abwab al-madinat.* Beirut: Dar Ibn Roushd, 1981.

———. *Wujuh baydaʾ.* Beirut: Dar Ibn Roushd, 1981.

———. *The Lost Memory.* Beirut: Institute for Arab Research, 1982.

————. *Al-tasbit wal mawdu^c*. Beirut: Institute for Arab Research, 1984.

————. *Time of Occupation*. Beirut: Institute for Arab Research, 1985.

Khoury, Enver M. *The Crisis in the Lebanese System: Confessionalism and Chaos.* Washington D.C.: AEIPPRFAS 1976.

Khoury, Gérard. *Mémoire de l'aube.* Paris: Publisud, 1987.

Khoury-Ghata, Vénus. *Au sud du silence.* Paris: St.-Germain-des-Prés, 1975.

————. *Les ombres et leurs cris.* Paris: Belfond, 1980.

————. *Un faux-pas du soleil.* Paris: Belfond, 1982.

————. *Vacarme pour une lune morte.* Paris: Flammarion, 1983.

————. *Les morts n'ont pas d'ombre.* Paris: Flammarion, 1984.

Khurasani, Ghada al. *Lu^{c}bat al-qadar.* Beirut, 1976.

————. *Hariq fil janna.* Beirut, 1977.

————. *Al-Harb wal-hubb.* Kuwait: Dar Al-Siyasa, 1983.

Kissinger, Henry, *Years of Upheaval.* Boston: Little, Brown, 1982.

Knapp, Bettina. *Andrée Chedid.* Amsterdam: Rodopi, 1984.

Kodmani-Darwish, Bassma. *Liban: Espoirs et Réalités.* Paris: IFRI, 1987.

Kvitachvili, Monique and Serge. *Du tabac et du sang: Le drame du Sud-Liban.* Lebanon: Editions Tibnin, 1981.

Labaki, Georges. *The Lebanon Crisis (1975–1985): A Bibliography.* Maryland: CIDCM, 1986.

Labaky, Père Mansour. *Kafarsama: Un village du Liban.* Jounieh, Lebanon: Saint-Paul, 1983.

————. *L'enfant du Liban.* Paris: Fayard, 1986.

Laborit, Henri. *L'agressivité détournée.* Paris: UGE, 1970.

Lacan, Jacques. *Ecrits I.* Paris: Seuil, 1966.

————. *Le séminaire.* Paris: Seuil, 1975.

Lacase, Marie-Thérèse. *La fin des terres promises.* Paris: Syros, 1979.

Laffin, John. *The War of Desperation: Lebanon 1982–85.* London: Osprey, 1985.

Lamb, Franklin P. *Reason not the Need: Eyewitness Chronicles of Israel's War in Lebanon.* Nottingham: Spokesman for the Bertrand Russell Peace Foundation, 1984.

Lapierre, Jean-William, and Anne-Marie de Vilaine. "Femmes: Une oppression millénaire." *Alternatives non-violentes: Femmes et violences* 40 (Spring 1981).

Lartéguy, Jean. *Liban: Huit jours pour mourir.* Paris: Les Presses de la Cité, 1984.

————. *L'or de Baal.* Paris: Mercure de France, 1985.

Laurent, Annie and Antoine Basbous. *Une proie pour deux fauves.* Beirut: Ad-Dairat, 1983.

Leitenberg, Milton, and Gabriel Stehher. *Great Power Intervention in the Middle East.* New york: Pergamon Press, 1979.

Lelong, Michel. *Guerre ou paix à Jérusalem?* Paris: Albin Michel, 1982.

Lemsine, Aïcha. *Ordalie des voix: Les femmes arabes parlent.* Paris: Encre, 1983.

Levy, Bernard-Henri. *Le diable en tête.* Paris: Grasset, 1984.

Libanius (Nagib Dahdah). *Les guerres du Liban.* Beirut: Edition du Cèdre, 1980.

Libis, Jean. *Le mythe de l'androgyne.* Paris: Berg International, 1980.

Loheac, Ammoun Blanche. *Histoire du Liban.* Beirut, 1979.

Lohéac, Lyne. *Daoud Ammoun et la création de l'état libanais.* Paris: Klincksieck, 1978.

Lukács, Georg. *The Theory of the Novel.* Anna Bostock, trans. Cambridge: MIT Press, 1971.

———. "Realism in Our Time." In *Essays on Realism,* Rodney Levingstone, ed. David Fernbach, trans. Cambridge: MIT Press, 1980.

M. A. *Chemin de croix ou le destin d'un homme et d'un peuple.* Beirut: Dar al-ʿAmal, 1979.

Maakaroun, Elie. *Terre qui brûle.* Paris: L'Harmattan, 1979.

———. *Le visage et la soif.* Paris: L'Harmattan, 1982.

Macciocchi, Maria-Antonietta. *Eléments pour une analyse du fascisme.* Vol. 1, no. 1026. Paris: Vincennes, 1974–1975.

———. *Les femmes et leurs maîtres.* Paris: Bourgois, 1978.

Mahfoud, Peter. *Lebanon and the Turmoil of the Middle East.* New York: Vantage Press, 1980.

Makarem, May. "Avec la non-violence Laure Moghaïzel, l'autre visage du Liban." *L'Orient-Le Jour,* Beirut, March 16, 1988.

Makdissi, Samir A. *Financial Policy and Economic Growth: The Lebanese Experience.* New York: Columbia University Press, 1979.

Makhlouf, Issa. *Beyrouth ou la fascination de la mort.* Paris: La Passion, 1988.

Malik, Charles Habib. *After Iran: Enduring Hope for Lebanon.* Washington, D.C.: American Lebanese League, 1979.

Mallat, Hyam. *Objectifs politiques de demain.* Beirut: Al-Nahar, 1977.

McCullin, Don. *Beirut: A City in Crisis.* Sevenoaks, Ky.: New English Library, 1983.

McLauren, R. D., ed. *The Political Role of Minority Groups in the Middle East.* New York: Praeger, 1979.

Menassa, Béchara. *Dimitrov et les roses d'Arabie.* Paris: Galilée, 1980.

Mendel, Gérard. "La violence est un langage." *Violences et non-violence: Raison Présente.* 54, 2 (1980).

Meney, Patrick. *Même les tueurs ont une mère.* Paris: La Table Ronde, 1986.

Mernissi, Fatima. *Sexe, Idéologie, Islam.* Paris: Tierce, 1983.

Mikdadi, Lina. *Surviving the Siege of Beirut: A Personal Account.* London: Onyx, 1979.

Millet, Richard. *Beyrouth.* Seyssel: Champ Vallon, 1987.

Minkowski, Alexandre. *L'Impénitent.* Paris: Lattès, 1984.

Mitchell, Juliet. *Psychanalyse et féminisme.* Paris: Des Femmes, 1974.

———, and Ann Oakley, eds. *What Is Feminism? A Re-Examination.* New York: Pantheon, 1986.

Mitscherlich, Margarete. *La femme pacifique.* Sylvie Ponsard, trans. Paris: Des Femmes, 1988.

Mizrahi, Rachel. *L'un meurt, l'autre aussi.* Paris: Hachette, 1982.

Moi, Toril. *Sexual/Textual Politics: Feminist Literary Theory.* New York: Methuen, 1985.

Mokhtar, Khaoula. "Se libérer à Beyrouth," *Peuples Méditerranéens* 22–23 (January–June 1983).

Moraga, Cherrie. *Loving in the War Years*. Boston: South End Press, 1983.

Mouradian, Krikor. *Media, mass media et fonctions: Éléments de communication de masse au Liban*. Beirut: Lebanon University, 1981.

Muller, Jean-Marie. "Signification de la non-violence." *Violences et non-violence: Raison présente* 54, 2 (1980).

———. *Stratégie de l'action politique non-violente*. Varsovie: Krag, 1984.

Naaman, Abdallah. *Le français au Liban, essai socio-linguistique*. Jounieh, Lebanon: Naaman, 1979.

———. *Umm ʿIsa*. Jounieh, Lebanon: Naaman, 1980.

———. *Les levantins. essai d'analyse sociale*. Jounieh, Lebanon: Naaman, 1984.

Naaman, Nabil. *La guerre au Liban*. Jounieh, Lebanon: Naaman, 1979.

Nabaʿa, Roger, and Souheil al-Kache. "Récits éclatés d'une révolution manquée." *Peuples méditerranéens* 20 (July–September 1982).

Naccache, Georges. *Un rêve libanais 1943–1972*. Beirut: FMA, 1983.

Naʿnaʿ, Hamida. *Al-Watan fil ʿaynayn*. Beirut: Dar Al-Adab, 1979.

Nantet, Jacques. *Histoire du Liban*. Paris: Téqui, 1986.

Nasr, Nicolas. *Faillite syrienne au Liban*. 2 vols. Beirut: Dar Al-ʿAmal, 1980–1983.

Nasrallah, Emilie. *Tilkal zikrayat*. Beirut: Nawfal, 1979.

———. *Al-Iqla ʿaks al-zaman*. Beirut: Nawfal, 1980.

———. *Al-Tahuna al-Daiʿa*. Beirut: Nawfal, 1980.

Nordic Commission. *Witness of War Crimes in Lebanon: Testimony Given to the Nordic Commission*. Oslo, October 1982. London: Ithaca Press, 1983.

Owen, Roger, ed. *Essays on the Crisis in Lebanon*. London: Ithaca Press, 1976.

O'Zoux, Raymond. *Les états du Levant sous Mandat français*. Paris: Larose, 1931.

Pakradouni, Karim. *La paix manquée*. Beirut: FMA, 1984.

Palazzoli, Claude. *La Syrie, le rêve et la rupture*. Paris: Le Sycomore, 1977.

Patton, Paul, and Ross Poole, eds. *War/Masculinity*. Sydney: Intervention, 1985.

Peristiany, J. G. *Mediterranean Family Structures*. Cambridge: Harvard University Press, 1976.

Péroncel-Hugoz. *Une croix sur le Liban*. Paris: Folio, 1984.

Peters, Emrys. "The Status of Women in Four Middle East Communities." In *Women in the Muslim World*. Cambridge: Harvard University Press, 1978.

Pharès, Walid. *Le peuple chrétien du Liban*. Beirut, 1982.

Picard, E. "Science politique, orientalisme et sociologie au chevet du Liban." *Revue française de science politique* 27, 4–5 (1977): 630–42.

Pierce, Judith. "Outside the Tribe." *The Middle East* (London, September 1983).

Pinter, Frances, ed. *Social Science Research and Women in the Arab World*. Paris: Unesco, 1984.

Poliakov, L. *De Moscou à Beyrouth: Essai sur la désinformation*. Paris: Calmann-Lévy, 1983.

Poole, Ross. "Structures of Identity: Gender and Nationalism." In *War/Masculinity*, Paul Patton and Ross Poole, eds. Sydney: Intervention, 1985.

Qubaysi, Zulfiquar. *Lilmawt lahja Lubnaniyya*. Beirut: Manchurat Mu'assasat Al-Inma' Al-Sahafi Wal Tiba'i, 1976.

———. *Ba'dal harb, Lubnan ila ayn?* Beirut: Manchurat Mu'assasat Al-Inma' Al-Sahafi Wal Tiba'i, 1977.

"Questions sur la guerre du Liban." *Les temps modernes* 435 (October 1982).

Rabbath, Edmond. *La formation historique du Liban politique et constitutionnel*. Beirut: Lebanese University, 1973.

Rabinovich, Itamar. *The War for Lebanon, 1970–1983*. Ithaca: Cornell University Press, 1984.

Raburn, Terry. *Under the Guns in Beirut*. Springfield, Ill.; Gospel Publishing House, 1980.

Rafa'iya, Yasin. *Al-Mamarr*. Damascus: Ittihad Al-Kuttab Al-'Arab, 1981.

Rahib, Hani. *Alf layla wa laylatan*. Damascus, 1982.

Rahmé, Georges. *Coordonnées de la crise libanaise*. Beirut: Cèdre, 1979.

Randal, Jonathan C. *Going All the Way: Christian Warlords, Israeli Adverturers, and the War in Lebanon*. New York: Vintage Books, 1984.

———. *La guerre de mille ans, jusqu'au dernier chrétien, jusqu'au dernier marchand— La tragédie libanaise*. Paris: Grasset, 1984.

Reardon, Betty A. *Sexism and the War System*. New York and London: Teachers College Press, 1985.

Reich, Wilhelm. *L'irruption de la morale sexuelle*. Paris: Payot, 1981.

"Religions et non-violence selon Gandhi." *Alternatives Non-Violentes: Religion et Violence* 64 (July 1987).

Rihana, Sami. *Histoire moderne de l'armée libanaise*. Beirut, 1984.

Riquet, Michel. *Une minorité chrétienne: Les maronites au Liban*. Geneva: Avenir, 1977.

Rondot, Philippe. *Le Proche-Orient à la recherche de la paix*. Paris: PUF, 1982.

Rondot, Pierre. *Les institutions politiques du Liban: Des communautés traditionnelles à l'Etat moderne*. Paris: Institut d'Etudes de l'Orient Contemporain, 1947.

de Rougemont, Denis. *Love Declared: Essays on the Myths of Love*. Boston: Beacon Press, 1961.

Rouleau, Eric. *Les Palestiniens: D'une guerre à l'autre*. Paris: La Découverte, 1984.

Roy, Jules. *Beyrouth: Viva la muerte*. Paris, Grasset, 1984.

Saadawi, Nawal el. *Al-mar'ah inda niktat al-sifer*. Cairo: Dar el Addab, 1977. Translated as *Ferdaous, une voix en enfer*. Paris: Des Femmes, 1981. Translated as *Woman at Point Zero*. London: Zed Press, 1983.

———. *Al mar'ah wal jins*. Cairo: Al-Sha'ab, 1972. Beirut; Al-Mu'assasat Al-Arabiya Lildirasat wal-Nashr, 1972. Translated as *La face cachée d'Eve: Les femmes dans le monde arabe*. Paris: Des Femmes, 1982. Translated as *The Hidden Face of Eve: Women in the Arab World*. Boston: Beacon Press, 1981.

Saïd, Laila. *A Bridge Through Time*. New York: Summit, 1985.

Sa'igh, Nasri. *Al-Kharab*. Beirut, 1983.

Salam, Nawaf, and Linda Sadaka. *The Civil War in Lebanon: A Bibliographic Essay*. Beirut: AUB, 1982.

Salibi, Kamal Suleiman. *Cross Roads to Civil War: Lebanon*. New York: Delmar, 1976.

Samman, Ghada. *Bayrut 75*. Beirut: Ghada Samman, 1975.

Saoudi, Fathia. *L'oubli rebelle*. Paris: L'Harmattan, 1986.

Sarner, Eric. *Beyrouth, Beyrouth à vif*. Paris: Encre, 1985.

Sartre, Jean-Paul. "Black Orpheus," Préface de *L'Anthologic de la nouvelle poésie nègre et malgache de langue française* de Sedar Senghor. Trans. by S. W. Allen. Paris: P.U.F., 1948.

Saudray, Nicolas. *La maison des prophètes*. Paris: Seuil, 1983.

Sayegh, Raymond. *Le Proche-Orient et le Liban*. Cousset: Delval, 1986.

Sayegh, Rosemary. *Palestinians, from Peasants to Revolutionaries: A People's History*. London: Zed Press, 1979.

Scarry, Elaine. *The Body in Pain: The Making and Unmaking of the World*. New York: Oxford University Press, 1985.

Schiff, Zeev, and Ehud Yarri. *Israel's Lebanon War*. New York: Simon and Schuster, 1984.

Segal, Patrick. *Viens la mort, on va danser*. Paris: Flammarion, 1979.

Selim, M. A. *Le problème de l'exploitation des eaux du Jourdain*. Paris: Cujas, 1965.

Seurat, Marie. *Les corbeaux d'Alep*. Paris: Gallimard, 1988.

Shaker, Fouad. *Fire over Lebanon: Country in Crisis*. Hicksville, N.Y.: Exposition Press, 1976.

Shapiro, William E. *Lebanon*. New York: Watts, 1984.

al-Shaykh, Hanan. *Intihar rajul mayit*. Beirut: Al-Nahar, 1971.

———. *Faras al-Shaytan*. Beirut: Al-Nahar, 1975.

———. *Wardat al-Sahra'*. Beirut: Al-Nahar, 1979.

———. *Hikayat Zahra*. Beirut: Al-Nahar, 1980. Translated in English as *The Story of Zahra*. New York and London: Readers International, 1986. Translated in French as *Histoire de Zahra*. Paris: Lattès, 1980.

———. *Hask al-Ghazal*. Beirut: Dar Al-Adab, 1988.

Singer, June. *Androgyny*. New York: Anchor, 1977.

Slater, Philip F.. *The Glory of Hera: Greek Mythology and the Greek Family*. Boston: Beacon Press, 1968.

Souriau, Christiane. *Femmes et politique autour de la Méditerranée*. Paris: L'Harmattan, 1980.

Spiller, Roger J. *"Not War but like War": The American Intervention in Lebanon*. Fort Leavenworth: Combat Studies Institute, 1981.

Stephan, Wafa. "Women and War in Lebanon." *Al-Raïda* 30 (Beirut, 1984).

St. John, Patricia. *Liban, l'amour possible*. Paris: Ligue pour la Lecture de la Bible, 1984.

Subh, Alaouia. *Nawm al ayam*. Beirut: Muassassat Al-Abhath Al-Arabiya, 1986.

Suleiman, Michael W. *Political Parties in Lebanon: The Challenge of a Fragmented Political Culture*. Ithaca: Cornell University Press, 1967.

Sullerot, Evelyne. *Le fait féminin*. Paris: Fayard, 1978.

Tabbara, Lina Mikdadi. *Survivre à Beyrouth*. Paris: Olivier Orban, 1977. Translated as *Survival in Beirut: A Diary of Civil War*. London: Onyx Press, 1979.

Tavernier, René. *Tentation de l'Orient.* Paris: Albin Michel, 1977.

Theweleit, Klaus. *Male Fantasies.* Volume 1: *Women, Bodies, Floods, History.* Minneapolis: University of Minnesota Press, 1989.

Timerman, Jacobo. *The Longest War.* New York: Vintage, 1982. Translated as *Israël au Liban: La guerre des consciences.* Paris: ISBN, 1983.

Tuéni, Ghassan. *Peace-Keeping, Lebanon, the Facts, the Documents: A Presentation.* New York: William Belcher Group, 1979.

———. *Laissez vivre mon peuple!* Paris: Maisonneuve, 1984.

Tuéni, Nadia. *Liban, vingt poèmes pour un amour.* Beirut: Zakka, 1979.

———. *Archives sentimentales d'une guerre au Liban.* Paris: Pauvert, 1982.

———. *La terre arrêtée.* Paris: Belfond, 1984.

Union des Juristes Palestiniens, Association Internationale des Juristes Démocrates. *Livre blanc sur l'aggression israëlienne au Liban.* Paris: Publisud, 1983.

Vallaud, Pierre. *Le Liban au bout du fusil.* Paris: Hachette, 1976.

Vial-Mannessier, Thérèse. "Fascisme et mystification misogyne." *Alternatives non-violentes: Femmes et violences* 40 (Spring 1981).

Victor, Barbara. *Terrorisme.* Paris: Stock, 1986.

Vieille, Paul. *Marché des terrains et société urbaine.* Paris: Anthropos, 1970.

———. *La féodalité et l'état en Iran.* Paris: Anthropos, 1975.

———. "L'Etat périphérique et son héritage." *Peuples méditerranéens.* 27–28 (April–September 1984).

———. "Du transnational au politique-monde?" *Peuples méditerranéens* 35–36 (April–September 1986).

———. "Le chaos du monde et les nouveaux paradigmes du mouvement social." Manuscript, forthcoming.

———, and A. H. Banisadr. *Pétrole et violence.* Paris: Anthropos, 1974.

———, ed. "Liban: Remises en cause." *Peuples méditerranéens* 20 (July–September 1982).

———, ed. "L'Etat et la Méditerranée." *Peuples méditerranéens* 27–28 (April–September 1984).

———, ed. "Fin du national?" *Peuples méditerranéens* 35–36 (April–September 1986).

de Vilaine, Anne-Marie. "La maternité détournée." *Alternatives non-violentes: Femmes et violences* 40 (Spring 1981).

de Villiers, Gérard. *Les fous de Baalbeck.* Paris: Plon, 1984.

Vocke, Harold. *The Lebanese War: Its Origins and Political Dimensions.* London: Hurst, 1978.

Wahba, Mourad, ed. *Proceedings of the International Seminar on Rural Women and Development.* Cairo: Ain Shams University, MERC, 1980.

Waring, Marilyn. *Women, Politics and Power.* Foreword by Robin Morgan. Wellington and London: Unwin, 1985.

Wehbé, N., and A. El-Amine. *Système de l'enseignement et division sociale au Liban.* Preface by V. Isambert-Jamati. Paris: Le Sycomore, 1980.

Williams, Raymond. "Notes on English Prose." *Writing in Society.* London: Verso, n.d.

Woolf, Virginia. *Three Guineas*. London, New York, and San Diego: Harcourt, Brace, Jovanovich 1966.

Yared, Nazik Saba. *Al-Sada al-makhnouk*. Beirut: Nawfal, 1986.

———. *Kana al-amsu ghadane*. Beirut: Nawfal, 1988.

Yermina, Dov. *My War Diary: Lebanon June 5–July 1, 1982*. Boston: South End Press, 1984.

Yétiv, Isaac. *Le thème de l'aliénation dans le roman maghrébin d'expression française*. Sherbrooke, Canada: CELEF, 1972.

Zamir, Meir. *The Formation of Modern Lebanon*. London: Helm, 1985.

Ziegler, Jean. *N'oubliez pas . . . le martyre de Sabra et Chatila*. Geneva: Coopi, 1982.

Zoghbi, Elias. *Le Liban, juge et bourreau*. Jounieh, Lebanon: Saint-Paul, 1979.

Zoghbi, Farid. *Le gage de satan: Liban 1975–1976*. Jounieh, Lebanon: Matabiᶜ Al-Kuraym Al-Haditha, 1976.

Zubian, Ziyad. *Jurh ᶜinda khasirat al-bahr*. Beirut, 1980.

Index